Home Already

In the Heart of Now

Glenn Francis, Psy.D.

In the Heart of Now Publishing

For more information, visit: www.IntheHeartofNow.com

ISBN 979-8-9946394-1-2 (Paperback edition)

ISBN 979-8-9946394-2-9 (Hardback edition)

ISBN 979-8-9946394-0-5 (Ebook edition)

Cover design © 2026 by Joel Lesko

Cover image by Zoltan Tasi

Grateful acknowledgement to Jon M. Sweeney & Mark S. Burrows for reproduction of their version of Meister Eckhart's poem *Our opening and Your entering are one.*

Every effort has been made to contact copyright holders. If copyright holders have not been properly acknowledged, please contact In the Heart of Now Publishing and we will be glad to rectify the omission in future printings of this book.

Dedicated to the source we cannot not be,

no matter what.

Contents

PREFACE: PIXELS   1
Perfectly personal pixels   2

INTRODUCTION   6
Home already   6
  Time out   8
  Undivided dividedness   9
  Nothing but change   10
  Pointing at us   11
  Through the veil   12
  Now, again   13
In the heart of now   14
A story right now   15

Part One
Foundations

FOUNDATIONS   21
Right about now   21
  The architecture of remembering   21
  Knowing now   22
  Limitless now   23
  Deep now   24
  Wise now   25
  The fabric of now   27
  All is well now   28
Now is awake   29
Preliminaries: Nuts and bolts   33
DIRECT EXPERIENCING   37
  We are our own authority   39
  Dismantling the layers with direct
  experiencing   40
  Identifying our experience prior to thought   41

We think we know everything (because
thought says so) 42
Existence knows existence 44
Mystic child 45
RESONANCE 47
The wellspring of resonance 48
A guide in dark places 49
The call of the uncaused 50
Pausing in presence 50
Saving my own life 52
SENSING OUR BODY 54
Living breathing star stuff 54
An inescapable connectedness 55
Separate images 56
Butting up against belief 56
Inside this clay jug 57
The perceived cannot perceive 60
A practical practice 63
The hill of separation 65
MEDITATION 67
Living meditation 72
VULNERABILITY 73
"You mistake vulnerability for weakness." 73
Vulnerability = Connectedness 74
Born through dying 75
Time for the undying now 76
Vulnerability's resonant truth 78
NEGATION 79
Using the sharpest tool 79
Now is all there is 84

Part Two
Unfolding

UNFOLDING 89
The knack of being 89
Easy now 89
Our silent companion 90
Real beliefs 92

The before-belief knack 92
Not-two, gazing together 93
A vibrantly alive pool 95
The knack of noticing 96
Hearing ourselves revealed 97
Sensing ourselves 98
Seeing ourselves 100
What we cannot not be 101
Silent seers: knowing, knowing knowing 102
Knowing nothing 104
Crashing from grace, into grace 104
I am the seeker 106
Of course we search 107
Amazing 110
Answers in the basement 111
Now ≡ Awake 113
Teachings in titles 115
Before we go on 116

Part Three
The heart of now

THE HEART OF NOW 123
WE ARE THE HEART OF NOW 123
Benediction 123
Our natural home 128
Only *now* is real 131
"Heart" 132
Already awake in the eternal now 132
Pierced by dying 133
No time here 136
Time no longer 136
It is 136
The siren song of time 137
Now is inconceivable 138
In the heart lies the deathless 140
Time is thought 140
A subtle delicacy 141
Oh, there is no time 143

Only now *is* — 145
An answering hand — 146
I don't know — 149
Not it — 151
Home in the heart of now — 152
Let's stop calling it "now" — 153
Let's *really* stop calling it "now" — 154
Infinity of the heart — 156
"Our opening and Your entering are one" — 157
PRACTICAL POSSIBILITIES — 158
Noticing noticing — 158
In no particular order — 161
Causeless love — 163
   Awakening noticing — 163
   Radical awakening — 164
   Before thinking decides for us — 165
Your experience is…? — 166
I am conscious — 168
The natural state of nobody — 172
Everything is perfect — 173
To be still — 176
It makes no sense — 178
Everything is in my heart — 181
We can't get there — 182
This will fade from view — 183
Radical stillness — 185
In quietude — 186
Be here now, redux — 188
Every breath a blessing — 191
Following the breath — 192
Vehicle, gas, driver — 194
Driver, gas, vehicle — 197
Three steps to where you already are — 199
Staying — 201
   Thing-time — 202
   The seeking-glitch — 203
   Glimpses — 205
   Stay — 206

Never having left 207
Burst out laughing 207
The heart of the matter 208
God laughing 209
The cosmic joke 209
A wrinkle in the cosmic joke 211
The seen is the seeing 213
Before the punchline 217
Chasing two truths 219
Countdown to luminosity 222
Wouldn't it be amazing? 226
INFINITY 229
Infinite now 229
Always home in the heart of now 230
You are here and nowhere else 232
Not realizing 236
Occurring by itself 237
The undying heart of the now-moment 238
What this is like 240
Non-duality is the mothership 242
Being here now…again 243
We are a gift of the infinite 244
Everything is included 247
The heart of Buddha-nature 249
Infinite identity 252
Intuition 254
SEEKING 254
Built-in benediction 254
Nonsensical benediction 255
Home free already 256
Stephen Levine: "Pretending to be real" 256
Effortless 258
Why "Stop searching"? 259
What you're pursuing ain't it 260
This can't be searched for 260
RELAXING 261
Thinning veils 261
I am is relaxed 263

There is just nobody   264
There is only now   266
Easy is right   268
REFLECTIONS   269
This which it is   269
The dilemma of the heart   270
How hard can it be to be still?   272
Inescapable us   273
THE HEART OF REALITY   276
Immersion   276
A million times   278
Douglas Harding and the open space of seeing   279
The Headless Way Mini-Kit   280
God is right behind our eyes   282
We don't recognize "ourselves"   284
The greatest mystery   287
  Going NowHere   289
  Inclusive immensity   290
  Searching for what cannot be lost   291
Oh, it's love   293
The journey of return   296
  Only one way   298
  This very moment of now is love   299
  The only time   300
Only "love" will suffice.   300

Notes   303
Acknowledgments   305
About the author   307

Preface: Pixels

On the screen or page, millions of dots convey a picture.

Georges Seurat laid down thousands of dots of color on canvas to convey a warm afternoon by the Seine, a picture we can gaze at endlessly because we are looking at the marvel of the true nature of what we're seeing, and the artist has vanished, enabling us to see directly into timeless reality. This sense of true nature can be seen, or, most importantly, felt.

The words, sentences, paragraphs, pages, and sections in this book are dots of color endeavoring to convey just such a picture. There is some linearity to the book's structure, but much more it resembles a pointillist painting. Reading one chapter you may find yourself saying "But didn't he already say that in a previous section?" And he probably did. The scene in Seurat's picture would be recognizable with only a tenth of the dots—but we wouldn't be affected by the picture in the way that we are. Conversely, the pointillism of this book means that we can dip into it here and there and still get a sense of what the whole of it conveys.

The invitation here is to let ourselves be affected by this offering. It is written more in the spirit of a song than that of a philosophical treatise and we listen to songs for pleasure, for the implicit revelation they give us of the real world, always here, yet often seemingly hidden.

~

Perfectly personal pixels

The many pieces of writing constituting this book emerged by themselves over the last couple of decades. While I lived in the UK, India, Japan, Germany, Holland, Canada, then in California, the book was slowly cooking, in the dark. As continents, work duties, and time zones shifted, and love relationships came and went, I surfed along a wild ride of circumstances that continues to this day. Jon Kabat-Zinn's wonderful phrase "*Full catastrophe living*" comes to mind.

I was a student, then a seeker, and alongside that, a bicycle store owner—then a devotee, later a heavy equipment mechanic, and beyond that, a deep tissue bodyworker, followed by becoming a personal coach, ending up with my role these days as a licensed psychotherapist.

The most important part of many of those days came in the morning, sitting down quietly with a cup of tea (and in earlier epochs, a cigarette), contemplating: What is the inescapable nature of this life? What is really happening here, deep beneath the habitual waves that thinking provides to explain it all?

Over these years, part of the morning was to send a greeting to a longtime friend, along with a quotation plucked from my quotation collection, almost all of which consists of remarks by people who have some degree of realization of the deep nature of reality.

A quotation is only in my collection because it has for me a quality I call "resonance," meaning, the distinctive luminosity of the words reflects wisdom already within myself that I have not quite yet been able to put in language. Yet here is the luminosity, appearing in the words of another, words that shimmer with truthfulness, and move me; there is shining beauty and happiness.

Consequently, many of the pieces of writing that make up this book come in a flow with quotations that they both derive from, and contribute to the sense of. Resonance is, perhaps, one of the most salient signals of the field of experiencing, quietly announcing its limitlessness.

I am a pilgrim in this limitlessness (although a pilgrim would be a separate appearance, which is one of the most marvelous, even miraculous productions of the limitlessness). Sometimes I seem to myself to be one more in the endless net of jewels that reach towards the light—that is their own light. At other times, I appear to myself as an utterly separate person, with all the above autobiography true, and it would then be accurate to describe me as the author of this book.

If I say I wrote these pieces it will not be entirely accurate, any more than it is fully true to say these pieces wanted to be written. That the limitlessness yearns to discover itself is unmistakably true; just so, like stepping stones, quotations give voice to the satisfaction of this longing. Every piece of writing herein comes from the very same source.

The book has taught me a good deal. Each piece of writing composing it reflects some moment or period of insight, but to give overarching expression to it in the form of a small phrase, *Home Already* has been a helpful encapsulation and reminder.

The additional subtitular reminder, *In the Heart of Now*, points at any one moment to the center of my chest. Then, when even this heart becomes translucent to the ever-present eternity of the center of all of us—to the essence of our true nature, home already, in the heart of now—the title sings the truth of itself, to itself.

Buddhist realization and commentary figures extensively in these pages: the resonance of Buddhist wisdom comes from the closeness of its observations to the truth of reality, which turns out to be *now*.

Now contains the central secret of every enlightened mystic who has ever lived. As all those mystics have said, this secret is intrinsically and freely available to each one of us at all times, no exceptions.

Perhaps we've read *ad nauseam* about the fact that now is really not that minuscule fragment of time in between the past and future. But very few people find themselves compelled to penetrate that speck as the gradual unfolding of the recognition that the kernel of now is all that really exists.

This speck, this kernel, is quite profoundly obscured by concepts, or the astounding cleverness of concepts hide the simplicity of the heart's clear nature-as-now. Concepts imply the existence of a world that does not actually exist in the way it is implied. Our human preoccupation is with concepts—I, me, mine being the most compelling of these—and we tend to only rarely notice the pearl beyond price that is unendingly here in the heart of now; intrinsically present every instant, even in obscuration.

Introduction

Home already

We are already home.

Except, we have never left. Except, leaving is impossible; completely, utterly, totally impossible. (This can be noticed, and eventually will be noticed, even if the ultimate realization of it happens in dying.)

Leaving is impossible because *now* is home, and *we* are home —and home is us. We are inseparable from home, and always have been. This inseparability is a mystery to thinking, but to the core heart of us, is the clear nature of reality.

The phrase *"Home already"* itself has two meanings; one of them implies that we intrinsically constitute home itself all the time, already—while the other meaning points to the fact that we are resident in that home at all times: the "we" that is resident is nothing other than the home itself.

But "we" have misidentified ourselves (and the mistake is inevitable, natural, and universal—as well as merely a mirage). We, never-ever-leaving, have come to believe we are solely some-thing—and indeed, the "thing" will die and rot, or burn; all "things" do. But "we" are not a thing, and never have been a thing.

"We"—what we are—is not subject to dying and is outside time entirely. We have always been outside time, effortlessly outside time. We are outside time this very moment, and this can readily be noticed—by turning attention to where we see from. If this reversal of the direction of attention happens from the space of the heart, this noticing of the timeless undying will be much more vivid.

"We" are timeless no-thing. "We" always have been timeless no-thing, and if attention reverses as we read these words, so there's noticing of the space of seeing, the timeless no-thing will be apparent. It never changes: this is us, and this is home, and the seeming-two of these, "us" and "home" are not-two, and never have been two. The heart sees this directly and immediately.

"We" have never changed or altered one iota. Change or alteration is as impossible for us as leaving is. "Our" change-lessness and timelessness makes it possible to notice all change, and all time. Our utter inseparability from all-and-everything makes possible the profound relaxation that is being, forever now: quite literally; being home already.

What follows is based purely on what each of us can notice by giving close attention to the life we already have. Looked into deeply, life reveals itself as the miracle we gradually learned to neglect and eventually forgot. Then we seem to be lost; nothing but solo-separate-selves wandering through time, searching for fulfillment.

But all the time, we are home already—and leaving home, it turns out, is completely and utterly impossible.

Our journey of looking deeply at life for ourselves is paradoxical, for it is never possible to be somewhere other than our destination, yet our travels continue. When time is stood aside, as it were, even for a moment, there can be the sheer revelation of our already-destination, and we are it.

This being "stood-aside" from time is *already* our reality, for it is the nature of now, which we never for a moment leave. The heart knows only now; time itself is a construct of thought.

Time out

The difficulty with measuring the passage of time—actually, the *impossibility* of measuring time's passing, which we consider to be measuring time itself—is that *no such entity exists.*

Every single means we have to measure seeming-time-passing is nothing but counting *events*; the sun's shadow at one point, then at another, the sequential tick-tocks of a watch, or the 9 billion-and-counting pulses emitted by a particular kind of substance under very precisely controlled conditions. These are all *events*, from which we abstract time. (Physicists are in complete agreement with these perspectives here, remarking that nothing in known physics corresponds to the passage of time; time, they say, simply *is.**)

---

* A United States government agency, the National Institute of Standards and Time states, on the agency's website in 2024: "Time has no physical properties to measure." Paul Davies, Regents' Professor at Arizona State University and director of The Beyond Center for Fundamental Concepts in Science wrote, in 2014: "Nothing in known physics corresponds to the passage of time. Indeed, physicists insist that time doesn't flow at all; it merely is."

*You have just to understand that time periods have no real exis-
tence; hence the attainment of the vital intuition occurs neither
within nor without a five-hundred-year period.*

— Huang Po

Leaving aside the profoundly useful utility of time, what remains? What is always here? What effortlessly endures, absent the past that is no more, and the future that is not yet?

We call it "now," but we are so convinced it is just the tiniest speck of time that we don't examine it. We tend to neglect some simple realities of now, such as: that *it* is *never* not now—and *we* are *never* not now. "It" and "we" are not divided.

Naturally, we tend to think of ourselves as separate, but this is entirely an artifact of time, which is built-in to our human functioning. Nonetheless, time does not exist other than as an essential element of our human cognition; the unlimited kernel that is behind thought lives eternally *now*.

Undivided dividedness

The following parts of our exploratory journey can be easily summarized: life as we live it is completely undivided, and this non-dividedness is our eternal home. *Life* is never not now, and *we* are never not now, and these seeming-two, "life" and "we" are not two, and never have been two—except in thinking.

*...all attempts to arrive at where you already are are going to
fail.*

— Paul Hedderman

In reality—which includes thinking, but is different from how thinking presents it—there is quite simply undivided now, and we are intrinsically it, *for there is no dividedness*, except in the marvels wrought by thought. Thought is like magic, an astonishing miracle conjuring the spell *that there is something other than now.*

Even so much as to call it "now" is to pretend it is a thing, the way words, ideas, language and concepts completely imply the things that seem to make up our world. But when there is complete silence of thought, or we carefully observe a non-thinking being like a lizard or a fish, what we call "now" goes on quite simply being as it is: absolutely dependable, never not here, solid as a mountain.

Now being "dependable," "solid as a mountain," and "never not here" again makes "now" sound like a thing; like a thought-of thing. But in these paragraphs here, we are amidst a winding descent out of thinking, closer and closer to the directly-experienced reality of now in the heart; and what we can notice is that despite being absolutely dependable, never not here, and solid as a mountain, now is nothing but change.

Nothing but change

Turning our noticing to different parts of our experience, unceasing dynamic change is perfectly evident: eyes flicker and light constantly varies as the visual world unfolds before us. What we might call sound or hearing is defined by alteration—and even a perfectly consistent and continuous "C" note is made of ripples that can be subtly felt. The constant fluctuations of taste and smell bring us to savor a great meal, entirely distinct from the whiff of cigarette smoke drifting outside the restaurant. The sense of touch is encompassing, almost synonymous with existing, yet when we bring close and curious attention to any part of our feeling sensations, they will readily be noticed to subtly tingle, shimmer, twinkle and ripple.

The part of our experience we call "thinking" is perhaps the most dynamic of all. Thoughts show up ceaselessly, and in sleep, become dreams, fabricating worlds that vanish like mist when we wake in the morning. Thinking seems able to do just about everything, and anything.

For instance, thinking can try to do the undoable (the way these words are doing): to embrace, describe and encompass now, even though thinking (these very words here) knows this is impossible.

Pointing at us

Why is this task undertaken by thinking impossible? *Because reality is undivided*—as we can know directly from our heart, perfectly clearly, without thinking.

Now cannot be adequately thought about, for the simple reason that thought always lumbers along in time behind the moment of now, which goes on dancing merrily ahead, just as it is, and just as it will. This dancing is life's pleasure and life's joy, even if it also contains pain and suffering; it is as it is, undividedly.

> *The Seeker is the found,*
> *The found is the seeker,*
> *As soon as it is apperceived*
> That there is no Time.
>
> — Wei Wu Wei

Thinking is *dividedness*, a trick of human cognition so powerful that almost any heaven, or any hell can be created by it. One thought above all insists on the reality of this dividedness: "I."

"I" is the most prodigious miracle in this whole assembly of marvels we call "life." "I" is woven from the timeless in total intimacy with time (or may I also point in the direction of us both, and say "We are woven"?)

The timeless is now; undivided reality, nothing but change. From this womb of time emerges the colonizing-claiming that there is *only* an I-in-time that is identical with my body; a long-lasting, separately-existing somebody who is born only to die. As we grow up out of childhood, I-in-time, or thought-I, becomes solely and totally who we believe ourselves to be, and the intrinsic peace, majesty and eternality of our timeless nature is lost to view.

Undividedness—timeless, perfect and unceasingly whole—appears to get *replaced* by dividedness. Eternal-I becomes camouflaged by time-bound-I, and when this cloaking is complete there is only the anxiety and depression of a solo-seeming lonely creature, in time, who knows for sure they are going to die.

Through the veil

Once this veiling has concealed reality, we are gripped by a certain kind of unreality that we are unable to dispel, because the only means now at our disposal is dividedness: thinking. Seeming to be exclusively time-beings, searching for fruition which endlessly eludes us, we appear to loop and loop in time until we die.

But perhaps we are fortunate, and there are moments in our lives when we catch a note that is purely sweet, or we glimpse a truth from we-know-not-where, wisdom that momentarily sings to us, even if thinking does not at all understand it. Perhaps love, grief, great beauty or unbearable anguish pierce us, and we glimpse the undying at our core.

Phrases that have endured down the ages seem luminous, even if the light of them cannot be adequately comprehended, just yet. "*From the very beginning, not a thing is,*" remarks one such phrase, while another, longer exegesis begins "*The great way is not difficult, for those who have no preferences.*" Another venerable wisdom teaching remarks "*You overlook the heart and fill yourself with desire.*"

Quite what it is that calls to us from these unfamiliar depths we do not know—but what may be dimly apparent is that the innermost reach of our being has gone nowhere—indeed, calls out to us with an intuitive luminosity impossible to ignore and completely inaccessible to thought. Never not here, yet outside time, this ultimate depth turns out to also be the vivid surface of things; in fact, there is nowhere to turn that it is not. Our word for it is "now." Now is the home of our heart.

Now, again

Now is completely undivided. This undividedness is behind the palpable goodness of it, underpinning the simple fact that when people facing a problem are asked "*But what about right now?*" they will invariably say that indeed, right *now* is okay—but what about the problem, coming from the past, and looming in the future?

Now can be no other way than it is, *this* very moment. Yet the marvelous, close-to-miraculous cognitive technology of time, woven in total intimacy with timeless now, endlessly brings the new into being.

This technology is so dazzling in its power and effectiveness that it entirely usurps the space of our attention, as if time is all there is. But now is all that *is*, in reality, and time (as well as all concepts) are born within now's timelessness.

Crucially, timelessness and time can seem distinct and separate *but they are not-two*. This is known immediately and directly through the heart. Life is *inherently* undivided; this non-separateness cannot at all, ever be undone—there is no such thing as dividedness, no matter how compelling the appearance of things. Life is one as we live it, and "we," despite appearances, are the totality of this living now. There is nothing else, and never has been. We are not just "at" home; we *are* home itself and cannot not be.

In the heart of now

You're never going to get it because you are it.

— Paul Hedderman

In the Heart of Now affirms we are home already—and being anything other than home is absolutely impossible. This "home" (which, in the ancient East, they pronounced with a London Cockney accent, as in "*Om*") can only ever be *now*, for there is nothing else. We are in the heart of now already.

We imagine now has something to do with time, but this is the mental version of now; the now we live, always and ever, is outside time. Only the heart deeply relaxes in this timeless reality, not at all the time-spinning head; now is intrinsic to the heart, for there is nothing else. The heart of now is the reality of life; the vivid, can-be-felt actuality that is the miracle of our lives.

For the time-weaving thought-mind of the head, now is just a springboard to get somewhere; to reach toward peace, contentment and happiness. This striving has astonishing power (typing on this laptop would be an example of this potency at work)—but it also has an unequalled capacity to prompt misery in the form of perennial chasing, *as if we are not already at home.* The heart knows that home is nowhere other than now; knows that leaving is impossible, and that pursuing something that does not exist camouflages this reality.

We have been taught that time-being is our sole nature, and until we look as deeply as possible for ourselves, this conviction does not dissolve. When the chasing pauses, or finally stops, in the complete failure of it, everything that was ever pursued turns out to be right here, right now: in the heart of now.

~

A story right now

The personal stories appearing in the inset sections—like this one—are intended to provide some leavening. "Facts tell, and stories sell" remarks an old marketing adage, pointing to what interests and motivates us.

My hope for these narratives is to illustrate wisdom—an energy all of its own and not belonging to anyone—poking through the fog of life's confusion; the story of such moments can be evocative, and provoke resonance. Books of this kind tend to seem offered from on high.

Perhaps in part this is because life is grubby, humbling, and filled with difficulty. We are powerfully drawn to the possibility of there being some sought-after depth in life that is luminous without conditions, even in great darkness.

Home Already

Life is like getting onto a small boat that is about to sail out to sea and sink.

— Suzuki Roshi

Paradoxically, those sages, yogis, avatars and mystics who talk about any kind of progression along this journey tend to talk more about bliss than about suffering. Seekers after awakening tend to be bliss-chasers. Relatively few paths to this fruition flat-out say that the end of the journey is exactly right here, at the beginning of it.

But if this truth, this reality can be gently borne in mind as we follow the story unfolded here, we can both appreciate how these things unfold in time—and perhaps see reflected our own journey of discovering, more and more deeply, that the fabled promised land is forever here-now (only we seem not to be).

All distress in life gestures in the direction of this truth: suffering inherently points to the end of suffering. "Suffering" is a term that appears dozens of times in these pages. Mention of suffering is never intended to misrepresent life, which is full of joys as well as sorrows. Counter to New Age preconception, the wisdom traditions are clear that 10,000 joys and 10,000 sorrows are the nature of life; what isn't generally spoken about is the tension and distortion we experience within ourselves when we try, in any way forcefully, to get the joys up to 15,000, and the sorrows down to 5,000.

This kind of trying is inherently full of suffering, even if it is supposedly in pursuit of more joys. This book is not at all about trying to change in this way; when life just as it is is welcomed, or even just allowed, our inherent luminosity begins to become gradually apparent to us.

It is here, in the very midst of life, as it is, that a certain kind of impeccable sovereignty is discovered to be unceasing and beyond harm. This "impeccable sovereignty" is absorbing the meaning of these words, this moment.

A further nuance about seeking is a paradox: anyone giving this book any more than a cursory glance will likely be impelled by what is sometimes in Buddhism called "the way-seeking mind." They will have an aspiration to awaken, or to resolve their suffering, or to understand the real nature of existence.

This aspiration is not voluntary, but our deepest essence singing to us—in the only way possible. When this essence is found to be timeless, and intrinsically limitless in space, there can be an understanding of the phrase "This that exists through itself is the Way." And this, the Way-seeking mind, calls our attention to these pages.

If you are the type of person who is looking for this sort of thing, you are the type of person who will find it.

— Kōten Benson

Abundant quotations appear in these pages; quotations are a very important source of resonance. A quotation may resonate when first seen, but be very puzzling. When insight deepens, the puzzlement will resolve in a most satisfactory way. In this resolution, the resonance and the remark quoted become deeply confirmatory of each other.

Many of the more challenging to comprehend quotations herein come from Wei Wu Wei, who published a series of books between 1958 and 1974 offering, in fresh form, the insights of a Westerner steeped experientially in the contemplative intuitions of Buddhism and Taoism.

Wei Wu Wei remarks: *"Authority is comforting, let us seek it."*

Indeed.

Part One

Foundations

Foundations

Right about now

The architecture of remembering

We may have begun to notice, however fleetingly, that now is not something to attain, but what we already are—timeless, undivided, intrinsically awake. This buoyantly-present recognition invites us deeply toward ourselves, with all the power of yearning in our heart.

This journey—always to NowHere—is into the wisdom at the core of us: the unceasing, unstoppable open-secret intrinsic to our being. Along the road of it, we may come to discover that this that exists through itself is intrinsically the way—and that the journey is illuminated from within itself, at all times. Our curiosity comes to rest on aspects of this inherent lambency, and the following sections in Part One reflect this light.

Knowing now

We all know now. Female, male or something else, Black, brown, beige or white, rich or poor, young or old; whether our language is Russian, Greek, Mandarin or English, now is our universal possession. Non-literate people possess now with just as great an abundance as the most scholarly. Babies, before language develops have an immediacy and nowness about them that's unmistakable.

Or perhaps we are universally possessed by now: now seems to be the deepest possible meaning of "something existing." For something to exist, it must exist now and this is true of trees and puppies, of clouds and birds—and books, words, and ideas. Snails and microbes appear and disappear in now, and while I may be able to remember a particular snail I saw yesterday, the memory only has meaning now.

We possess now, and we are possessed by now: both are simultaneously true. Language tends to suggest that "we" possess "now"—or "now" possesses "us." Both seem equally true, but the concepts start to fragment and vanish as we move closer to the inescapable mystery of the moment. Now needs no concept whatsoever to exist: isn't now always here, even before the thought of it?

Put another way, now is unbound by concepts. Now is fresh, and if we check carefully and repeatedly for ourselves we will find that now is never not fresh. Concepts are stale, while reality is ever new. Reality, what we are-and-are-possessed-by, what we call "now," is sublimely indifferent to whether concepts are trying to encompass it or not. Reality itself seems to possess an unlimited freedom to be just as it is.

Limitless now

As we explore now it will be helpful to remember that the word and concept are not what is perennially here, always changing. Now is conventionally regarded as the momentary doorway between past and future, a brief instant of time sandwiched between two immensities. But when those immensities vanish for a moment—think of orgasm, a car accident, the moment of a sneeze, or falling deeply in love—now is as it is: timeless, limitless, and completely free.

Perhaps saying "limitless" can seem exaggerated, particularly if we fully believe the conventional view of things in which there is a limited "me" looking out at a world that is "other." But the closer we move to momentary now the less we will find those conventional distinctions being true. Some kind of inherent, essential me-ness persists in the middle of momentariness, but it has no separate nature from everything, until concepts come up and claim separation.

There is only now.

— Scott Morrison

This inherent, essential me-ness is very enriching to explore within ourselves, experientially, now. It is self-existing, and although it can seem like it belongs to Jane, Richard, Dave or Camille, it's here before those concepts make a claim to any such belonging. Convention says it belongs to me, Glenn, elderly, and sitting in front of my computer—but when conventional logic falls silent, as it does in between every thought, this intrinsic awareness goes nowhere; it is causeless.

"I am" has been proposed as the only adequate way to give language to the inconceivable mystery in the middle of now's momentariness. Contemplating "I am" is a deep meditation close to the heart of now. But when we strip ourselves as conceptually bare as possible to go even closer to this heart of existing we find something more like am-ness; sheer being.

> *Ordinarily we say 'I am'. In that state, when you are deep in love with yourself, 'I' disappears. Only amness, pure existence, pure being remains.*

> — Osho

Deep now

At this depth of exploration—amidst "deep now," we might say—we are no longer using clunky sequential concepts that always come along later, too late to be useful in this immensity of nowness. Intuition, direct apperception (the latter a word that is sometimes defined as "inner awareness"), or immediate direct experiencing start to become our way of knowing and sensing. While we can give voice to our intuitive immediacy, direct experiencing comes first and language second. Direct experiencing is that which occurs at all times by itself, with or without thought.

For instance, in the heart of now we may begin to discern that this being-ness, this am-ness has an immediately evident and miraculous quality: it knows itself. There is no division between knower and known at this level of immediacy. Being-ness, existing-ness cannot help but also be knowing-ness, or awareness. Concepts say things exist apart from awareness: in the heart of now is a miracle in plain view: no such dividedness.

Awareness can only be apperceived, i.e., realized by a knowing that is beyond perception. Apperception liberates one… and exposes one to infinite freedom. Apperception is the proof that consciousness is all there is.

— Stanley Sobottka

Another miracle: this undividedness is the nature of everyone and everything; sometimes it is called "true nature." True nature, the heart of now, is without dividedness—not two. "Two" only comes later, when thought casts its spell.

The miracle of undividedness in the heart of now has the quality of a divine gift when it begins to be noticed consciously. All of us exist helplessly now, and the essence of now, the very heart of it, is this undividedness. From the very beginning, we are all, without exception, undivided.

My eye and God's eye are one eye, one seeing, one knowing, one love.

— Meister Eckhart

Equally miraculous is the unending great perfection of the heart of now. This perfection is not by comparison with any standard, but perfect in immediacy, as it is, when the trailing shadows of thought and judgment are stood to one side.

Wise now

Recognizable too, here in the heart of now, are many foundational truths endlessly elaborated in the great wisdom traditions of the world. Impermanence is the most obvious of them, for nothing in the heart of now can be secured or held.

Intuitive apperception also makes it apparent that now is nothing but the eternally permanent flow of impermanence.

Freshness and aliveness are also unmistakably here in the heart of now, along with the endless upwelling of the unexpected. Impermanence is aliveness and vitality, but we only have to go out into nature to notice that the vibrancy of spring is indivisible from the deathly downturning of winter. Undividedness doesn't just reunite knower and known, but also life and death.

Here too, in the vivid immediacy of the heart of now can be found the most profound and surprising implication of Buddha's discovery of impermanence: the self, separated from the world, is only one of the infinite number of reifying spells cast by thought. Nothing, not even the "self" has any permanent essence.

> *The now-moment in which God made the first man, and the now-moment in which the last man will disappear, and the now-moment in which I am speaking are all one in God, in whom there is only one now.*
>
> — Meister Eckhart

Buddha is believed to have sat down underneath a particularly accommodating tree and said, we might imagine: "Enough already, I'm through with people teaching me things; I have to find out for myself, and by myself. I will sit underneath this tree until I've realized the deepest truth of everything."

We are following the same process here, using the same means. When we dive into the heart of now—which is any moment when the dictatorial conceptual mind is silent or ignored—there is a dawning realization, available to direct experience, of the gift of existing being intrinsically aware of itself.

The fabric of now

And the fabric of this gift? Love seems to be most obviously its nature, although because we identify as separate beings who are sometimes loving and sometimes hateful, love seems able to come and go. But whenever we reside in the heart of now we will find that being here now is helplessly love.

Perhaps "love" is too loaded a word for us to use. We might instead become present to the sensations of our body, because they, too, are palpable in the heart of now. We call them sensations but perhaps a broader term for our immediate apperception of this is "energy."

We have energies divided into categories like "seeing," "hearing," "tasting," and "touching," but the moment we dip closer to deep now and the labels can fall away, a torrent of energy becomes noticeable. Except conceptually, we cannot find a boundary where sounds stop and bodily sensations begin: all is energy.

The visual realm is where dividedness is most compelling to us. If we sit quietly without switching on artificial light, as the day ends and the light goes down, we may find that the distant hills, as well as the features of the room where we sit begin to dissolve into a sea of dancing points of light. These are shimmering just the way the energy of our body tingles.

When darkness is complete—or right now, if we subsequently close our eyes and inspect what we notice behind closed eyelids—we will find experientially a field seemingly composed of an uncountable number of infinitesimally tiny light particles. *Where* these exist is impossible to know, except conceptually. By what are they known? In the heart of now we may discover that any such distinctions can only be conceptual, not existential.

This question of where do things occur only has one answer: here. Things have location relative to one another—but separate things are not the nature of the undividedness in the heart of now. Separate things, with their possibility of having location relative to one another, are conceptual add-ons. The idea and image of "me," here, looking at these words, is one such add-on.

There are many ways to explore what "here" means, and all such roads of exploration lead to limitlessness. Turning our gaze 180° or pointing our finger towards the place from which we look, we can contemplate in the heart of now the experiencing so revealed. We gaze directly out of limitlessness—but please, don't take my word for it, we have to look for ourselves. This limitlessness is the obvious meaning of "here," although it gently erases all but conceptual meaning to "here," the finite distance between two demonstrable entities.

Turning attention to the energies of our body we can see if we can discern where our backside stops and the chair supporting us starts. Not only will we find no such place apparent in direct experience but the dimensions of this energetic realm are completely impossible to determine—except in terms of the conventional conceptual map which offers a clearly demarcated boundary where "myself" ends and "the chair" begins.

All is well now

Now has one singular and remarkable property: all is well in the heart of now. Animals seem not to have access to anything other than now. Walt Whitman, saying he could turn and live with animals, remarks that "*Not one is respectable or unhappy over the whole earth.*" Could it be that the cheerfulness displayed by my dogs is simply because they know nothing else but now is real, and all is well in the heart of now?

In the heart of now—our universal reality—there is undividedness. All is as it is—flowing, fluid, impermanent, perfect and sheer blessing. Another word for undividedness is wholeness, and wholeness is the root meaning from which the word "healing" comes. Healing is not, in the depth of itself, anything but a return to undividedness. This return happens whenever going anywhere ceases, whereupon healing is intrinsically revealed to be the nature of now. "Going anywhere" is the domain of the thinking mind, which can only access the past and future, memory and imagination. Now is the whole.

Now is awake

Now is awake. But we don't go there, because mind has nothing to do there. Or rather, "go *here*," because we cannot go here, to now: we *exist here* all the time, without exception, the only utter and complete certainty of our lives.

This is a massive paradox. We exist in the arms of goodness at all times—yet we can be tortured by a stream of thoughts constantly promising to take us to goodness, once the desires behind the thoughts are fulfilled. A different stream of thoughts and experiences fight back badness.

We don't go here partly because mind has nothing to do here, and partly because we are unfamiliar with the nature of our own being, which is here-now and nowhere else. So it can be helpful to become familiar, or more familiar, with what our own being is like.

Nowness-awareness is the authentic, unfabricated Buddha.

— Dudjom Rinpoche

The only way to find this out is through our own experience. We can play with turning towards what we notice, and be curious there. We can find out for ourselves if thinking a lot and constantly being busy with the past and the future leads to the same quality of relaxation as the effortless simplicity of being exactly where we are, right now.

Am I something other than this nowness? I have definitely been heavily trained and also have extensively practiced being something else, but I personally must confess at this point, in a long lifetime of such practice, that I am a failure. Being something other than this nowness has not worked out for me. The peace I was seeking in that other, separate, and practiced way of life has eluded me. But this practiced separateness, and the failure of it, has left behind the discovery of the non-seeking peace intrinsic to this nowness.

We can live this nowness but we cannot possess it. In order to pretend to possess it we have to turn ourselves into something separate from it, and then we are so deeply miserable that our only seeming option is to obey the dictates of the mind that says it has the solution for getting out of this misery. But the real solution is to eliminate the problem at the root of it; take the no-journey back to nowness and find out if our pretending to be separate from it is reality.

Pretending will make us miserable. Being in reality is happiness, because reality is already happy and can be no other way. We can have plans, by all means, but if our being is conditional on the outcome of the plans, beware. Our being is always here, now, and the plans are playful and creative—or serious and destructive—but always lovingly-supportive of creature-survival.

However, we make a giant mistake: we believe our conceptualized past-and-future self *is* solely our self.

This conditioned misidentification will be default unless we become more familiar with what our own being is like. So let's take a look at it.

We can approach this a few different ways. One of them is to recognize that "our own being" was here when we were born, at a time when we were wordless. When thought is silent, or suspended, or we look over the shoulder of it, our being is obvious, although we may find it difficult to give words to it. Effortlessly implicit in the noticing of our being is the here-nowness of it.

"Our being" can be confusing; is this like "our stomach," or "our shoes?" Something is here that is unmistakably very much ours—but so much so that it is more like "us" than "ours."

What we are—"us"—cannot see what we are, any more than we can bite our own teeth, or our eyes can directly see our own eyes. There is an experience, however, but this experience has no experience-er; it is whole and undivided and complete, moment by moment.

We can't get away from it (although we can seem to, by using thought-which-comes-later). It is always now, or rather, it is nowness itself. Before we can think a thought about it, it is already here; already whole, already perfect.

We can also reverse the direction of our attention, and notice that the core and essence of us is completely empty and silent. Again, when words about this fall away, the miracle of non-separate being is clearly revealed. There is no dividedness between this empty clarity and everything that fills it. Only the convictions of thinking and the propulsion of going some-where hide this reality from us.

Home Already

The secret key point of mind is that its nature is a self-existing, original wakefulness.

— Tulku Urgyen Rinpoche

We can engage the meditation of seeking awareness, then find that it is discovered only when all seeking activity comes to a halt. In the silence that ensues, everything is known to be just as it is; immensely peaceful and without limits. When words fall away, when seeking stops for a moment, the encompassing immensity may stagger us.

If we follow powerful and inspired intuitions or insights—such as the one given to me 20 years ago that *What I seek is now*—we will find the intuitions were emanations from the greatest depth of ourselves, where awakening is already buoyantly drifting upward to the surface. This buoyancy is the unstoppable nature of awakening.

In what follows, *now*, periodically in italics, refers to this very moment, before there can even be a thought about it. It is always here, no matter what. Each time *now* occurs in the following pages, we can be reminded *we are already within this moment*, exactly as we live it. The nature of our heart *is* this withinward total intimacy—and the outward world. Undivided.

～

Preliminaries: Nuts and bolts

Truth is.

— Osho

What is really true is wordless. It exists—it is real, but the moment we give words to it, it becomes something else. For instance, unless we've explored what it's like to be aware, we might firmly believe our universal human story, which is the presence of an observer—ourselves—looking at the outside world from within ourselves.

But when we explore being aware we find that the story always comes after the fact, in a thought. In the middle of *now*, where we always already are, that story isn't true. However, the moment we do give words to what's true we'll find the "really true" has vanished from view. It gets replaced with concepts, and while these are enormously useful, they also create a great deal of trouble.

Everything in this book is already within our own experience: this book is about now, and we are always already here, *now*. But to pay attention to parts of our experience we may not have noticed asks for a certain attunement, and these preliminaries provide that.

Perhaps **DIRECT EXPERIENCING** is the most essential of these attunements. Now is available to us through experiencing, or more precisely, *now is* direct experiencing. When this experiencing is re-told through the lens of concepts, timelessness vanishes from view and time enters the picture. But the experiencing available *now*—direct experiencing—is always here, always available, always pristine and new. Repeatedly touching into direct experiencing gradually dissolves the compulsivity of the lens of concepts.

Little of what's in this book is given to us in our conventional conditioning and education. However, the world is full of an infinite diversity of thoughts, beliefs, and perspectives: how do we listen for the views and voices that are true for us, really true, in a way that ushers us toward our own direct experience? How do we discover our own authority in a world full of seeming-authorities?

Cultivating **RESONANCE**—intuition amplified and grounded by sensing our bodies—will help us discern teachings that are right for us, as well as distinguish what is really true for us from ideas that seduce by their bright shininess and promises, but are often false.

Cultivating resonance is also cultivating awareness of inner space; and flowing out of that cultivation, progressively finding and trusting our own true and unique compass bearing. Gradually, this knowing emerges into clarity; it was always here, but hardly noticeable beneath the white noise of habitual thinking.

A perfect example of experience hiding in full view is available in the practice of **BODY SENSING**. We may find that in the beginning of sensing our body, we will tend to compulsively refer to the images, thoughts and concepts *about* our body that we have been conditioned to believe *is* our body. Leaning again and again, with persistence and curiosity into the difference between this mental activity and actually sensing our body substantially expands awareness as well as giving us access to a source of wisdom that has been evolving for many millennia.

This source of wisdom—our sensed body—is our biological connection to now, quite simply because our body exists now, and only *now*. The images of our bodies, and the beliefs, thoughts and concepts that make up the conventional "sense" of our body all make reference to time, past or future. All that is quite different than the actuality of *now*, accessible through direct body sensing.

When we go out into nature we may recognize that the natural world exists solely in this timeless time of now, and is absolutely at ease with birth, life, and death; with catastrophe and with blessing. The natural world can open a door to the nature of *now* that can be directly known through immediate sensing. Our sensed bodies are equally just such a doorway.

> *It is a common idea that feeling differs from knowledge, and that its content is less clear. The alleged unclarity of feeling means nothing more than that it cannot be expressed in conceptual knowledge. It is not that consciousness in feeling is unclear, but rather that feeling is a more subtle and delicate form of consciousness than conceptual knowledge.*
>
> — Nishida Kitaro

MEDITATION has a vast range of meanings in our world. When we sincerely try out a few of these approaches—focusing on a mantra in TM style, giving zazen a go, or closing our eyes and affirming abundance—we may find ourselves confused. The ancient roots of the word "meditation" say that something in this activity is quintessential for discovering the nature of being, but give few clues about it.

"*Regarding the basic nature*" is how one old Chinese sage alluded to meditation, pointing us in the direction indicated by words like "contemplation." Modern sages like Jean Klein say pithy and provocative things, such as that the only purpose of meditation is to discover that there is not a meditator. Should we sit down and look for the meditator—whereupon we will only be able to find *thoughts* of such an entity—we are then potentially open to the universality and globality of "*regarding the basic nature*," which turns out to be everywhere. And deeply mysterious.

> *Meditation . . . is a way of investigating for yourself—in your own body, in your own mind, upon your own authority, upon the authority of your own experience.*

> — Adyashanti

This kind of profound and objectless curiosity— *What the heck is really going on here?* —calls on direct experiencing, employs resonance and the amplified truthfulness of body sensing— and makes obvious that meditation is not only something done during formal practice or at particular times. Rather, meditation is the inhabitation of a certain kind of ongoing curiosity fueled by the deepest longing to come home—as well as suffused by an intuition that this coming home is already actually here, and already the case.

The basic nature—our basic nature—is unshakably anchored in *now*. Now and the basic nature turn out to be identical to each other. "Awareness" is another term for this basic nature, but let us be reminded that any sense of this being cut off from the content of awareness runs the grave risk that the words (awareness + content) might imply that there are two separate things *in reality*, when this isn't true and never has been.

The penultimate section of these preliminaries is about **VULNERABILITY**, but it could just as well have referred to connectedness, authenticity, sincerity, or reaching deep into ourselves. Any really muscular exploration of who and what we are asks us to have skin in the game.

There's a riskiness about this inquiry that asks us for the highest level of rigor we are capable of. Without this rigor, known to us as vulnerability, sincerity, and deep authenticity, we'll be too tempted to default to what we've been taught to believe. Rejoining the familiar collective of beliefs is comforting in a certain way, but it can also be a betrayal of what we set out to do, which is to find out what's really happening here.

Finally, **NEGATION**, here called "the sharpest tool." We learned very early in life to identify ourselves as someone and something. These identifications were all erroneous, without exception, but in order to belong, taking them on was inescapable.

We want nothing but the safety and protection of being a member of the tribe, and this desire is not optional, but baked-in biologically. *But we are not, and have never been what we have identified ourselves as*—and a pervasive misery that has no discernible cause quietly tells us so. Negation is very simply "What I can notice *cannot* be me." All our identifications are *noticeable*, and once we begin to inhabit the experience of identifications vanishing through negation, what remains is impossible to say *but is unmistakably what we cannot not be.*

DIRECT EXPERIENCING

Of every direct perception, however luminous it may be, we should know that to the majority of the readers of its expression it will appear nonsensical, to a minority a mystery, and to a very few a faint reflection of a luminosity that glimmers within themselves. For it is the nature of such expression to appear impenetrable to the deductions of the objectivising mind.

— Wei Wu Wei

Direct experiencing is a marvelous porthole into the micro-minutia of experience. It's an opportunity to find out what is really here.

Frankly, this section is something of a trick. Any suggestion to find reality is inherently tricky, because what is sought is already here. In direct experience everything is as it is. This is the end of the Zen search; finally arriving at the culmination of the path, and discovering that what we essentially are is always here, every step of the way. Right *now*.

But that's not how we live most of the time.

We inhabit a world constructed according to *thought*. Many of us have wonderful and deep relationships with those who do not live in this world of thought—babies, pets, horses, wild creatures. We may feel something akin to reverence for the ordinary-yet-sacred space they inhabit with such grace. However, most adults, most of the time, seem to live else-where. This "elsewhere" is the world of *thought*.

> *It may seem we are on a path, but we are always back where we started.*
>
> — Rupert Spira

The thought-world certainly gives us a remarkable gift: we can draw from the past, from memories. We can create abundant possibilities in an imaginary time we call the future. This extraordinary capacity has led to our becoming the planet's predominant species. With this, we are the only creatures on the planet that experience the anguish that comes from mistaking our creatively-brilliant fantasies of future possibility with the nature of our essential essence.

Only direct experience can provide the platform from which this writing proceeds. Direct experience is wordless: as inti-mate as it is possible to be; never not here, and the very core of our life. Here, words are used as tools of expression, not as the root and ground of experience.

In these pages we'll often be welcomed to discover what is so in our own direct experience. We are invited to a realm of ourselves that is always here and now—before thought tells us what's so.

We are our own authority

How do we enter this realm of here-and-now? By staying with and not going away from our experience—and landing down and down and down within it until we can go no further, finding ourselves in the now, the inescapable now. *Thought* can no more represent this changeless-yet-infinitely-changing realness than a valley-echo can convey the timeless majesty of a mountain scene in the deep wilderness.

We enter this dimension of ourselves by recognizing that we are our own authority. We inhabit this authority quite simply by becoming fed up with the endless circling that is all that thought can provide as a guide to the truth. Of course this is not in any way to deny the utility of thought (such as for writing this book): it is essential to the revelation of our own being.

> *The eternal present, the now-moment, the interval between thoughts, which we normally never perceive, alone is real. Past and Future are a duality of which Present is the reality. The now-moment alone is eternal and real.*
>
> — Wei Wu Wei

As for our own being, thought is *included* in it, but pretends to encompass it entirely. An analogy uses a toaster, a TV and thought. The toaster cannot know the electricity grid upon which it is dependent for its functioning. Nor can a character on a TV screen have any possibility of knowing the totality of the television experience. Thought is a toaster, or a character on the TV screen: it is known, but it has no self-essence of its own. But it pretends to have. This pretension is what we take to be who we really are.

But, again, we are our own final authority. This is very different from dogmatically asserting our opinions, or recycling those of others. For, in the end, the authority that we are can only be *what* we are; what we truly and inescapably are.

Nothing except our own authority will enable us to deepen our self-knowing wisdom. Scriptural revelation or the wisdom of anybody else, no matter how true and profound, is utterly puny and without power compared to the palpable heft of what we discover is true for ourselves.

Dismantling the layers with direct experiencing

So we go into directly experiencing. We inhabit the immediacy of experiencing, repeatedly exploring being-before-thought. "Repeatedly" because the spell woven by thought is remarkably powerful and persistent. To gradually dissolve this spell is to little by little dismantle the dominance of what we have imagined our own self to be.

This mantle of supposed-self has many layers, and each must be repeatedly pierced with direct experiencing. What does the "I" of thought consist of? A listener, a viewer, a feeler, a taster, a smeller—and a thinker.

Direct experiencing gives us an opportunity in the middle of the moment to really notice for ourselves. *Is* there a listener taking in sounds? *Is* there a hearer distinct from the sounds? Or is there, subsequent to the sound, just the thought of such an entity weaving the camouflaging cloak of a thought-self where there is actually nothing of the kind?

Pierce again. *Is* there a viewer seeing the sights of visual perception? Or is this a combination of simply seeing plus a subsequent thought? The chapter *The knack of being* explores this question, bringing experience unfiltered by thought to the forefront. This opens up the most remarkable and yet most often unnoticed mystery in our very midst—that of presence; what we are and cannot not be.

Identifying our experience prior to thought

Now on to the one who feels. What if we were to directly explore this feeling-I? The range of experience claimed by this segment of 'I' is all the way from the prick of a pin (*That hurt me!*) to disabling levels of rage, envy, fear and shame (*I was so embarrassed I wished the ground would open up and swallow me!*). Although some of these experiences require deeper investigation, we can make a profound beginning with just the simple sensations of our bodies.

Our body tingles. We can feel the shimmering sense of it by resting attention anywhere we ask ourselves to. And the implication is—as attention moves to our lips, our hands, our eyes —that "we" are the one doing the sensing. We can try it for ourselves right now.

In any given moment of our sensing isn't there just simply and only sensing? Then a thought is tacked on subsequently that says *I'm doing this*. Is there ever any more to the sens-er, the feel-er, than this thought?

Tasting and smelling can be similarly pierced by penetrating below the level of the familiar picture woven by thought. Here we can identify that experience consists of nothing but direct experience itself—ungraspable, nothing-but-now, a painting on the surface of water, the momentariness of the swallow's flight. What we take to be normal life consists of this immediacy endlessly woven into the dreaming textile of "thought-coming-after."

We think we know everything (because thought says so)

What about the thinker? As we use direct experience to investigate whether there really is a thinker (because we really think there must be), we can identify two completely distinct aspects of thought-experience.

Firstly, if we practice watchfulness, mindfulness, or meditation (see the section *Meditation*) we begin to notice the distinct existence of thoughts; their facticity, or their quality of being factual.

As our noticing becomes more discerning and clear, something becomes startlingly obvious: these thoughts come from nowhere. They simply arise by themselves. That they might arise from a thinker turns out to be just another thought. Even to say they come from nowhere is a thought. "Thought" is a thought.

The second aspect of thoughts is the world they weave. We think—because of thoughts—that when we use words like "nowhere" that we actually understand what nowhere is. There is something (or somewhere!) called nowhere and we have used the right word to label it.

We think we know everything, because thought pretends so. Yet J. Krishnamurti delivered a whole teaching that gave voice to a deep yearning in us in just the title of his book: *Freedom From the Known*. Similarly, Zen master Seung Sahn's teaching-by-book-title is called *Only Don't Know*. In it, he explores what early Christian mystics called *The cloud of unknowing*; our foundational conscious nature, just like that of the animals living spontaneously wild, across the planet.

The world woven by thought convincingly persuades us that we are separate beings, with separate consciousnesses, existing in something we call "time." We are onlookers *separated* from a material world different in nature from us, from our own selves, from our own interior awareness. But is this actually so?

Thought a million billion times over identifies a thinker of these thoughts, cobbling together this biological experiencing, and the mélange of seeing, hearing, sensing, tasting, and smelling into the supposed time-bound thinker that we tend to identify as "I."

The first aspect of thoughts, the unmistakable existential *happening* of them, occurs always and only *now*. But thoughts weave a world of there-and-then, not here-and-now. They knit an other-than-now world out there in time and space that offers the seeming possibility of choice, as well as of biology enduring as biography; life as story.

> *The past and future are both far from God and alien to his way.*
>
> — Meister Eckhart

Consciousness, often believed to be enclosed in the brain, gets included in the story despite it remaining a total and prodigious mystery, the hardest of hard problems, even to the most venerable psychologists.

Emeritus professor Stuart Sutherland's entry in respect of "Consciousness" in the 1989 *International Dictionary of Psychology* reads:

> *The term is impossible to define except in terms that are unintelligible without a grasp of what consciousness means. Conscious-*

ness is a fascinating but elusive phenomenon; it is impossible to specify what it is, what it does, or why it evolved. Nothing worth reading has been written about it.

Despite this unequivocal statement being some 35 years old, the latest science does not at all contradict it. In 2025, when AI was asked *"Has 'the hard problem of consciousness' been solved yet?"* the response was:

"No, 'the hard problem of consciousness' has not been resolved yet...the fundamental question of why we have subjective experiences remains a significant challenge, and there is currently no resolution to 'the hard problem of consciousness.'"[*]

Could the reason for this possibly be that consciousness is prior to absolutely everything else? Explanations of consciousness from occurrences downstream from consciousness (such as thoughts) would be akin to characters on a movie screen delivering beliefs and opinions about the nature of the screen, the light, and the film—when they are, in fact, simply, marvelous characters in a movie, or a dream. Their very manifestation is, nonetheless, *indivisible* from the entirety of the film, the light, and the screen.

Existence knows existence

Inhabiting direct experience is not easy, but profoundly rewarding. In *The Literary Essays of Thomas Merton*, Merton remarks that the Zen practitioner is not engaged in what we

---

[*] A human writer, in a 2026 *Scientific American* summary on consciousness research remarks "…researchers can't even agree on what consciousness is, let alone how best to reveal its secrets." https://www.scientificamerican.com/article/what-is-consciousness-science-faces-its-hardest-problem-yet/

ordinarily think of as meditation but rather, "*...enters into a purifying struggle against conceptual knowledge...*"

The person "sweats out" his connection with reality that comes through images, ideas, and various forms of believed-in thought. Through this labor of love the person yearning to live fully "*...seeks to recover an immediate, direct intuition: not so much an intuition 'of' being as an intuition which is rooted in and identified with his very existence: an intuition in which the existence knows existence, or 'isness,' while completely losing sight of itself as a 'knowing subject.'*"

Unfiltered direct experiencing—including the recognition of the thoughts drifting unbidden through this awareness space called "I"—is completely at ease with this mystery, this undivided wholeness that is here before thought chops it up into arbitrary conceptual pieces.

> *Is not life one as we live it, which we cut to pieces by recklessly applying the murderous knife of intellectual surgery?*
>
> — D.T. Suzuki

When we are invited here to enter direct experience, it is this ground of being—where in reality we can never not be—that we are invited toward. In reality, in this very moment, we are already here and cannot not be. But thought says otherwise, because the world it weaves is always of a time other than now. But *now* is the only time there is.

~

Mystic child

At around six years old, lying in bed at night before

sleeping, some experiments with a mystical flavor began in my life. I could say "I began" these experiments, but what actually occurred is these things happened by themselves, and they were compelling, fascinating, and sometimes terrifying.

My felt-size could spontaneously expand, all the way to infinitely large. Of course, this must have been an inner sense experience, but at six years old children don't have these distinctions very well nailed-down, between actual physical size and inner imaginal size; I could just become infinite.

I could also become infinitely small, an experience so terrifying that I can still feel the echoes of it in my abdomen when I recount it today, in this writing. Nobody taught me these maneuvers and my parents were, for all intents and purposes, perfectly ordinary middle-class people without the slightest leaning towards the mystical.

Nor did anybody suggest to me the subsequent experiment in which I tried to see if I could predict what the next thought would be, suggesting a degree of presence at a quite early age that can be seen in almost all young children. When you look into a child's eyes you can see a palpable intelligence and perceptiveness that is open to an extent rarely seen in adults: perhaps as children are, I was just a child very awake to everything, my burgeoning mental processes included.

The next experience I can remember didn't come back to me until I did intensive training in shamanic body-work in my forties. This work opens locked-away experiences by deeply and painfully touching the places in one's body where they are held.

During one particularly agonizing session on the body-work table, I suddenly and vividly remembered the time in kindergarten when I had found that becoming a certain version of myself in my head closed down the helplessly-open vulnerability to everything I had hitherto experienced. From being unalloyed openness —available for love, laughter and ecstasy just as much as for agony, grief and despair—at five years old, I became "someone" with only one mission in life: survival, no matter how life was dulled as a consequence.

~

RESONANCE

…what we're seeking is an experience of being alive, so that our life experiences on the purely physical plane will have resonances with our own innermost being and reality, so that we actually feel the rapture of being alive.

— Joseph Campbell

Our essential nature is infused with mysticism. Resonance is the quiet announcement of the presence of our intrinsic wisdom and effortless depth. Resonance silently affirms that what we may not yet be able to give our own words to is nonetheless unmistakably and deeply true—because another person is giving words to it, and their words could *only* sound and feel sacred owing to their coming from precisely the same source from which our own sense of resonance emanates.

Resonance is the gradual inhabitation of a truth-sense that has nothing to do with logic and absolutely everything to do with the reality in our heart, which springs into vibrancy in the presence of poetry, dance, music or particularly sublime expressions of truth.

Resonance is deepening discernment:

- Does this stir me?
- Does my heart sing to read or hear this, as if the seed, the soil and springtime have suddenly found one another, and blossoming is palpably imminent?
- As I trust resonance, do I effortlessly slip past some formerly tempting things—words that used to seem true, ideas that are now self-evidently hollow—and dive more and more deeply within myself?
- Is this deepening fruitful, gradually infusing my life with the obviousness of the truth?

The wellspring of resonance

The above explorations of the truth of resonance actually reflect a foundational resource that is hidden until we start to draw from it. It is as if something—we know not quite what—urges us to seek a wellspring just below the surface of things. When we start to drink, and there is the blessed meeting of longing and its satisfaction, we realize it was thirst that drew us to the water.

This chapter could have been called "The truth of intuition" because intuition is, in reality, the inner pathway that opens, and then goes on opening the deep nature of experience to us. Yet intuition alone can have a hard-to-pin-down cerebral, unearthly, or floating quality about it. Resonance is intuition amplified and grounded by sensing our body.

As we cultivate sensing our body we are also growing our intuition. We are tuning the finest discernment in ourselves, questing the wisdom to be found not only in the marvelous brain between our ears, but also in the greater brain that is our heart and the immense enteric brain of our gut.

Our heart and our gut live and exist only now. Could our heart beat yesterday? Does the centrality of our belly's sense of this moment truly reflect anything but *now*?

A guide in dark places

This is not in any way to deny the grave difficulty many of us face in the form of anxiety about the future and prolonged grief about the past, and the way "a knot in my guts" and "a heavy heart" may echo and even affirm these anticipations and memories.

In the section *Sensing our body* we'll find a way to clarify such experiences, drawing closer to them *as experience*, tuning into the nowness that is the hallmark of our body's existence. As we repeatedly turn to this experience-now, even if it seems to be about there-and-then, we'll find our attunement to the moment deepening, widening, and growing. This attunement is the gift offered us by our body's amplification of intuitive experience. This is cultivating resonance.

Resonance has many forms. We are unhappy, for instance, and we cast about within ourselves for the source. We discover that changes need to be made: in our diet, in our job, in our relationships, in where we live, or how we spend our time.

Despite making these alterations—and things may improve because of the changes—a subtle sense draws us deeper and deeper within ourselves. Something foundational is not quite right, something that cannot be ameliorated by modification of circumstances, nor by medication or psychotherapy.

Riding resonance—beneath the surface level of our thinking mind—we find ourselves questing deeper and deeper.

The call of the uncaused

Some sense of suffering exists that resonance says quite clearly is not intrinsically the nature of life. Perhaps we find ourselves turning to something; *A Course in Miracles*, the Upanishads, *The Power of Now*, or we find ourselves attending a meeting where a spiritual teacher talks, and in the mirror of the wisdom words we can clearly sense the taste of truth.

Resonance has accurately discerned this deep level of suffering, and resonance has just as faithfully drawn us closer to our own deeper, even unconditional existence, glimmering in the words where the truth is spoken. Resonance distinguishes between the misery of an ill-fitting job and the intrinsic unhappiness of being only a separate self.

With resonance as our guide, we can enter into the realm where separateness vanishes and resonance, again, celebrates the wholeness it was always calling us towards.

Pausing in presence

So resonance is a guide, an echo amplified by the sense of our body revealing more and more deeply what is true for us.

"*Does that resonate?*" I will often ask my clients and students, inviting them to notice if there is a glimmer, a brief distinctive wave of vibrating energy welling up out of nowhere in response to something I said. What was said was generally my best effort to discern and then to speak the energy of the moment.

Participation in this encompassing field—it has been called "the awakening field"—is actually best understood by splitting the word "nowhere" into its component parts, "now," and "here."

To engage resonance is simply to attend inclusively and with open interest to *now* and here. This is pausing in presence, slowing and softening the hard-charging get-somewhere busyness of mind in favor of a gentle open interest that invites what is here to become known.

The unthought known.

— Christopher Bollas

This pausing in presence has four distinctive aspects:

- Including our sensed and felt body.
- Letting ourselves be in the unknown.
- Open interest, or curiosity.
- Slowing down.

Cultivating the combination of these is a knack, the pleasure of which is discovering that something difficult turns out to be also profoundly natural: walking, talking, swimming and riding a bicycle are examples.

Zen practice integrally includes body sensing, but tends to have large cultural overlays. Somatic and body psychotherapy have body sensing as a central technique but naturally incline to a focus on the resolution of trauma and difficulty, not the opening to our true nature that is the invitation of cultivating resonance.

The knack of noticing resonance reaches inward to illuminate the unthought known. Outwardly, resonance highlights sources of wisdom, encouraging connections and helpful avenues to explore. In due course, resonance compellingly invites and encourages the noticing that inward and outward only seem to be two things conceptually, but are undivided in reality.

The only fitting sequel to reading these pages about resonance is to ask the question "Is there resonance here?"

~

Saving my own life

My career fog cleared briefly in 1969 and then descended again. I had graduated from the UK equivalent of high school with qualifying exams in math and sciences. The hard-fought battles of the exams and studying for them behind me, I duly decamped for the University of Essex to study electronic engineering. I was 18 years old.

My father had once wanted to be an electronic engineer. The project of my studying electronic engineering seemed like a default continuation of the same absurd process of career choice that had been going on since I was 10 years old.

At that point it began to become apparent a) that everyone around me expected me to know what I wanted to do as an adult, and for the rest of my life and b) that I had not the slightest idea, or, only fanciful ideas: airline pilot-racing car driver-fire chief-TV repairman; that level of ideas. But choice was demanded, so electronic engineering emerged out of the haze of my teenage interests in fiddling with the interiors of disassembled radios, and my vague practical proclivities for mathematics and physics.

The lectures in physics, mathematics, programming and electronics at the University of Essex were astonishing to me. I felt like someone landing in a class taught in Mandarin, with only Greek at my disposal. My covert glances at my classmates told me that not only were they comprehending it, but lapping it up. How could that be? The classes were all in Chinese, and made no sense whatsoever.

If the lectures were in Mandarin, my social life was from another planet altogether. I was housed in a bed-and-breakfast in Clacton-on-Sea, 15 miles from the university. As my fellow students and co-guesthouse-residents and I went back and forth between the university and the institutional smell and stern atmosphere of Mrs. L. Smith-Dutton's Clacton establishment, I did my increasingly despairing best to sound as if I too was full of a kind of racy-sounding confidence about every deeply puzzling aspect of life; about girls and sex and romance, about alcohol and eating right and dancing, and the impossible assignments piling on us. I was completely perplexed how on earth I'd ended up here, doing this, completely overwhelmed and under-equipped for any of it.

At midday on a Thursday two months into this catastrophe I had the first lightbulb moment of my own life. In one brilliantly crystalline instant, walking dispiritedly from one incomprehensible lecture to another I realized: *I can leave.* Mercifully, there were no thoughts of consequences beyond relief and the astonishing discovery of the power contained within planting my own flag, and to heck with the consequences. I had just saved my own life.

(The story continues in *"The hill of separation."*)

~

SENSING OUR BODY

In the evolution of the senses the sense of touch was undoubtedly the first to come into being...Touch is the parent of our eyes, ears, nose, and mouth. It is the sense which becomes differentiated into the others...touch is the earliest sensory system to become functional in all species thus far studied, human, animal, and bird.

— Ashley Montagu

Living breathing star stuff

Despite our seeming separateness, our bodies are intimately interwoven with the wider world. We were born out of this world, emerging from nowhere as this distinctive form, a journey of recombining primal star stuff in never-to-be-repeated ways.

Our parents likely could not in a million years have anticipated the particulars we bring here: how we like our sandwiches cut, the phone ringtone we choose, our preference for sleeping on our back rather than our side.

Despite these particulars we are all part of the universal necessities of embodiment: deprived of our shared life-giving oxygen-rich atmosphere, each one of us will die in a few minutes. Without water our body will die in about a week; deprived of food we might last two months.

When our movements are restricted and environmental stimulation is limited, hallucinations, extreme anxiety, bizarre thoughts, and depression set in very swiftly. Even social isolation can lead to significantly deteriorated mental functioning and shortened life.

An inescapable connectedness

No part of this world functions separately from the whole of it. The clouds scudding by outside my window move in invisible concert with the temperature of the far-off Siberian plains.

The tiniest details of the trillion root hairs through which trees drink from the downpour of cumulus are essential to their offering up part of the atmosphere in which the clouds float. Our bodies breathe, eat, and drink from this intricate and inescapable largeness. The consequences of actual disconnection start in seconds with suffocation and are far-reaching: death, anguish and madness.

All of this declares our intimate connectedness with an extended world that we mostly feel distinct and separate from. Science unequivocally confirms that our bodies are inextricably interwoven with our whole world: could we begin to know more of this wholeness by sensing our bodies?

"Mr. Duffy lived a short distance from his body" wrote James Joyce in *Dubliners*, naming a hidden truth for most of us. In my twenties a woman teaching Reichian bodywork said to me in astonishment *"You are* so *in your head!"* I had no idea what she was talking about, just as Mr. Duffy might have been perplexed.

Shortly thereafter a senior process group leader told me I was too tense for him to be able to work with, and that I needed to get intensive deep tissue bodywork to remedy the situation. Somewhere around the tenth session of Rolfing, my bodyworker told me that he had done everything he could to get my shoulders to drop: now it was up to me. And, somewhere before the eleventh session I discovered I'd been holding my shoulders up near my ears all those years, and gradually becoming aware of the tension, found the possibility of releasing it. When awareness grows, everything changes.

Separate images

Invited to sense their bodies most people default to consulting an image they have of their body in thought. These images can create havoc because they imagine a body which is limited and separate, which is not at all our direct experience of our bodies.

Thought works with limitation, separation and division, but when we come experience-close to our bodies we are seeking out the most intimate possible connectedness with a world that is almost limitless, and whole.

Thinking is miraculously rapid. We can go as fast as light from London to Paris—in thought. But sensing, always *now*, here long before thought began to predominate our experience, is far slower, more diffuse and less separating. We can think of our left big toe far more swiftly than we can notice the sheer sensation of it blossoming into awareness.

The separate images we carry of our bodies, fostered by a cruelly competitive culture, tend to devastatingly override wholeness. Lonely misery, alienation, isolation, and shame are the outcome, except for Ms. and Mr. Universe—and even they live in anxiety about losing their winning form.

Butting up against belief

Butting up against our believed-in sharply-outlined body edges can go on for a long time. Visual reality points to the air being here, an inch out from my skin surface, and the two being definitively separate. In a photograph I am clearly delineated as separate from my dog, she of the fuzzy silken-coated edge.

But when we turn to sensing—to feeling our bodies from within, right *now*—we can find only fuzziness at our perimeter, a subtle vibrating or tingling field of experiencing completely belying what our visual sense and body image say is true.

As a quote earlier remarks, touch is the parent sense of all the other senses, in all species so far studied. Touch is also the only mutual sense: I cannot touch you without you touching me. Hence, this origin-sense displays to us what is always here, *now*: our primordial interdependent undividedness.

Inside this clay jug

As body sensing deepens, the remarks of mystics about the body may begin to resonate more richly; Rumi firmly points us inward:

> *There is a force within*
> *Which gives you life-*
> *Seek that.*
> *In your body*
> *Lies a priceless gem—Seek that.*
> *O wandering Sufi,*
> *if you want to find*
> *the greatest treasure*
> *don't look outside,*
> *Look inside,*
> *and seek that.*
>
> — Rumi

Buddha says that the way to this profound revelation is found by going within:

Friends, I proclaim,
it is within this very fathom-long body,
with its perception and inner sense,
that lies the world,
the cause of the world,
the cessation of the world,
and the path that leads to
the cessation of the world.

— Buddha

And Kabir goes right to the heart of love:

Inside this clay jug
there are canyons and pine mountains,
and the maker of canyons and pine mountains!
All seven oceans are inside,
and hundreds of millions of stars.
The acid that tests gold is there,
and the one who judges jewels.
And the music from the strings
no one touches,
and the source of all water.
If you want the truth, I will tell you the truth:
Friend, listen: the God whom I love is inside.

— Kabir

Meanwhile, Saraha affirms the universality of the wisdom-mystery we all inherently bring with us in simply being alive:

Here in this body are the sacred rivers;
here are the sun and moon
as well as all the pilgrimage places...
I have not encountered another temple

as blissful as my own body.

— Saraha

❧

You are invited here to explore your own direct experience of your body, with my accompaniment. The sections *The wellspring of resonance* and *Direct experiencing* will be helpful backdrops, particularly since we will likely come up against beliefs about, and images of our bodies as we lean into and begin to inhabit the more immediate and unfiltered truth of sensing.

Let's begin:

> Bring your attention to your upper lip. Not the upper lip exclusively in thought (although thought may help you to direct your attention to the sensed area just south of your nostrils) but the physical sensation by which you know your lip is there. Pause there—really pause, being present. Notice what you are noticing as you do this.

> Might it be accurate to describe the sensations you're experiencing there as a cloud, or a pillowy gathering of energy that, when you zoom in on it, is subtly vibrant, softly tingling or very gently buzzing? Take enough time to notice for yourself, in your own experience.

> If your experience in no way resembles this, check to see whether thought, image, or belief has crept into your exploration. If your own direct experience is different than mine, trust that, and let yourself deepeningly explore it.

Remaining present to the area of your upper lip, start
to notice the different waves of sensation going
through your experience there as the breath comes
and goes through your nostrils.

Inhalation slightly cools the upper lip and when the
warm air of your exhalation flows over the lip, you can
feel the shift in temperature. Although this has been
going on since you first began breathing on your own,
it may be the first time you have become conscious
of it.

If you'd like to play further with the experience you
can slide aside the labels of "cooler" and "warmer"
and just become present to the unending waves of
sensation going through the space of you: take in the
ceaselessly varying experience that the labels call
"warmer" and "cooler."

The perceived cannot perceive

A deliberate practice of body sensing starts with doing exactly
what we're doing now:

- being in the unknown,
- letting ourselves be interested without agenda, and
- slowing down to take in the gradual blossoming of
  our experience.

When I began this practice I often found my thinking mind
forcibly asserting the habitual fixed position of belief: *This is
stupid. And pointless. My lip is exactly like I can see in the mirror, or my
yearbook photograph. It's a limited thing—sheesh, anybody can see* it's
just a lip!

But I persisted. For one thing, I had become aware that I was noticing something—my body—and although I'd always taken that to be myself, this could not be: because I was noticing it, deeply and intimately. As the Zen master Huang Po put it, "*Let me repeat, the perceived cannot perceive.*"

Whatever this directly sensed tingling, buzzing, vibratory energy is, it cannot and could not itself be the source of perception *because it is itself perceived.*

Our universal and worldwide belief is *I am inside and the world is outside.* Yet here we are palpably noticing that what we take to be "inside," our inner sense of our body, is nothing but another perception. Precisely the same noticing reveals again and again that thoughts are themselves perceived, and so they cannot be the source of perception. More on this later.

Other aspects of directly sensing our bodies are potentially fascinating: let's go back to our upper lip and explore some more:

> Bring attention to your upper lip again. Pause in quietude long enough to be presently curious, letting the insistence of belief and image subside a little so you can become present to what you notice directly, *now.* Let your attention wander back and forth, as it were, in and out to see if you can find an edge in direct sensational experience where your lip stops and the air starts. Is there any such place, except in imagination? Can you give adequate explanation or definition to this fuzzy territory without an edge?

> Bring your lips gently together. I say "lips" so there should be two of them. But outside of image, without invoking thought or belief, can you actually find a place where one lip stops and the other starts? What

thought says is two things, upper and lower lip, turn out in direct sensing to be experientially undivided.

Of course, if you asked your mouth whether there are two lips it would say this is absurd; both lips originate and return to these corners—but again, you cannot find two corners in direct sensation. Buzzy, blurry sensation, but not two, at least in the way there are visibly two monitors on this desk in front of me.

Nor, if you turn attention to your right hand and bring the same quality of presence to it, can you find five digits? Rather than a glove, the *sensational* experience of your still hand more resembles a mitten.

If you wiggle your fingers the perfectly sensible distinction of fingers and hand—in thought—makes no sense at all in your direct experience of sensing. Energy moves, although just like one cloud contiguous with another, there is no true separation between them. Place the palms of your two hands together for a moment or two, pause, and see if you can distinguish by sensing whether there are still two, or whether they are palpably simply one.

Bring attention to where your backside meets the chair you are sitting on. That should be two things, right? (Says thought.) But isn't the experience one single sensation? Although thought may have a lot to say about this, your direct experience of sensing remains as it is, doesn't it?

A practical practice

A body sensing practice provides a consistent way to come back to *now*—where our body actually lives. "Here" is naturally included in this practice, and these two together are the fulfillment of one witty Buddhist definition of sanity: to have our mind where our body is; always here, now.

Body sensing practice also cultivates presence, substantially increasing our capacity to notice everything in awareness. Attention grows through using it, consciously and deliberately. All day long we can have short moments of attention to our body, momentarily (or longer) dropping out of the there-and-then stream of thinking to notice our here-and-now sensed-body.

This can happen in the shower, while eating, petting our cat or dog or talking with our boss. We can play with it while we drive our car, drink coffee or lie in bed in the morning after waking up. When we do we will find ourselves quite rapidly shifting from a dutiful and regimented quality of practice to it being something we quite simply play with because it's vitalizing, enjoyable and real. *Now* is where our body lives, and reality is whole, and beneficent.

What are these benefits? We'll have access to a grounded and real sense of ourselves. Sitting in the seat of our own body, we can come back to here-now reality really fast, which is tremendously helpful for tempering agitation and distress with nowness.

We'll tend to find that with more presence to our body the time between being triggered and being conscious of it gets shorter and shorter. Then we don't have to have the shocked realization a week, month, or a year later that something really affected us. We also healthily sidestep having to deal with the way we may have acted out prior to noticing what was actually happening in us, in our own experience.

Nor do we have to wait so long before we say something about it, and when we do, we can speak it from a place of responsibility because "This is the experience I'm having...." is simply a natural place of reporting what's showing up in awareness, and quite remarkably objective, neutral, and true. It's our truth, in our awareness and speaking of what's happening in our experience.

A contemporary Buddhist teacher, Gil Fronsdal remarks: "... *mindfulness of the body is one of the best windows I have into my inner life.*"

This is after he extensively quotes the Buddha who said: "*There is one thing that when cultivated and regularly practiced, leads to deep spiritual intention, to peace, to mindfulness and clear comprehension, to vision and knowledge, to a happy life here and now and to the culmination of wisdom and awakening. And what is that one thing? It is mindfulness centered on the body.*"

Elsewhere, Buddha said: "*If the body is not cultivated, the mind cannot be cultivated. If the body is cultivated then the mind can be cultivated.*"

Having quoted a number of mystics and realizers in this section, Jiddu Krishnamurti's remark on the words of others will be helpful to remind us that every part of this journey is based on our own experience, and that is our only true guide:

"*It is through self-knowledge, not through belief in somebody else's words, that a [person] comes to the eternal reality, in which his being is grounded.*"

Making use of our gathering sense of resonance, we can find out for ourselves what is true, for us, in our own words, in our own experience. Resonance—intuition amplified by the sense of our body—is a vital guide in this journey. We can readily cultivate sensing our bodies as a primary navigational tool for our travels.

$\sim$

The hill of separation

Six months after dropping out of my derailed electronic engineering career, I left a high school reunion with a new girlfriend and a hangover. Trudging in a daze beside the girl who had broken my heart two years previously and now was, perhaps equally numbly, accompanying me, we made our way to where we could hitchhike to what passes for warmth and tropical breezes in England, to Cornwall in the southwest of the country.

Rounding a bend as we walked, I saw a hill some miles in the distance, a soft outline in the hazy early summer afternoon. A question from I-know-not-where, some confluence of the emotional conflict and distress-pleasure I was experiencing in her company, alongside a premonitory visitation from years in my future floated acutely through my mind: "Why on earth do I feel so separate from that hill?"

A question like this has significance far beyond its own simple linguistic meaning. The fog of our normative state of separation is so ingrained and customary that a question of this sort could simply appear absurd and not be given a moment's further attention. But it was a striking question, to me, one arising from a dimension inexplicable, fascinating, and completely off my mental map up to then.

I still don't know what grace it was that compelled me to attend to that question with complete devotion, but as I write about it now I think it's time I made a pilgrimage to that hill, because the emergence of the question that afternoon was the harbinger of an awakening that has continued to infuse my life ever since.

In Cornwall a farmer let us stay in a dilapidated caravan amidst the fields where I harvested his crops of cabbages and turnips, and thought long and hard about my possibilities in life. About how little of all those years in school had been interesting to me and how only one brief psychology course had actually really engaged me. I eventually applied to thirteen universities to study psychology and while twelve of them rejected me because I was a dropout from the University of Essex, the University of Southampton accepted me.

(The story continues in *"Crashing from grace, into grace."*)

MEDITATION

Osho says: *What is meditation? Is it a technique that can be practiced? Is it an effort that you have to do?*

Is it something which the mind can achieve? It is not.

All that the mind can do cannot be meditation—it is something beyond the mind, the mind is absolutely helpless there.

The mind cannot penetrate meditation; where mind ends, meditation begins. This has to be remembered, because in our life, whatsoever we do, we do through the mind; whatsoever we achieve, we achieve through the mind.

And then, when we turn inwards, we again start thinking in terms of techniques, methods, doings, because the whole of life's experience shows us that everything can be done by the mind. Yes —except meditation, everything can be done by the mind.

Everything is done by the mind except meditation. Because meditation is not an achievement—it is already the case, it is your nature. It has not to be achieved; it has not only to be recognized, it has only to be remembered. It is there waiting for you—just a turning in, and it is available. You have been carrying it always and always.

Meditation is your intrinsic nature. It is you, it is your being, it has nothing to do with your doings. You cannot have it. You cannot not have it. It cannot be possessed, it is not a thing.

It is you. It is your being.

— Osho

Might we cultivate, with curiosity and kindness our own willingness to look for ourselves to see what's true *in our own experience*? To gradually grow trust that despite this directly-experiencing going up against what we have been told is true, it is the ultimate trustworthiness, and always our own.

Each fresh wave of recognition—of the reality here, where the infinity of mySelf lives—reminds us that this was always known—and always, largely ignored. The wisdom-words reflecting it, the echoes from down the ages of sacred self-discovered luminosity tended to be passed by as "mere words." Perhaps like these words, here.

The unsatisfactoriness of the explanation of things given us by thought—uprooted from depth experience—and by our (global, human) culture prompts us more than a thousand, thousand times to look for ourselves. We look backward, with daring, persistence and directness into the nature of the looker.

Don't do anything.

— Papaji to Gangaji at their first meeting

We can do this too. We can do it right *now*. When we look in this way, our believed-in thoughts will tell us what we see. We will believe this is us talking to ourselves. *This is a lie*—and we will believe it, the way we believe we are nothing but a separate self; the way we believe our consciousness is separate, enclosed in our body and brain, and the way we believe all our thoughts are us, despite the fact that we are ever *the intimate noticer of them* (kindly don't believe that, since we can all find out for ourselves).

These beliefs are mirages. Everybody lives from them, so they are taken to be reality.

In meditation, every form of search must come to an end.

—J. Krishnamurti

Hardly anybody looks backwards to take in the perceiver, the believer: why should they? The beliefs—the profoundly compelling delusions of who we are—seem to completely explain who and what we are. In the face of this much certainty there seems absolutely no point in scrupulously examining our experience—by means of the presence we cannot not be.

Undistracted nonmeditation

— Tsoknyi Rinpoche

For one thing, this scrupulous, self-authorized examination would leave us feeling very alone—how could we possibly depart from the crowd, finding and following our own authority? The fact that every single one of us yearns to do just this is an uncomfortable truth in a culture bent on fitting in at all costs.

The true miracle of this can be said in words but it will need our participation, our own accessing of our own depth and truth to bring it alive as it always actually is. *This miracle is that this presence knows itself by itself.* Once this quality of knowing itself by itself is recognized in the nature of everything known —which is the infinity of everything—everything known is also known to be this same miracle.

Do not seek any God other than self cognizing intrinsic awareness.

— Dudjom Lingpa

This is the nature of self-knowledge; that the self knows itself. Nothing else in all the universe is like this: no object, no matter how supposedly conscious, knows itself. Even a marvel like my eye, an astonishing piece of biological technology cannot regard itself: only presence can regard it. This presence knows itself. There is no greater miracle in the universe than this.

Mostly we don't notice our own essence, our intrinsic conscious nature. We look outward, and the world we see powerfully supports our compelling belief that we are intrinsically that also: stuff, a thing amongst an infinity of things.

> *This is something I can't give because you* have *it. It is ridiculous to ask for a thing which you already have.*

> — U. G. Krishnamurti

Only rarely do we turn our gaze in the opposite direction and recognize that all things only exist because of this core aware essence. This essence—the conscious knowing taking in these words right now—is radically and completely different than all the things that exist because of it.

Making this radical turn in our own attention is entirely accessible: rather than going outward towards things, even subtle things like thoughts, we can become curious about our own direct experience of what notices things. Shifting the direction of our attention—from the things that are known (squeal of tires, backside in chair, taste of coffee, familiar littered desk) we can notice the knower of things, our hidden-yet-open secret, imperturbably within.

Attuning to this takes some time, and a gradual shift of perspective: we are regarding an absolute miracle about which we can do nothing, which is beyond harm, beyond even death; which is causeless and completely free. Nothing in all the world of things remotely resembles this, yet the world of things inter-depends entirely with it.

*When there is understanding of "what is" then there is no need
for control.*

—J. Krishnamurti

The shift of perspective is that all things can be experienced
—buildings, love, cardboard boxes, grief, and clouds—but
this experiencing is simply the true nature of the experiencer, loving all things experienced with an undivided
intimacy.

*In the understanding of "what is" there is neither despair nor
hope.*

—J. Krishnamurti

And this intimacy is so close, so complete that things are
nothing but this knowing, and knowing is nothing but these
things. "*Form is emptiness,*" says the Heart Sutra, "*and emptiness is
nothing but form.*"

… "what is" is the most mysterious thing in life.

—J. Krishnamurti

Why the *Heart* Sutra? Because these truths have long ago
utterly escaped the corral of logic. They have nothing to do
with the world of cause-and-effect. They exist and reflect a
reality that includes cause-and-effect but is utterly beyond it—
and the heart intrinsically knows this.

*As long as there is a meditator, there's no meditation. When the
meditator disappears, there is meditation.*

—Jean Klein

Living meditation

I had just come back from living at a Zen priory in the north of England. Northumberland is a peculiarly cold place in winter, and no matter whether I was digging ditches in pursuit of restoring the septic system, reciting sutras before mindfully eating rice and pickles for breakfast, or trying not to nod off during sitting meditation, I felt thoroughly chilled.

The Reverend Hofuku Hughes, my Zen teacher in London, reminded us that Zen had flourished in Japan (a very cold place) because at its core Buddhism has the warmth of the heart. Myself, I felt discouraged— my efforts to reach somewhere less screwed-up feeling than what seemed like my usual state of being had thus far failed.

I knew there was something to this meditation busi- ness, but quite what it was eluded me. What does the heart have to do with any of the issues of living that trouble me, I lamented, amidst my late teenage thought process? And what's with all these cold places?

My school friend Steve had faithfully followed the arrow of his only interest from that time of (largely completely uninteresting) scholastic endeavor, and become a potter. The day I came back from Northum- berland, he invited me to visit him at Heal's in Tottenham Court Road, an upscale store which had one of its display windows filled with an electric potter's throwing wheel, at which my friend sat, making pots in public view.

I stood amidst the onlookers and watched him, leaning over the wheel as he spun the shape of a graceful bowl out of a lump of clay dashed, seemingly-casually, into the center of the wheel. His head wove minutely back and forth as his hands guided the clay into a shape at once practical and beautiful.

I was suddenly struck by a realization: whatever I had been pursuing, sitting meditation on my cushion, he was already fully embraced by; his head, eyes and hands perfectly forming the moment of creation in a dance that suddenly fully informed me why he had eschewed the more orthodox route I had taken and gone directly to the fulfillment of the arc of his passion.

Throwing pots was meditation.

Meditation could be throwing pots.

~

VULNERABILITY

"You mistake vulnerability for weakness."

There is no point in writing this section about vulnerability unless I'm willing to be vulnerable as I write it.

Emotional vulnerability is personal. To be vulnerable means to allow ourselves to be at risk emotionally, to open to the possibility of being wounded; the word *vulnerable* comes from a

Latin word, *vulner* meaning wound. To be vulnerable is the only way of really telling the truth about ourselves, opening to the possibility of being fully seen and felt by another.

Vulnerability = Connectedness

Many synonyms for vulnerability are very negative and carry the implication of weakness. But research affirms the connectedness implied by the few positive synonyms: openness, possibility, accountability. Tenderheartedness is not mentioned, but it is certainly one of the overtones that affirms that vulnerability can be both positive, and essential.

Brené Brown, a much-heard voice expressing the research says: *"Vulnerability sounds like truth and feels like courage. Truth and courage aren't always comfortable, but they're never weakness."*

Telling the truth about ourselves takes a lot of courage, although we may not feel very courageous when we realize we could posture, defend, prevaricate or protect ourselves—or we could tell the truth. Telling the truth tends to be vulnerable, and uncomfortable, yet it makes us real, to ourselves and for others.

There is a profound truth in the middle of this very personal activity of being vulnerable. The protections we have—all of us, without exception, and without blame or pathology for having them—insist that we will be harmed and possibly wounded if we are vulnerable. The risk, the threat is so severe that the protections sometimes say I will die if I don't hide behind them. So sometimes to be vulnerable is like risking dying.

Born through dying

I have found without exception that each time I'm willing to step into the uncomfortableness of being vulnerable I become aware of something in me which cannot die. I have, after all, risked a certain kind of death, the death my protections are certain I will suffer without their shielding.

But it turns out that the truth, emerging in the moment, fully embodied and real is beyond harm. More deeply, the essence of myself beyond definition—yet never not here—is once again found to be invulnerable to death.

I wrote the following note some years ago as part of a book that never emerged because such protective fear came up that I could not bear the vulnerability. Yet the truth is still here.

Vulnerability: what does it mean, to "grow yourself"?
What is "widening, deepening, and maturing yourself"? What is "yourself"?

The only reply I can offer is from my own experience:
when my protections are less powerful, or absent,
when the habitual ways I camouflage my true feelings
in relationship to another are less effective, when unfiltered love or grief or fury burst through my coverings,
revealing the fact that I am just as I am, no more and
no less, then "myself" shows up. The "story" of who I
am with all its apparel of past and future vanishes in a
wave of authenticity, of complete sincerity that unmistakably issues the clear ring of truth to anybody
nearby.

This vulnerability is sudden and beyond harm. The
redolence of truth intrinsic to it is so powerful that
nothing can infringe it. But there are degrees of

vulnerability: any time I risk deliberately stepping into territory delineated as forbidden by a protective part of me, I will experience the discomfort of transitional vulnerability, somewhere in between the habitual dead-but-invulnerable state that most of us live our lives in, and the nakedness of utterly being myself.

Cultivating this transitional vulnerability takes the practices of spirituality out of the temple and the exercises of psychology out of the therapist's office and brings them into the potentially mean streets of ordinary relationship.

We will be uncomfortable if we practice deliberate vulnerability. If we allow the moments when we are uncomfortable because we are allowing truth to be more important than protection, we will gradually come to realize that we are moving the fulcrum of our being further and further away from that habitual deadness, towards the unfiltered "myself" we intrinsically long to be.

Every millimeter of this movement will be uncomfortable, queasy and provocative of retreating and shutting down. Every time we allow it, we'll grow ourselves. There will be more of who we really are, and less of who we mistook ourselves to be. This is the practice of vulnerability.

Time for the undying now

Let's glimpse ahead to some of the pages to come. That which we cannot stop being—presence, awareness, conscious-nowness—is always available for whatever is *now*. One of the things it's available for is our ordinary human sense: time-bound, frightened, and limited.

> *The extent to which we can allow ourselves to confront—to experience and be responsible for—the pretense and trying, the avoidance and fear, is the extent to which we can be who we really are.*
>
> — Werner Erhard

These seeming-two live intimately intermingled in every moment, but one of them, the born-to-die entity of biology and biography, the separate-seeming self, really just has one preoccupation: to get rid of the disliked, to get more of the liked, and to avoid the boredom in between these two.

Vulnerability is not welcome to this one because vulnerability is the antithesis of getting what I want and avoiding what I don't want: it is being true. Vulnerability, carried through moment by moment would be risky-feeling for this separate self.

The other, existing-without-cessation aspect of our being is the quintessence of vulnerability. No matter what comes in life, this deeply-open intimacy at the core of us unhesitatingly welcomes it.

How can it do that? If we are beyond harm, if we can't die, if our nature is nothing but immortality, the essence of presence beyond thing-ness, we will laugh at all threats, welcoming them in. We cannot be harmed—even death has no sting.

Vulnerability is the truth of this eternal aspect of our nature, with the exception that "able to be wounded" simply doesn't apply. But any moment in which human emotional vulnerability is pierced is a moment of potentially glimpsing that indwelling undying essence of us that cannot be bloodied; of suddenly noticing something in ourselves that is beyond harm, and the central essence of truth, although it may be unsayable.

~

Vulnerability's resonant truth

The initial subtitle in this section was said to me in a no-holds-barred encounter group 50 years ago: "You mistake vulnerability for weakness." Recognizing the profound truth-resonance of these words, for years afterwards I worked with the edge in myself where I mistook vulnerability for weakness.

Gradually, as I was able to recognize the rigid, block-like believed-in mental conditioning constituting the flashing alarm signs WEAKNESS! DANGER! WEAKNESS! I could begin to discern the uncomfortable somatic experiences beneath the belief that vulnerability is weakness.

I began to be able to recognize this belief as nothing but the billion-times repetition of that mental conditioning. Because I'm male, and because I was brought up, as many boys are on a steadily-shaming diet of "Boys don't cry," my inherent vulnerability had been shut away, necessarily.

With each further step into vulnerability I could recognize anew the simple fact that to be vulnerable is to be connected. To be vulnerable is to offer one's isness, one's immediacy and beingness to another, or to oneself. To be vulnerable is to be real. To be vulnerable is to risk hurt in this human existence—for glimpses of the eternity in the core of myself.

The practice continues for me—50 years seems like a relatively short time for the changes I've noticed to happen. Yet I'm also frequently staggered by how much of my life is lived from biology and biography, and I both dread and welcome the moments when vulnerability offers me the chance to pierce this skin and open further into the infinity which I really am.

~

NEGATION

You are the seeing of what you're not.

— Paul Hedderman

Using the sharpest tool

The sharpest tool was given us by the venerable Zen teacher Huang Po, who spoke about it emphatically and personally: "*Let me repeat*," he remarked, "*That the perceived cannot perceive.*"

What does he mean? We don't really know, of course, because he said this about 1,200 years ago, and most likely in a dialect that no longer exists. But this little phrase, "*The perceived cannot perceive*" is sometimes known as "timeless wisdom," so we can use it now just as well as ever.

Whatever can be perceived cannot itself perceive. What we can notice naturally fascinates us—but we neglect the perceiv-*ing*, forever unchanging amidst our captivation by the perceived.

Anything noticed is perceived—including thinking we have gotten somewhere by naming "the perceiv-*ing*." But naming "the perceiv-*ing*" in this way is to turn it into the perceiv*ed*. Yet the perceived cannot perceive. Nonetheless, perceiving is happening; boiled right down to it, life or sentience means "perceiving."

How to use this tool? The key is in the word "*cannot*" in Huang Po's statement. Just as much as the perceived cannot perceive, so anything we can notice *cannot* be myself—for it is being noticed. The noticed *cannot* notice.

> *…what you are cannot be described, except as total negation. All you can say is: "I am not this, I am not that".*

> — Nisargadatta Maharaj

Again, if we say "I am the noticing" we have turned "the noticing" into the *noticed*. The noticed cannot notice. (We can also say "I am the noticing," then negate that, since it too is observed. We will find we have gone nowhere, although our interim definition of ourselves, "I am the noticing" has lost all its power via the negation.)

An invisible outcome awaits us when we rigorously apply "The noticed cannot notice" as far as possible, and then pause, and see. The invisibility thus uncovered is sometimes called "true nature" or "self-essence." It will not be perceptible in the ordinary way we sense our external world, but will be unmistakable, the essence of "you." Did Shakespeare perhaps consult Huang Po?

> *…But man, proud man,*
> *Dressed in a little brief authority,*
> *Most ignorant of what he's most assured,*
> *His glassy essence, like an angry ape*

Plays such fantastic tricks
before high heaven
As makes the angels weep

— William Shakespeare

We may, for instance, in this moment be aware of a swirl of thoughts (and perhaps experiences in other sensory channels) that we ordinarily take to be ourselves. They are noticed. A further thought may then occur, something like "Huh, all of that is perceiv*ed*, so cannot possibly be me." *This thought too is perceived, and also cannot be you.* This is as far as it is possible to go: we can now pause, and notice. Going further than this is quite literally impossible.

...the very act of perceiving shows that you are not what you perceive.

— Nisargadatta Maharaj

"Cannot" is negation. "Cannot" applies to the obvious content of "myself:" all the thoughts and sensations that seem like who I am. Then "Cannot" is applied to the negation itself, for that too is perceived. Now, we can take a moment.

Nothing remains—and this nothing is no different than it ever was, is, or will be. The whole conscious-cartwheeling entirety of life continues exactly as before. This conscious-cart-wheeling entirety seeks nothing, unfolding continuously without any cause, or care. No separate self can be found in it, although it is miraculously aware.

Nothing but dynamic change is the fabric of it—and the unalloyed feel of the fabric, just as it is, is subtly blissful. This feeling is heart-feeling, for truth can only be felt, not summarized in words; only feeling is the intimacy, the subtle and delicate level of consciousness that is intrinsic to the heart.

Everything is exactly the same as it is in our ordinary day to day lives. The burbling of me-me-me continues, but the transformative tool of Huang Po has done its work for good; all of that separate-seeming-self is percei*ved*, and cannot possibly perceive. The "wooden puppet" of the Taoists, or the "action figure" of Paul Hedderman is revealed. All that can be perceived cannot possibly be me, and, in the pausing beyond the double negative, I remain; *now* as "I am"—now liberated from solely *I am Glenn*.

I am liberated, too, from the need for liberation. Liberation is unceasing, once this sharpest of sharp tools has made its cut: liberation is the nature of life itself, and has never been any other way—unless we take ourselves to be exclusively what we were trained into in early life: someone separate and independent, inhabiting a body, born to die (and seeking liberation). The tool cuts all that away in a moment of negation, then negation of the negation—and pure causeless freedom is revealed: the heart of everything.

> *There's never been a single thing;*
>
> *Then where's defiling dust to cling?*
>
> *If you can reach the heart of this,*
>
> *Why talk of transcendental bliss?*

> — Hui Neng

This freedom is entire and complete. It can be felt, but not cognized (despite these cognizing words)—terms such as "infinity" and "eternity" are the perfume of it, the impossible-to-pin-down scent of the moment.

The nature of this moment of *now* foretold all this; perfectly clearly, this very instant is impossible to capture with thought and so is utterly undivided, and cannot be divided—and is unhesitatingly where we live and have our being: no matter what, no matter who, no matter when.

A multitude of the already-intuited aspects of this flood in: the sheer unalloyed emptiness, ever on display, seemingly behind our eyes, inexplicably intimate with the everything-ness. Time-lessness is obvious, intimately woven with time, which is the dreamt-theater of the dreaming of it.

This is the natural territory of the heart, the untouched (and untouchable) landscape of it. This is the "What is" of J. Krishnamurti, the "As it is" of Tulku Urgyen Rinpoche, "The gift you receive, that you are" of Jean-Pierre Weill, the "This is it!" of Alan Watts and the "All there is" of Tony Parsons. And, this is the end of all seeking, of which Huang Po himself remarked *"Having many sorts of knowledge cannot compare with giving up SEEKING for anything, which is the best of all things."*

> *Once you have understood that you are nothing perceivable or conceivable, that whatever appears in the field of consciousness cannot be your self, you will apply yourself to the eradication of all self-identification, as the only way that can take you to a deeper realisation of your self. You literally progress by rejection —a veritable rocket.*
>
> — Nisargadatta Maharaj

Conceptualization is a miracle within the dreaming, leading eventually and inevitably to the concept of the long-lasting independent self that so captures our attention that it can only be the repository of the final suffering, propelling its own dissolution. Spiritual seeking can be nothing but the signal-flare of this distress, the last desperate grab by the total failure of separateness. Entirely paradoxically, separateness eventually fails by *virtue* of the tool of separation, the sharpest tool, sometimes used only once: "*Let me repeat, that the perceived cannot perceive.*"

~

Now is all there is

My good friend had just come back from studying with a European teacher by the name of Jean Klein. As she shared her experience with me she remarked in a rather matter-of-fact tone that now is actually all there is.

Our friendship goes back over several decades of deep trust in each other's psychological and spiritual exploration and I was aware that she was simply saying how things are for her, not imparting teaching or doctrine to me. I was very affected, by a truth that hitherto I had heard but not been able to absorb in any significant way.

Subsequently in a chapter about meditation in one of Jean Klein's books I read his—to my knowledge unique—proposal that the only purpose of meditation is to discover if there is a meditator. Somewhat ruffled and my self-assigned status as a meditator piqued, I took the book and a cushion out to the hills behind my house and sat down to discover if I could find the meditator.

I couldn't. There are just thoughts and these masquerade as the meditator. No matter how long we sit on our cushion no meditator can be found. An endless stream of thoughts—the most problematic of which are thoughts seeming to come from a putative meditator trying to meditate better—is all we can ever notice that might even constitute a meditator. But if we are a "good meditator" we will know full well that no matter their composition, the thoughts cannot be us.

These thoughts imply an enduring person who sits down to meditate, notices their thoughts and makes progress based on deepening noticing. Indeed, noticing can deepen as a result. But noticing also deepens if we simply follow the profound curiosity in ourselves about our inmost nature. Over time there's the gradually dawning recognition that this that is curious is absolutely not different than the "I" it is curious about.

This recognition, sometimes spoken as "The seeker is the sought," or "The observer is the observed," is also the gradual collapse of belief in the reality of time as existing objectively in a reality outside of ourselves. Only in the theater of time, furnished entirely by concepts, can there be a separate observer and observed, or seeker and sought.

In *now*, before thought throws up the separation that we take for granted as reality of observer and observed, there is nothing of the kind: no dividedness. *Now* is the only reality there is, as well as the indubitable reality of the heart. Anything else is conceptual; brilliantly useful, yet wrought by thought and time.

∽

Part Two

Unfolding

The knack of being

Easy now

Truly, in one way there is nothing much to say about this now, or nowness; this where we always are—effortlessly. This is where we cannot not be; now. Yet for all its seeming-momentariness, it is atomic in nature and expands infinitely in loving attention.

When we attend to it lovingly for ourselves we will immediately recognize the easeful space of being that waits for us always here, *now*. Try it, and discover that the wearisome habitual busywork of trying to get somewhere in life can pause. In this cessation—and it is totally okay if it is just a moment—the ease of being that is everywhere is suddenly apparent.

If the trees live this, and the clouds, and my dog and the rivers and hills, how difficult could it be?

> *After all our futile efforts to transform our ordinary minds into idealized, spiritual minds, we discover the fundamental paradox of practice is that leaving everything alone is itself what is ultimately transformative.*
>
> — Barry Magid

But by dint of long practice we've got things upside down. What is actually quite difficult (like ignoring now, which never goes away) seems natural and easy while something inherently easeful seems like it needs seeking in order to find it. When actually, it is never not here.

To clarify my stance, writing this: I am not an expert

pronouncing on how things are. If anything, this writing is simply the reporting of what is found to exist when the effortful is peeled back and the easeful gradually revealed.

This immersive experience of myself yields to curiosity, revealing itself layer by layer to be very different to the story that was already firmly in place when I first noticed the dreadfully familiar suffering of separation.

That story—which we all believe in so deeply it seems like reality; obvious reality, beyond doubt—is that solely a separate-I exists and is now sitting here speaking these words and looking at the computer screen. There is no doubt about the existential reality of a large part of that story: I could take a photograph of myself right now, showing my body sitting here. A video would reveal someone I identify in the mirror as "myself," speaking these words.

What neither the story, the photo, nor the video reveal is the silent companion to all this, namely the remarkable and completely inexplicable *presence* of consciousness.

Our silent companion

If we were to subtract consciousness there would be nothing at all: no myself, no photo, no video, no section of writing. On the other hand, subtracting an element like the computer screen, or the particulars of my British accent makes no difference whatsoever to consciousness, which goes right on imperturbably simply being here, *now*.

Our believed-in story even incorporates consciousness by saying it lives inside the container of my skin body, principally in my brain, in my head. So there is consciousness here, inside my head and a dead material world out there. A lonely business, no doubt about it. The story tells itself, and is believed to the point of complete lifelessness. The world, once magical in childhood and without limits, has become overgrown by knowledge, and is thereby suffused with dullness. This dead dullness is the effect of a story that is not true, but is infused as the sole reality during an inevitable colonizing process we call "growing up."

The story lives in thought. The I of this story lives in time: something like *As yesterday was, so tomorrow will be.* Time is very much connected to a sense of incompleteness which promises to be completed in the future, a promise that is achieved by pulling good experiences towards myself and trying to keep bad experiences away. The bad, I hope, is not me, and the good is me; I will eventually be happy, I hope.

> *Thinking that there is somewhere to go, that there is something that must be attained, is the basic illusion.*

> — Thomas Merton

But the aware is-ness that is backdrop to time has no such partiality: everything, including the story, all of time, and every last atom of experience is welcomed by this isness. This isness welcomes the human busy-ness of stretching towards good experiences and recoiling from bad. In the moments of this like-don't-like kind of living the imperturbable existence of the isness, of presence suffusing everything seems quite well camouflaged.

How can we know this presence? Our initial realization of it often involves a spiritual teacher, who, however, is just pointing out something we've always known is here. If any sort of guidance exists from how this has tended to unfold for me, there may be a prolonged period of repeatedly gazing at what seems like indubitable reality before, in the presence of curious, still noticing, it begins to become porous, and there is gradually some freedom from the imprisoning net of beliefs. More simply, this gazing is curiosity in the space of suspended belief.

Real beliefs

To make that practice of "gazing" concrete, I'll name the two realities all of us are familiar with, one on either side of the apparent divide of observer and observed. Looking in toward ourselves there's consciousness. We don't know what it is, but without exception, even without thought, everybody can say *I'm conscious*. We believe awareness, sentience is enclosed within the biological envelope of our bodies. Only very rarely does somebody turn back towards this consciousness and gaze, and gaze, and gaze to find out in direct experience whether this deeply believed-in conviction of enclosure is true.

Looking outward, there are things, the material stuff of the universe, the outside that is the counterpoint to the conscious inside. One of our most bedrock beliefs is that these two, inner and outer, conscious and material *are actually divided one from the other*. We might even find ourselves saying that the belief reflects the reality of this dividedness, but the only way to be completely sure about that is to see what's actually true *before the belief sways our experience*.

The before-belief knack

Just how do we check what's here before belief tells us what's true? Belief can always be detected as some kind of thought or experience—sometimes merely a subtle image, other times a barely discernible sense in our body, and probably, in addition, the more familiar blatant repetition of sentences affirming a reality—that everybody knows to be real, do they not? It couldn't be any other way, could it, than that consciousness or mind is enclosed within my head and body? How on earth else would things be, other than that the observer is divided from the observed? That I am a separate observing consciousness fundamentally divided from the world in which I live?

Just in case we wonder if anything exists before all these thoughts, consider a young baby. Infants have very profound perceptions, responses, behavior and even distinct individuality—but only later do they learn the capacity to divide the world up into conceptual chunks. Only much, much later do they find themselves completely imprisoned as adults by the belief that these conceptual chunks (like observer and the observed, like consciousness inside our bodies) describe how the world *actually is*.

So this gazing-before-belief is actually very simple—it is natural for babies—although not necessarily easy. What we'll be doing in the next few pages is gazing at the reality represented by these two beliefs—"enclosed consciousness," and "the subject-object divide" and finding out what's true, for ourselves, in our own direct experience. Discovering this is like a knack, and just like the knack of riding a bicycle or swimming there can be a tremendous excitement when we discover *This is built-in; I can do this as if it's absolutely natural to me.* We might call it the knack of being.

Not-two, gazing together

Perhaps I might invite us for a few minutes to gaze together; this experiment will absolutely include me. To do this we'll be going to the edge of the springboard of words, bouncing up and down gently in ruminative contemplation for a while and then diving off into the pool of utter silence where thought is absent.

The paradoxical fact that I'm going to comment on this silence using words is simply the irrevocably strange nature of this use of the finite to reach toward infinity. If we bear with the process, we can see what happens in our own experience —in that, is (or is not!) the proof of the pudding.

The walls of belief are made of thoughts. Just as the bricks that build a wall are separate one from another, so thoughts have gaps between them: how else could we distinguish one thought from another? In those gaps, thought is absent.

As said earlier, infants seem to be thought-free, and since we were all once young children, this possibility must be inherent in us, since it is naturally present before the conditioning of language overtakes us. We are born absent of thought.

If we examine thought closely and meticulously, with great alertness, and notice the sequence of life and thought we will more and more clearly discern that thought always comes after life. Life, the now-instant of it, *happens* and thought chases after it, endeavoring to catch up but never succeeding. So thought is *inherently about* something that happened in the past, even if it's the just-past. Or thought is busy turning memory on its head and anticipating the future. But the one place thought cannot go is the middle of this moment of *now*.

To check this, we can snap our fingers, or rap a knuckle on a piece of furniture: in the middle of that sound, in the very now-moment center of the sound, can thought be there? Or does thought show up afterwards? While thought and imagination might be very good at putting together a series of raps to make a fine dancing rhythm, it simply does not have access to the very middle of the moment.

A vibrantly alive pool

This is the pool we can dive off into: occupy the middle of the moment.

Two things about this: the first is that the middle of the moment is always present—is it ever not *now*, where experience is taking place? The second is that this process here called "gazing" truly is natural to you; although we don't have their report we can clearly feel the energetic signature of this experience when we're in the company of horses, dogs, lizards, trees, clouds and rivers. Gazing is a natural amalgam of curiosity, being still, and a suspension of believing what thought says is so in favor of our direct present moment experience. Sometimes this suspension of believing is called "letting go"—when we release what we believe is true in thinking, and are curious and quiet, what is here? *Right here*, in the very middle of *now*?

The first thing we might notice is how astonishingly full experience is; rich, vibrant and overflowing with energy. Traffic humming down in the valley below; the tingling of my body; this brightly lit desk scattered with pens and connecting cables and notebooks; the flavors of tea in my mouth; the drifting scent of a neighbor's barbecue.

Wherever our attention alights—whether this be in the form of seeing, hearing, touching, tasting, or smelling—this experiencing is an effortless brimming over of vitality, of life itself. We don't have to do anything, do we, for all this experience to happen? If we are completely still and quiet for a moment, everything goes on, doesn't it?

As we become more still, we can gradually enter the quiet of what is here in the middle of the moment. We may find the odd bubble of thought popping up, but each such bubble, recognized as an ambassador from the world of "past" and "future" helps us to notice more and more deeply the nature of now. The past and future is also the world of observer distinct from the observed—to take the true gift of thought is to step delicately from thought's confining of the real to the openness of direct experience itself.

The knack of noticing

The knack of being shows up in noticing the difference between thought, and direct experience: at first it may not be so apparent that there is a difference between {the experience of bird song + the label "bird song"} and the untrammeled, unconfined energy that is consciousness as bird song; completely open and magically free, observer-intrinsic, abundantly filled with aware presence not different than the song.

We are so accustomed, so habituated and automated to ceaselessly place labels on things that it seems that the universe *consists* of the *things* named by the labels: a material existence, distinct from the naming consciousness, or so we deeply believe. This capacity for naming is quite possibly one of the greatest miracles in creation—when we twig to it, starting at birth, with it gradually becoming compelling over the next 7 years of life, we have discovered the root of all the technological and creative marvels each one of us is heir to.

Unfortunately, but absolutely necessarily, what we also start to absorb in that early innocence is what seems like a reality: that *I am exclusively my body*, that *my body contains consciousness*, and that *outside my body is the separate material world*.

This interpretation of reality is necessary because this is what all of our global tribe believe, and live by, and our joining the tribe is baked-in biologically; adopting this perspective of "the way things are" is inexorable.

Yet there is also a deeper realm to this universal interpretation of reality: the suffering it inevitably brings, in due course provokes the journey of return to the deep truth, one form of which is the expedition we're undertaking here.

The practice of gazing—of simply noticing what is immediately and directly so in present experience unfiltered by thought—can readily reveal something rather astonishing about ourselves. When we notice it we may not believe it, or our mind may prefer to shred it, pooh-pooh it, or otherwise dismiss it. But it will still be true every time we come back, and again notice what is so in the moment of *now*.

Hearing ourselves revealed

Look, gaze with this quiet, curious stillness to find ourselves. This is a classic instance of using thoughts to jump off into a quite different, almost secret existence, never not here, right alongside our present life, yet hidden from us by labels. Where does our attention go as we look to find ourselves?

We may notice our body, its visual outline, the tingling of our cells, vibrantly alive. We will almost certainly hear a repetitious screed of thoughts that say *this-is-me this-is-me this-is-me this-is-me*. But what if we pause these thoughts for a moment, gaze with curiosity and quietude, alert in all our senses to what is experientially so when this labeling is paused?

Everything keeps right on happening without the thoughts. Hearing continues unabated, in fact becomes more acute—because aren't sounds always and only *now*? Somebody listening—that would be "me," according to the thought—is simply something added by thought, isn't it? Although this thought is deeply believed, it remains simply a thought. In our direct experience of *now* there is just listening or hearing.

Can we actually find a hearer, in direct experience or is there just effortless listening, or hearing? When thought falls quiet for a moment what remains? What shall we call it, that which is left when thought is quiet?

It is here, now, unstoppably vibrant and dynamic, appearing from nowhere, without dimensions yet unmistakably present. Thought says "bird song-computer fan-traffic-breathing sounds: all heard by me." But take away those boxes for a moment and just be. Notice for ourselves what is here *now*.

> Please remember that nothing offered here is from an expert perspective: reading this, we are together exploring this gazing meditation-inquiry-contemplation, in which writing is just a readout of direct experience.

> Writing this from my own present moment experience is my own invitation to myself, to pause, to slow down long enough and be contemplative so that the familiar contrails of thought dissipate and reality is left vividly open. The discoveries we are making here are not made in an instant: if they were, our fast-paced world would be full of them.

Sensing ourselves

Because we are mostly mentally distracted from the actual this-moment experience of our bodies by our believed-in body-images, we don't very often check to see what's really and truly here in sensing. So we tend not to notice that the *sensation* of our body is quite remarkably amorphous and diffuse.

What belief says is the edge of our body is directly-and-experientially nothing whatsoever like that; on the contrary, what thought and image declares is the edge, the boundary, the sharply differentiated skin-air or skin-clothing border is, in direct experience, very fuzzy-feeling, and quite indistinct. In this fuzziness we certainly can't feel a clear division between the clothing or air and our skin. Can we, right now in direct experience, find any such clear dividedness?

Similarly—and we can check in with ourselves about this; notice our own direct experience—we might become aware that where our backside meets the chair, or our feet rest on the floor, or our hand touches this book or our phone or screen/mouse/trackpad—in fact wherever there is twoness *in thought*, we will discover only *one* sensation in directly-sensed reality, *now*, unfiltered by thought.

Wherever thought says "I am/resting my feet on the floor/sitting on this chair/musingly stroking my chin as I read this and investigate whether it's true,'" there is just *one* sensation happening in each case. We can't distinguish feet from floor, in our unfiltered experience of bodily sensation. We can check this out for ourselves. And {my backside + the chair I'm sitting on} turns out to be, in direct experience, one single sensation. Even my hand thoughtfully stroking my chin is a single experience, not {hand + chin}.

If you find yourself disagreeing with these statements please, deeply explore your own experience—as much as possible uncontaminated by concepts and thought—before you dismiss the invitation of this writing. Should the discovery emerge that there is no separate listener, yet there is hearing, and should you quietly notice there is no separate recipient of sensations, yet there is sensing, and should you find that these discoveries awaken consternation and bewilderment, or awe and astonishment in you, read on.

Seeing ourselves

We *very* strongly believe that seeing is done by particular, localized, individual lookers. Everything—accepted biological science, common sense and the *this-is-reality* conviction of billions of people—affirms this belief. Only very rarely does somebody explore visual reality persistently enough to find out what's really true.

To begin to dismantle the walls of this particular imprisoning belief we'll need a doubling up of our tools. We'll continue to see what's here in the instants when thought has nothing to say on the subject, and we'll add in the recognition of what we discover, in unfiltered direct experience *when we turn our inner gaze to visual gazing itself.* We'll look nakedly at looking; looking noticing itself.

Finding and then using this second tool will also enable us to discover for ourselves, in our own direct experience, if consciousness *is* contained within our biological interior, as another of our bedrock beliefs says it is. This second tool will also help us clarify the mystery—and make clearer the self-evident reality—of hearing without a hearer, and of sensing without a sensor.

We can turn our attention now 180° from its usual outward direction of looking and become as alert as we can to what we are noticing: we can gaze back, as it were, toward the gazing itself.

We might find it helpful to point a forefinger at our face, but once we have done this, bring in our first tool, becoming alert and curious to what is directly experienced here *now* when thought isn't running the show. What is this from which we've always looked? This we've always called me or I ("*my* body," "*my* mind," "*I* can hear," "*I* can feel"): *what is it actually like in our own present moment directly-noticed experience?*

The late Douglas Harding, who originated this very helpful pointing experiment, used to say that almost everybody sees the reality their finger points to but relatively few people believe what they see. But our first tool helps greatly here: we point our finger, or simply reverse the direction of our attention—then pause the habitual there-and-then momentum of our thought stream, or look over the shoulder of it. We take our time; we are openly curious.

What we cannot not be

We be here *now* and allow what we cannot not be to take in what we are noticing. This is akin to the effortlessness of listening, or the ease of sensing. Isn't what we're noticing with our pointing finger or our reversed attention utterly and completely effortless?

Remember, if we are convinced this about-turn of attention simply points to our eyes, or our face, or our brain, we have been lassoed by thought; without referring to what we believe, without bringing in what we have learned or have been taught, without reference to imagination, leaving aside even feeling, what is this that we're noticing?

Because adequate description may be very hard, or impossible to come by, instead we can let ourselves bathe in the sheer noticing for a while. Perhaps we'll find curiosity gradually spilling over into wonderment because the more we honor our direct present moment experience, the more remarkable this becomes.

Thought always does an end run around this, routinely a million times a day mumbling in the back of awareness "I-am-looking-out-of-my-eyes-which-are-connected-to-my-brain-which-is-inside-my-body-which-is-where-localized-conscious-ness-is-contained." When everybody believes this as if it is absolutely true, how very difficult it can be to look for ourselves.

We may find the ordinary momentum of thought profoundly uncomfortable with what we are noticing, and ourselves unable to stay for more than a second or two in this gazing at reality. We may find amazement, awe, wonder, a profound sense of mystery—or possibly, the experience that thought is so entrenched that anything but "I-am-looking-out-of-my-eyes-just-like-everybody-else-is" seems like the silliest silliness.

Silent seers: knowing, knowing knowing

Perhaps we might feel encouraged by noting what the *Katha Upanishad*, one of the most ancient and venerated spiritual documents on the planet says on this subject (this version has been slightly adapted to reflect the gender-free universality of what the teaching points to):

God made the senses turn outwards, people therefore look outwards, not into themselves. But occasionally, a daring soul, desiring immortality, has looked back and found themselves. They are the imperishable among things that perish.

Could it be that in this turning back, in this naked looking *at* our own experience by means *of* our own experience we are beginning to discover the real nature of ourselves—and perhaps even find intimations of our own immortality within it?

Perhaps encouragement could also come from reporting some of my own experience, for I am following along with this exploration, taking my own invitation to directly look into the place from which I'm seeing, just as I'm now inviting here. Is my experience anything like yours?

There is a particular kind of nothing here, where my reversed attention, my looking back reveals a hard-to-describe openness. About this openness, I can do nothing whatsoever. This open spaciousness is conscious—that is, effortlessly alert, present to everything—and entirely without dimensions.

I say "here" but if I obey my own injunction to slip out of thinking for a moment this small word of location, "here" turns out to be a thought, and sliding free of it I can find absolutely no edge to this openness, nor location. In immediate direct experience, no edge or boundary can be discerned to this openness I call by the familiar term "here."

"Here," as I very well know, conventionally refers to where my body is, or the building I'm in, or my town, or country, even planet or universe. But the backdrop to this infinite range of meanings of "here" *in concepts* is truly this here-less-ness in direct experience, about which logic, rationality and intellect are completely at a loss.

This open here-less-ness can be known, but this knowing is not the knowing of an object by a subject. Rather, it is the greatest of all miracles—which is that this knowing knows itself. And —thinking mind overlooked, labeling fallen quiet—this knowing noticing itself manifestly cannot possibly be confined. The very nature of knowing, aware of knowing is unlimitedness.

If instead of "knowing, noticing knowing" I said "awareness cognizant of consciousness" or "presence conscious of awareness" it would be easier to parse in rational thought, as in, one thing being conscious of another. But when mind's labeling is put aside and this knowing, knowing knowing is contemplated in thoughtless curiosity and quietude there is palpably neither time nor edge to it. All things known are quite simply this knowing, knowing knowing.

Knowing nothing

The risk of talking about "knowing" is that it may seem like some-*thing*, yet when we turn curious experiencing towards it, it is the essence of all that is gossamer: completely airy, insubstantial, utterly beyond harm.

Because it is beyond harm, because it is causelessly here, because we can do absolutely nothing to move it, change it, modify it, hurt it or destroy it, it paradoxically is also the quintessence of what we mean when we say something really exists.

Every-thing that exists, borrows, so to speak, its existing from this imperturbable ceaseless causeless knowing. Insofar as existing means to endure, this possibility comes from the only truly enduring reality, this open knowing; luminously conscious, formlessly and seamlessly intimate with all possible forms.

Where might I find I, myself, in this world turned right way up? Could it be, as the *Katha Upanishad* remarks, that the essence of the very depth of this deathless knowing beyond harm is what I really, really mean every time I say "I"?

~

Crashing from grace, into grace

From the get-go at the University of Southampton I was an accomplished student and applied myself with great enthusiasm and energy to the study of psychology. When, three years later, the final examinations for my B.Sc. arrived on the horizon, my professors, certain of my exam performance, had already obtained a postgraduate place for me at University College London, or UCL.

UCL was one of the best psychology departments in the country, and my professors had found me, along with the placement, a generous stipend for the expenses of studying for a Ph.D. I hazily anticipated a career in academia, because I'd loved few things in my life as enthusiastically and generously as the endless under-graduate hours in the University of Southampton library, slicing and dicing ideas, my intellect a-sparkle. Earning the ultimate goal of all the work of those three years—the bachelor's degree—depended almost entirely on my performance in that week of final exam papers.

Like my professors, I had little doubt of my first-class result until, in the examination hall with hundreds of other students, at the proctor's signal I opened the first question paper on the desk in front of me. And had a breakdown, a sudden ripping and tearing of the stur-dily assembled (and until that moment) dependable reality of the previous three years.

I realized that all that my three years of study had prepared me to do was regurgitate data from my memory banks onto the paper before me. Below my neck nothing whatsoever had changed in those years in the library. My degree status rested entirely on not-very-important data that I had memorized, and on ideas that were just ideas, no matter how brilliantly I could cut and thrust with them.

The dots took years to connect, but in that moment of

the floor of my life falling away in the examination hall, I became implicitly aware of the existence of transformation, and even more crucially aware that whatever I had been so enthusiastically focused on in the form of psychology was not transformative.

The question "What is missing from psychology?" was born, simultaneously with the transmutative death of a part of me that had grown strong and confident about my intellect in those three years of undergraduate study.

With help from the tranquilizers given me by a doctor I visited immediately after that first exam, I limped dispiritedly through the rest of the papers, squeaking an upper-second degree and thereby saving my postgraduate spot.

But the stuffing was knocked out of me. I couldn't any longer pretend that psychology—at least, the unadventurous empirical-experimental flavor of British psychology at that time—contained what I had been unknowingly looking for.

(The story continues in *"Answers in the basement."*)

I am the seeker

That's it—my whole identity as separate-seeming, is that *I am looking for something*. The absence of this would be to be free—and now—since the looking-for-something takes me away into time.

Or so it seems: the unlimited immensity of immediacy, of what now *really* is—infinite every moment—would be, so to speak, freed up to live as me. This much can be glimpsed in the moments between thoughts. It may be a terrifying prospect (to myself-as-thought-mind); of no-control, of surrender, of non-volitional living (it is also the less-obvious dawning of ease, peace and causeless happiness—but those are not the qualities that bare their fangs and growl at me when this is glimpsed.)

In my seeking I have turned lately to the wearisome observation, a thousand, thousand times that I (!) still very much believe in an "I" who lives in time and will one day find fruition. This version of I seems so much more pleasant to live with, so much more predictable and under control than the deathly risk of everything being dictated by forces beyond my control, or some such locution of how life is apparently currently lived. Yet is any element of life, whether it be climate, thoughts, feelings, news and social media items, relationships or health, is there really any control, beyond fond imagining?

This feels arduous: sitting quietly for 30 minutes, noticing the swirls of identity, recognizing the blips of fear when another possibility is glimpsed, is now going to be swallowed up by breakfast, and the reading of the news; comforting actions so riddled by familiarity that the whole topic of these few paragraphs will conveniently vanish from view.

Of course we search

Our searching is the most natural thing in the world. Coming up out of the complete fulfillment of infancy, we gradually find ourselves inveigled into the adult model of happiness being elsewhere, in time and space. There seems no other solution for the misery that gradually envelops us; intrinsic happiness is lost, and we must find it.

Decades will possibly pass before we realize that it is the searching for happiness that has made us miserable. It may take us even longer to engage in the most radical exploration of all: to give up seeking and see what is here.

During these decades we learn how to acquire, use, and then practice, practice, practice being someone separate. Or *seeming* to be apart; we gradually forget our early experience; forget we once knew ourselves to be intrinsically interwoven with everything. Our primal perceiving of undividedness gradually disappeared from view as we assiduously practiced separate-selfhood.

And, separate-seeming selfhood is not a mistake, but a blessing, in myriad ways—as well as a curse. Equipped with the idea of time (now taken to be reality) we can dream up marvelous buildings, and construct them for our comfort. We can also dream up that whole groups of other people are detestable, and destroy them, also for our comfort. But the misery of our loss of intrinsic-interwovenness—and the unhappy empty searching prompted by it—are our faithful companions, and they never leave us.

So our searching is entirely natural: this is what we have been taught to do, to solve the problems of our life. If we are seekers we apply ourselves with tremendous intensity to the quest. Like the great avatars of religions, like a Jesus, Buddha, Lao Tzu, or Mansour, we search and search until, perhaps we encounter a venerable teacher whose words resonate at the deepest level within us. The translation may be misleading, the patina of time obscuring, but the import is unmistakable: stop searching, and relinquish conceptualizing, and you are home; the Buddha mind is everywhere you are (and "you" are not solely the separate-seeming entity you were taught you are.)

This takes a while to sink in—plainly; all we have been taught, all we have been conditioned to do, and the example of every single person around us tells us to search and to seek. Time is vastly more important than nowness, which we have also been taught is nothing; only the transition between past and future, an inexplicable blip in time.

Perhaps someone mentions infinity and eternity, someone respected, someone whose voice sounds like it comes out of the timeless. Perhaps there are momentary glimpses; that infinity and eternity could not possibly be anywhere and anytime than here *now*.

These glimpses are of reality, a kind of implicit recognition that what is momentarily seen is precisely and exactly what was lost—as if seeking-for-something overtook, camouflaged, and then buried intrinsic-being early in childhood. (It did.)

But it is arduous to take the road less traveled, and singularly alone: there are companions, but most of them have not taken a breath for centuries. However, their words live on.

We resonate when Jesus says become again as little children. There is a flicker of recognition deeper within us when Huang Po suggests the cessation of seeking, even of conceptualizing. We know, even dimly, that he—and now we—may be on to something.

What is also vividly apparent is that this we are *now* does not exist in the world of concepts except as the tiny and evanescent notion of "now." It makes no sense to talk of deepening into now—yet that is our meditation.

We may recognize that everything we ever did that was intentional and effortful "meditation" was simply this; doing our best to stay close to now (which is paradoxically impossible to leave). We recognize, with increasing depth, power, and the resonance of wisdom, that in deepening into nowness, we are immersing ourselves in what we had to relinquish long, long ago—what we had to abandon in favor of searching, seeking and conceptualizing.

All of this may be accompanied by an intrinsic knowing: we have never, ever, for an instant or by the width of an electron been away from this nowness. "Being away" is no more possible than separating water from wetness, or heat from flame.

If I say the word "cow" to you, then try to describe her sight, sound, smell, and texture to you in an effort to evoke the animal herself, redolent with mooing and munching, I will fail. But as soon as we come into the barnyard to meet the cow herself, all will suddenly be clear. The word "now" is much the same—but the cow, the *now* herself, is here, real, and available: there's no need to be led into the barnyard to see for ourselves. Searching, natural though it is, cannot in any way find the now herself; when searching falls away, as it may, she is suddenly, vividly, immediately and obviously apparent. She is fulfillment: we never left.

Amazing

The extraordinary nature of this finding—potentially the end of the torture of seeking—is that when it is relaxed into, it turns out to be never not here. It was always here. It is always here.

Relaxed into, there is the astonishing felicity that what we were striving towards all those countless other times is inescapable; only striving camouflages it from us. Only our trying to find it hides it from us.

So when the great Buddhist teacher Huang Po suggests to stop seeking and cease conceptualizing, he is simply speaking from this reality: in the no-place, no-time where we already exist, no matter what (we call it "now," believing it to be part of time, which it is not), no conceptualization of it is possible. This moment (remember! Where we universally live, all the time, not a place to get to!) is inconceivable.

Anything said about it can only come from the system of dividing things up into concepts, which system is born from this infinity, but is only a child of it.

My dog looks at me with unstinting innocence and complete openness. From the woods next to my house comes bird song, and further down the valley, chainsaws. Conveying these experiences here is *only* courtesy of the miracle of language and concepts. Suddenly, via this miracle there appears to be time, and enduring things; my dog, for example, bird song, chainsaws—and "me."

Yet whenever I can re-member that all my seeking and striving—to understand, to describe, to convey—is an emergence from the great ocean that we call "*now*," there can also be a relaxing back into the warm beneficence of the ocean. It is amazing to float here, where everything and everybody lives, all of the time, perpetually tingling, shimmering and changing; this is conscious existing, effortlessly loving to be.

~

Answers in the basement

The stacks of the University of London Library had
the Eastern philosophy section in the basement. When
I trailed disconsolately out of the psychology shelves,
having found nothing there with the remotest spark to
correspond with the abyss glimpsed in my breakdown
(which was, as they tend to be, a break-through),
gravity and who-knows what else led me downward

into a cornucopia of wisdom I had no previous idea even existed.

Here were hundreds of teachers, mystics, practitioners, seers and yogis, all of them manifestly reporting a commonality, a perennial wisdom that immediately and obviously had the flavor of what I had sought in psychology, but could not name. Here were people talking about the experience of being separate—and not being separate—from the hill, while others celebrated the nature of profoundly transformative change in a realm entirely behind and beyond the mind. There was grace for me in that stack.

I didn't finish the Ph.D. but truncated it into a master's degree, which was the least of what I attended to in the next two years. At the new personal growth centers that were springing up in London at the time, I launched hungrily into an exploration of myself far enlarged beyond any ideas I had hitherto possessed.

Eventually, fed up with noticing the limitations of group leader after group leader who wanted me to expand no further than the template of themselves, I turned to Zen, sitting zazen meditation at the London Zen Priory under the direction of the delightfully-named Reverend Hofuku Hughes, and spending a lengthy spell residing at a Zen monastery in the north of England, cold, hungry and deeply perplexed about what this had to do with anything I was interested in. I began training as a Gestalt therapist with a tough student of Fritz Perls, Isha Bloomberg, who qualified himself as nearly as abrasive and offensive as his own teacher had been.

One feature of the London growth and meditation scene at that time was particularly irritating to me: amidst the advertisements for workshops and groups in the personal growth section of *Time Out*, the prime guide to London at the time, there appeared a weekly ad for a meditation center. This ad quoted Rajneesh's remark that for meditation to happen, the meditator first needed to throw out their madness in catharsis before stillness could descend upon them. Every week I read this and every week, from my newly-arrogant perspective of being a silent-sitting meditator, I pooh-poohed what I read.

The eventual award of my masters degree was completely overshadowed by my vivid explorations of what I'd come to see as my real study of psychology in the London personal growth centers, and then inside Zen. I ignored the award to the extent of calling my brother on graduation day and proposing we set up a retail bicycle store business together, a suggestion that morphed into a successful store in northwest London. Nearly a year after we opened our doors a policeman came into the store to tell us that our mother had died of injuries received in a car accident.

(The story continues in *"Pierced by dying."*)

Now ≡ Awake

"Now" and "awake" are identical. In our own immediate direct experience we *cannot* find where "now" stops and "awake" starts. "≡" is from math: it means "is identical to" or "not other than."

The more we relax with this reality (which is reading these words, this moment), the easier life is. This is life lived from the source, from the only place life itself really lives, which we call "now," but which we easily overlook is "awake now." This is the *only* "time" of our heart.

Becoming more attuned to this awakeness (that is identical to *now*) is easy—it is always here, for our noticing. Our noticing can rest into this intimate attunement more and more deeply. This resting feels like love, or our true nature relaxing, without end—into our true nature. Noticing, resting, and true nature are nothing but the infinite.

Words like "now," "awake," "intimate," "relaxing" and "love" are eddies on the surface of the limitless ocean we are. Yes: "*are*"—for all the other ways we think about ourselves and believe ourselves to be are also ripples and waves of this very same ocean. There is nothing besides this, and this recognition is intrinsic to our heart's knowing of reality.

So, it turns out, as this loving, curious, intimate and easeful noticing goes on, there is only this limitless ocean, and we are it. We have never left it, nor could we possibly ever leave it. We, awakeness itself, are it—*now*. "Awake" and "now" are indeed identical: the relaxation we feel when this is naturally noticed, then inhabited tells us everything.

In these pages this noticing is offered in a variety of ways— every single one of these ways being, in actuality, a glimpse of the whole ocean, offering itself; now as a "Hey, look at this: *no-one at all* separate here!" and then next minute, "Look over here! How'd ya like this timelessness?!?!" Perhaps most vividly, through the eyes of the heart of us these glimpses become sustained; illogical, inconceivable, yet unmistakable.

These kinds of recognitions are purely intuitive, or as they are sometimes called, apperceptive. Consequently, no language is adequate to them: the glimpses and episodes of seeing tend to occur when all seeking and all conceptualizing are stood aside —when all that is experienceable is recognized to be "the perceived"—which cannot, ever, in any way, perceive.

What remains cannot be perceived, is beyond harm, birth, and death, and cannot in any way be gotten rid of—only ignored, which is the meaning of "ignorance." Noticing it, words like "now" and "awake" may convey its flavor. It may take a leap to also notice it is eternity, in full view, and never not here: now≡awake≡eternity.

A further leap draws on a theme of this book, which points to the inherently-open-we that death will not destroy—the "we" reading this in this moment of *now*. Hence, the complete statement of this section is: now≡awake≡eternity≡we. All these identities are effortlessly subsumed in the intrinsic knowing of our heart.

Noticing this, we may notice—apperceptively, out the corner of our eye, in immediacy—that this knowing of itself, by itself, is the clearest possible indicator of infinity. We; the knowing of ourselves, the awakeness, and the being of us, completely configured in the unique way we are, are identically awake in the indefinable heart of now.

Teachings in titles

Spiritual teachers (or their students) tend to publish books—some of which have titles that are themselves concise teachings. Here are a few of those teachings-in-titles; read slowly in order to invite the never-not sunk-in to sink in:

> *Getting to Where You Are; Look for Yourself; Being-Time; Impermanence is Buddha-Nature; Open Secret; As It Is; I Am That; Nobody Home; No Boundary; Open and Innocent; There*

Is Only Now; All Else Is Bondage; This Is It; Great Doubt; Loving What Is; Call Off the Search; The Perfection of Nothing; Already Home; On Never Having Left; Only Don't Know; Doing Nothing; Eternity Now; All There Is; Face to No-Face; Open to the Source; The Tongue Tip Taste of Tao; The Cloud of Unknowing; The Discipline of Surrender; No-Gate Gateway; The Damndest Thing; Being Aware of Being Aware; Never Mind; Emptiness Dancing; How About Now?; Be As You Are; Flowers of Emptiness; Be Here Now.

Before we go on

What this book is about is impossible to say in words—yet the book consists of pointing to it in words.

What this book is about is *inescapable* for every human being, indeed, for every sentient being. One of the most obvious aspects of it we call "now," and it is a sheer miracle and has no time about it whatsoever, occurring by itself, ceaselessly. "Being at home" turns out to be nothing but this inescapable occurrence, vividly self-evident when the fictitious elements of time and separation evaporate in the clarity of inclusive noticing that is the most outstanding and obvious element of this flow of being.

Existence never asks you who you are.

— Osho

Time is one of the many appearances that occur in this miraculous flow—along with the seeming-presence of each one of us appearing to ourselves, by virtue of time and conditioning, as someone separate. This is not a mistake, but a feature of the miracle, provoking suffering (amongst other remarkable features, ranging from genocide to Gaugin) and potentially leading to awakening from the conditioning of seeming *exclusively* like someone separate.

Neither time nor this separate-seeming self actually exists—for nothing actually exists outside of the ceaselessly altering perpetual flow of ever-new *now*. Outside of this flow—or so it appears—are the "things" of this world that exist in "time." But neither "time" nor "things" exist the way concepts proclaim they do. The flow alone is real, and we are the flow, and cannot not be the flow—and intimately amidst the flow appear time, things, and what we ordinarily take to be "ourselves."

> *The one who is afraid is a false phenomenon, a false entity—an entity that is created by the feeling of separateness.*
>
> — Osho

The flow is entirely happy, absolutely without division, completely timeless, and the most ordinary and natural occurrence in the world, to which we have given the name "now"—thoroughly confusing ourselves by believing it is something to do with time. It is not. Time is the operation of a distinctively human cognitive capacity which abstracts "time" from the seriality of events. The flow alone is real.

These are not philosophical considerations, but simple practical observations accessible to each and every one of us, if we will but stand aside one of the other miracles of appearance—conceptualization—and see for ourselves. If we can also stand aside our habitual chasing-after—our customary searching, seeking, hunting, pursuing and chasing—it will very much help our seeing what's so for ourselves.

Seeing for ourselves, we can gradually discern that where our face is supposed to be—yes, right here where we are reading these words from—an openness of the most profound and inexplicable kind can be noticed, or glimpsed.

Here, especially, the words falter and fail. "Openness" offers only a faint echo of the deepest and most powerful experience a human being can have, for it is unmistakably the depth and power of what is glimpsed, *noticing itself.* There is no "human being" looking, at this level of noticing; there is only seeing. If you like, seeing is noticing seeing.

All of us have a believed-in, conditioned mental model of seeing which involves seer-seeing-seen (and, of course, the perspective of *time,* in which that sequence inevitably seems to occur.) The moment we turn attention backwards in the direction of our faces, noticing what's here for ourselves, immediately and directly from within (outside the oh-so-familiar restrictive web of conditioned concepts), what is plainly obvious is that the seeing has no such sequential components to it. There is no seer, nor seen: there is just *seeing.* The seeing is perfect, still, imperturbable, and exists *inseparably* from the infinity of occurrence that our conditioning has narrowed down to being something called "now."

This infinity of occurrence, this ceaseless flow of *now* was termed "impermanence" by Buddha, who is probably the most well-known person to have noticed all of the above. Instead of "openness," terms such as "the void," and "emptiness" have been used to talk about the experientially-noticeable open space vividly evident when we *see* for ourselves, instead of continuing to exclusively believe our conditioning.

Impermanence is itself Buddha Nature.

— Dogen

Unfortunately, the effect of these mysterious concepts—"impermanence," "the void," or "emptiness"—is only rarely that of looking for ourselves. Instead, we can tend to spend a long time in the conceptual wrinkles and folds of Buddhism (fruitfully, or not), unaware we can turn direct noticing backwards, that we can see for ourselves the most blatantly-noticeable reality in the whole world—and discover that what is looking is what is being looked at.

"What is looking" can be noticed directly and experientially, especially as the raw, direct *seeing* gradually predominates over the thicket of concepts camouflaging experience: "*It's my eyes, my brain, me; it's a biological process, it's me in time, etc, etc, etc.*" These are all useful fictions, *except and unless* we find ourselves passionately interested in awakening from the dreaming of the fictions (and the inevitable suffering+pleasure of them)—gradually finding ourselves in exactly and identically the same place, now transformed.

Part Three

The heart of now

WE ARE THE HEART OF NOW

Benediction

Wei Wu Wei said "...*perpetual and universal benediction*" is how life should be. So it is—when we are liberated from the need to be liberated, when the possibility *intrinsic* in our living experience is realized to be *already always here.*

My own journey with this must surely be the longest I've ever heard of; the most riddled with misunderstanding, endlessly hedged about with impossible conundrums and desperate searching. So anything I say in this piece of writing, or in my other writing, could only be the purest possible encouragement, for you are coming along much faster than I ever could.

However, questions about pace and progress bedevil this whole enterprise. As actuality is noticed, what is abundantly clear is that this was always here; just we were distracted from it by some very adamant convictions, so deeply installed in early life that they came to seem like reality itself.

We have, for example, to inhabit the conviction that *I am solely my body*, and that *I am exclusively within my body*, and furthermore, *that my body is somehow separate from the world in which it lives*, as well as *separate from the other people who are seemingly inside their bodies*—and then live within these convictions as if they are the sole reality.

These ideas together constitute our global worldview, our *belief* about reality, yet almost everybody lives them as if they are the nature of reality itself. Nonetheless, at all times and under all circumstances, the true nature of things (which is the true nature of ourselves) is completely accessible to us, and in no way at all hidden. We just have, as one old Zen wag put it, to believe what we see, not what we think.

As a preliminary step, we can notice that seeing is happening from nothing—in our own direct experience. This seeing is the purest openness, in which all the things of the world blossom. This openness has no cause, nor characteristics, and when our bodies die, this openness simply notices that happening, for it cannot die. Dying is not of its nature.

Dying is impossible for eternality, and that is the pure nature of this seeing, universal amongst us, absent in no one. We just have to look for ourselves, and see if it might be possible, by and by, to trust what we *see*, not what we *believe* we see.

The most obvious aspect of this open seeing is that it is entirely and completely *now*. It does not, in clear fact, have anything to do with time, although each and every nanosecond of time is as welcome to it as everything else. But of time itself, this has not one electron of that; it is the purest timelessness, or, the very essence of what we call now.

We can give ourselves a helpful boost in this process of exploring the obvious by coming to recognize that there is already a whole realm of our being where this only-nowness is the self-evident reality. Every single one of us were born in this realm, then had to gradually uproot ourselves from it (but only seemingly), so we could become yet one more of the innumerable mirage-bound people, the people convinced of their sole-separateness—and searching for the end of it.

Where is this natural realm, within ourselves? Quite simply, the heart of us. When seeing drops into the heart, what becomes immediately obvious is that the heart knows only *now*, and is intrinsically non-divided, so that the open seeing and the world of things are no longer divided, one from another.

The heart of now

To watch the universe emerging and subsiding in one's heart is a wonder.

— Nisargadatta Maharaj

This heart of everything is intuitively perfectly obvious; the innocence in a baby's eyes, in the open gaze of a horse, in the trusting unguarded presence evident in every dog's eyes. None are without it

This is "intuitively" discerned because rationality cannot go here. Rationality divides things, and here, no-thing is undivided from anything else—and most especially, we are no longer divided from the world, and we can have again the mystery and wonder that was intrinsic to us as children, before "adult reality" began to be necessarily imbibed; before tribal membership as a separate-seeming person had to be learned, arduously—and then the heart forgotten.

What we are undergoes a dramatic transformation in this minuscule journey of twelve inches, from head to heart. Where before we were the lonely solo traveler in profound pain about time—regret of time-gone, terror of future-time— now we find ourselves to be our true nature; utterly empty, luminous with eternality, and completely impossible to either describe, or get rid of. "Now" is what we call it.

What may remain is the remnants of the head, protesting "… *but-but-but…*" The hegemony of the head has vanished in favor of loving what is, in favor of the miracle of what is, in the depths of the profoundest of Buddha's truths: that there is, in purest truth, only nothing but changefulness. No separate self can be found, beyond deeply-believed ideas, compelling images, and blossoms of all kinds of bodily experience.

What also becomes clear is that any time the separate self-notion is needed, it can emerge from the rag-bag of conditioned functioning, and work perfectly reliably. Learning how to be a separate self—learning how to pretend ourselves as solely the fiction of a separate self, long-lasting, independently existing, and separate—this fiction does not disappear, in fact, appears with complete automaticity whenever there is need.

But there is a circumstance in which this need for the automaticity of the separate-seeming self is stood down. "*When two or more are gathered in my name,*" remarks Jesus, going on to say that then, manifest miracles multiply. The greatest of these miracles is quite simply life itself, as it is, this very moment. As the head knew, from its dim distance, from its separate-seeming perch: momentary life is inherently undivided, and cannot be rationalized.

The head, as is its way, being the servant of desire, desperately desires to grasp whatever this is that is undivided; this that cannot be rationalized, that we never leave. The mental process of imagining can substitute *pursuing* for *finding* until finally, the body of the host dies, and there is revelation when time stops—and only *now* is revealed to be the nature of the uncaused reality.

This is also the reason that the sacred heart of Jesus is a core symbol of what remains of his teachings. A Biblical "mighty angel" says that in heaven there shall be time no longer, and Jesus himself invites us to become again as little children.

Where in our current being is this open, timeless, innocent and deeply curious nature freely on display? When attention drops into the heart, when the familiar, agonized, excruciating process of trying to find something in time collapses into the reality of the non-divided *now* that is the simple home of the heart. Sometimes this dropping is abrupt, but more often, it takes place only gradually.

The heart turns out to be home, the amazing and miraculous home inhabited by no one, yet saturated by the most marvelous presence that has no cause. Sometimes called God, and sometimes, godliness, this intrinsically sacred presence is the nature of being in every particle of the minutest electron of it.

Great perfection reigns here, just as all the ancient masters and the profoundest scriptures have ever said. What tends to get missed in these scriptures, and in the hagiographies of the masters, is that all the customary machinery of the separate-seeming solo-self goes nowhere.

How could it? This machinery came into being as the brain developed, and as the inevitable shaping processes prevalent amongst parents and caregivers came to bear on the open space of innocence and completeness.

Shame is not optional, but an essential element of this brain-shaping process, and by and by a child is ashamed to admit that they can find no entity whatsoever corresponding to a separate self within themselves, no matter how hard they try, and all they can find is the openness.

No child can admit this seeming failure. A great deal of our familiar human pathologies come about because each of us has to make this deal with the devil; we have to relinquish our open innocence, our vivid intrinsic belonging to the world *as* the world, our deepest no-nature that is everything, in order to take up inhabitation as a solo fragmentary figment. We are supposed to be someone installed within a body, whose entire life is then dedicated to searching for fulfillment that can never be found, because the essence of it was camouflaged, then seemingly abandoned in the original bargain that had to be made.

The scope of this script is monumental—as are the profound power of the images and emotions essential to it. One avatar of the process ends up nailed to a cross, dying in humiliation and abject nakedness, but before he dies, he remembers himself as the heart, and in one last anguished moment of the deepest doubt, cries out to himself, to his own undivided nature, "*Have you forsaken me?*" before he is plunged into eternity, forever deathless.

Even in death we are not forsaken, or rather, even in death the forsaken bargain that we had to make as little children finally comes apart. Time vanishes, and the siren song of it stops. The shining deathless, ever here in life as the inexplicable no-presence behind our eyes, is suddenly known as the heart, through the heart of our indivisible true nature: forever intimately wedded with time, and in every instant, nothing but benediction, universal and perpetual.

Our natural home

Truth cannot be objectified. You cannot put it there and see it. You cannot hold it in your hand and see it. You cannot examine it from the outside—only from the inside, only by becoming one with it, can you feel it. Feeling is the only knowledge possible. Hence, those who know say: love is the way.

— Osho

Our heart is our natural home. We can clearly feel this. Or, our heart is the home of our nature, which is undivided.

To say "our" heart is not quite right, for it is some intimate confluence of completely personal and absolutely universal—otherwise, these seeming-two, the universal and the personal, would be divided—and this is the home of undividedness.

The heart of now

*...in the heart there is just pure knowing of that infinite bound-
less freedom of existence...*

— Kat Adamson

How is this known, that the heart is the home of undividedness? Feeling is the medium and the message—and these
words here give voice to the feeling, but the feeling is a more
subtle and delicate form of consciousness than concepts.

*Nothing like knowledge is needed—only innocence, a childlike
innocence. Vulnerable, open...*

— Osho

The heart being undivided, and feeling being waves upon the
truest ocean of being—I heard this wisdom from a teacher I
loved many years ago, with a love beyond forgetting.

At the time, listening to him, the response was a kind of
rapt thrilling; something of extraordinary significance,
almost completely hidden in the darkness within my being
was being voiced, by the man in the flowing robe on the
podium in front of me. He played the part with immaculate
totality; a long white beard, chauffeured in a Rolls-Royce,
every word spontaneously perfect poetry, from the heart of
wisdom. I could only sigh, and marvel, and hope for my
own fruition.

So the journey can be long; some of the quotations in this
book were spoken by Osho 50 years ago, while I sat in rapt
silence as he spontaneously spoke the text that would become
one of his hundreds of books. I did not know how to come
down out of my head at the time, and still these days, quite
often habitually live as if the center of my being is between
my ears and behind my eyes. I'm not unusual in this, I know:

isn't this who we are trained to be, and who we practice being, day in and day out?

At some point, perhaps about 25 years ago, an insight about the present moment inspired me to take that phrase, "*The present moment,*" and search the database of Osho's words for the occurrence of it. I found some 1300 instances, printed out perhaps the first 50 or 60 of them, and put them in a manila folder.

I could recognize the profound truth he eloquently repeated; that the heart lives completely in the present moment, and knows no other time than *now*. But the realization of this truth as the true home of myself seems like something on elastic—able to be effortfully stretched down from my head into my heart, but then being rapidly retracted, in a way that seemed impossible to regulate.

For a while, I dallied with this elastic-reaching as a practice, despite knowing full well that for myself, practices do not bring fruition, only the promise of eventual ripening. This is not entirely erroneous, as this very section demonstrates, for the journey reflected here has happened over decades, and at different phases of it, a lot of "practice."

But what becomes more and more apparent is that what is sought is already here—indeed, that the sought is nothing but the seeking—and one of the ironies of practice and seeking is that only pretending the sought is elsewhere in time hides its shining miraculousness from us already.

This could hardly be, surely? That the treasure I have always sought, always longed-for, always sorrowed over the seeming-separation from—that this treasure could always have been here, indeed, *is* here, *this* very moment?

Where? In the heart of now; in the *now* that lives uninterrupt-edly in the heart—in the *now* that is the sheer benediction of the infinite and eternal, *now* so intimate with form and time that a kind of quiet ecstasy radiates from it.

Truth is felt by the heart, by your totality.

— Osho

The ecstasy doesn't jump up and down, and wave its arms in proclamation; on the contrary, it is the deep peace of it that has the most powerful radiance. The word used in the East for this experience is *Ananda*, sometimes translated as "bliss." Sailor Bob Adamson calls it *"Loving to be,"* an inspired phrase from within the experience.

Only *now* is real

The divine will is a deep abyss of which the present moment is the entrance.

—Jean Pierre de Caussade

Only now is real. Only now is all right. Only now is whole and entire. Only now has nothing missing from it.

Only now is free. Only now is creative. Only now is beyond thought. Only now is outside time. Only now is free of the compulsion to seem solely like someone separate.

Only now is inescapable. Only now is universal. Only now intrinsically connects all beings, and all Being. Only now knows the freedom of only now—and knows it instantaneously and eternally, from within only now.

Only now knows the deepest secret: that within only now is eternity and infinity. Only now, infinite and eternal, births time, engendering suffering and prompting the illuminated discovery of only now.

Only now is reliable. Only now is trustworthy. True relaxation is possible only now. Discovery of what we are/not is possible only now. What we seek is only now.

Only now actually exists. Other than only now, everything is a fiction. Only now knows that fictions can sometimes be exceedingly useful and sometimes—like the belief in our being exclusively and only a separate-seeming-self who lives in time —excruciatingly torturous.

"Heart"

"Heart" is a literal metaphor; "heart" in metaphor means core, center, or essence—and, the moment we drop attention into our chest space, as if our eyes were in the midst of our heart, we can recognize that the heart knows only now, and nothing else. Now is the heart of life, and the heart knows only *now*.

The moment we notice Being—that our existence *at* the center of now and *as* the center of now is utterly inescapable —we also notice that we *are* the heart of being; the core, center, or essence of it, each and every one of us. This center, essence, or core is everywhere, all at once—and our intimacy with it (which can only, only, only be the intimacy with itself) is closer than close, and deeper than deep.

Already awake in the eternal now

Nothing can be done about this: we are already awake in the eternal *now*. We may just not have quite noticed it, or our noticing is unsteady. We are conditioned into our certainty that we are exclusively time-beings.

This belief hides from us our unmistakable true-nature—nonetheless, this true-nature continues at all times; uninterrupted, blithely indifferent to our ignorance, and utterly unaffected by anything whatsoever.

This true-nature is quite simply "now," or more accurately, "nowness." Resident here, the unending modulations composing what otherwise seems like time can be noticed to go on by themselves. Our conditioning (necessarily; inevitably; inescapably!) insists we cast off from this timeless residency early in life, setting out as solely separate-seeming entities made of time and biology. Then, we are thoroughly and completely distracted from our true-nature, for all we know to do is to search for the happiness we have lost—and searching is the best way of all to overlook what we cannot not be.

Perhaps most of a lifetime passes before we notice that we—our true, inescapable, essential nature—are intrinsic meditation itself. There is no other possibility; this stillness never went anywhere, and never could. The immemorial causelessness of it cannot be overturned. Without it, nothing could exist.

Wei Wu Wei remarks that "it" is "*...that universal and limitless interior...which is all we ever were or ever will be, and which is out of time.*"

~

Pierced by dying

Something broke inside me with the news of my mother's death; some boundary, some barrier hitherto utterly unpierced was suddenly overwhelmed and swept away. I could not stop weeping. It went on for more than a week. I was staggered, amazed, horrified, fascinated: something completely beyond my control had colonized me with the greatest force I'd ever known.

With the death of my mom I suddenly knew that whatever my Zen practice was, it could not in any way touch the depth of the experience that was sweeping through me with such imperious power. The irritating advertisements on the back page of Time Out for the dynamic meditations of Rajneesh (subsequently known as Osho), the meditations that I had sneered at before my mom died—these, I knew with sudden complete certainty, I needed to go and do instead of my Zen practice. My mother's death was a sharp left turn in my life.

At 6 AM the next morning, in the top floor of a converted warehouse in Chalk Farm, I had my first experience of "Dynamic meditation." In the 10 minute long stages, demarcated by music changing in coordination with the stages, chaotic breathing was succeeded by vigorous catharsis, culminating in a moment of complete cessation of movement, and after frozen stillness for 10 minutes, a haunting flute melody invited spontaneous dancing.

There were about 40 of us, in a huge room. We wore blindfolds, and the raw energy that poured through the top floor of that industrial building; the power, the dynamism of Human Being liberated from constraints bowled me totally over. Specifically, where at 6 AM I had what I recognized as my neck, by 7 AM was only a fluid space of complete freedom: it was the beginning of a long journey to come down out of my head and to be embodied. I had no clue how cut off I had become from my own nature: I was just beginning to find myself.

I went every morning after that to the dynamic meditation, very often emerging onto the 7 AM streets of London—which were filled with people going to work visibly disgruntled and burdened—amazed at the cleansing I felt from the meditation, the unbelievable revitalization, as if I had been dead and come back to life.

I went, too, to the evening meditations, involving allowing a kind of gentle shaking—and of course, dancing subsequently—and after about a week of this twice-daily practice my brother turned to me one day in the bicycle shop we owned together and said "What on earth has happened to you? You used to come in here and be so active and vigorous—now you sit behind the counter as if you are stunned all the time."

My life had indeed taken a sharp left turn: the meditations I attended morning and evening were my first visceral glimpses, so to speak, of trustworthy responses to my lifelong preoccupation with spirit, suffering, energy and being. I could not put this into words: my Zen practice was a stalled effort to get closer to it.

My mother's death blew the covers off the raw emotion of it. I was groping in the dark—and for the first time in my life, reaching my hand into the shadows, I found an answering hand holding mine.

(The story continues in *"An answering hand."*)

~

No time here

No time here, where I am. All the timelessness in the world, so that time can happen. And nothing here identifiable as space: infinite capacity, yes, for there to *be* space. But no space, of the kind in the manifest world.

Time no longer

We are where we are—can be nowhere else—and hardly ever notice what it's like.

What's it like, where we are? Stop. Simply notice what it's like: when we be *exactly* where we are. Where we are *already*. Where we cannot not be.

Location is implied by words like "where." If I asked "What's it like *when* you are," I would be endeavoring to point to the time dimension—but *when* we actually are is outside time.

Here is the "peace that passeth all understanding," along with that other quality of heaven that Jesus (or "a mighty angel") is supposed to have spoken about: that there shall be time no longer. For the peace that is here, *now*—that we discover ourselves unable to not be, when we finally come to it having searched everywhere else—is entirely inexplicable: uncaused, inescapable, impossible to explain, and yet at the core of everyone and everything.

It is

(The freedom of the heart)

…there is no one who could possibly do anything….

— Kat Adamson

It simply is. This the heart knows; from within the knowing, delighting in its own knowing. This is it, always it—the energetic electricity of it, whole and perfect, moment after moment. This, the heart knows, is it; it is.

It is just as intimately being as it is knowing; the dancing together of knowing and being with such intimacy that the heart thrills with their immediacy.

No-one separate exists in this immediacy (our usual name for it is "now.") And the moment there is total cessation of seeking for anything, perfection reigns, and complete freedom.

Getting to where you are.

— Steven Harrison

The siren song of time

We are timelessness.

Then, time is conveyed, installed, created. It is a sheer marvel.

Then, we get carried away in time.

Then the magnificence of our timelessness is lost from view. Then, we start looking for what we have lost.

Ultimately, we discover that the looking itself was an artifact of time, and we stop looking.

Then, we are the timelessness we always were.

But bear in mind, or in heart, that "timelessness" *absolutely* means "no-thing-ness."

Now is inconceivable

Nothing so much hinders the soul's
understanding of God as time and space.
Time and space are parts of the whole
but God is one.
So if the soul is to recognize God,
it must do so beyond space and time.

— Meister Eckhart

It's worth letting this sink in for a bit: *now* is absolutely inconceivable. In other words, where all of us live, all of the time, without exception, is impossible to conceive.

This inconceivable-ness is the only reality. Only now is real. What is real is the essence of the life of every one of us—and it is inconceivable.

"Inconceivable" doesn't mean that it could be conceived of if somebody bright enough or smart enough or supremely gifted at language were to give it a go at putting it into words. "Inconceivable" means that it is impossible to conceive what this moment is.

Consequently, there are no dimensions whatsoever to this moment. All dimensions, all boundaries, all delineations, come about through concepts—and no concepts whatsoever are possible here, in the center of this moment where all of us live, all of the time, with no other possibility.

We do have a word that encompasses this inconceivability: the word is "infinity." This doesn't mean "very large," but rather, "without limitation." Other words and phrases encompassing this inconceivability (that all of us are, all of the time) are sacred, divine, God, onlyness, one without a second, or, in the words of devout Jews, the unnameable, G-d.

All of us are this, all of the time because there are no limits to it; no boundaries, no delineation. The time-bound, dualistic world of me separate from you, and of each one of us separate from the planet we live on is a fiction—of fantastic survival, creative, and destructive power—birthed within the undividedness which is our true nature.

So anything conceivable which we could say about life is, amazingly, extracted from the inconceivable. Another way to say this would be to say that the inconceivable, longing to sing a song of itself, gives birth to conceptuality, so the song can be sung. The almost miraculous technology of conceptuality is born from a source utterly and completely without concepts— which we are, because we can no more not-be-*now* than we could suddenly turn into rocks, or fly to Venus.

We are home free, already. There is no other possibility, in this unsayable landscape of infinity. "We" are not somewhere, for there is no "somewhere" in the unlimited inconceivable. Our only possibility is to be the unlimited inconceivable—which we already are. But mostly, most of us live in a seemingly-perpetual state of misidentification with some-"thing" plucked out of infinity. Nonetheless, our true nature as undivided nowness never ceases, nor could it ever cease.

Time is another production within this unlimited wellspring. Now is entirely without time—yet *now* is the birthplace of time, without the slightest contamination by time itself. We are not separate beings in time, born to die: we are this unlimited, undivided timelessness that is the real meaning of the word "eternity."

The undividedness is always prior, always the real, always the uncaused inescapable. Only now is real, and it is inconceivable, and all of us are nothing but it.

In the heart lies the deathless

The one place the separate self cannot stand is the now. The one place awareness cannot stand is in time.

— Rupert Spira

Time is thought

Time is made of thought and memory: there is actually no such "thing" as time. There is unceasing change—in fact the present moment of *now* could simply be defined as unceasing change. Another way to say this is that in actuality there is only now. Now is all that actually exists.

All other times besides now are fabricated in thought, a fantastically powerful bio-technology able to use memory (snapshots of now) to anticipate outcomes—the past speculatively reassembled as a potential future (snapshots reassembled so they look very much like time ahead).

But despite the fact that time is a fabrication of thought, we are entirely familiar with living in time. We are brilliant thinkers, one and all of us; our lives seem to be an endless shuttling between what was and what will be, a pure gift of life loving itself in survival. The present moment of *now* seems to hardly exist, and besides, is utterly fleeting; an evanescent will-o'-the-wisp that nobody could possibly pin down.

Yet if there is only now—if that statement resonates in some way as true for us—that surely can somehow be known directly by us. Although we are intimately familiar with time we rarely notice that this familiarity is only possible because something even deeper and more intrinsic in us is timeless, that is, has about it the very nature of *now*.

What follows is an exploration of this way of knowing the timeless now. The short form of what's presented below is that what we call "our heart" is actually nothing but the domain of the *now*. Rather than being asked to believe this, we are invited to a journey of discovering what is true for us. To find out for ourselves. The suggestions below are one way to structure this exploration of the profoundest importance.

A subtle delicacy

Think about tomorrow. Think about what has to be done, the arrangements that have to be made, meals planned, journeys calculated, time and energy and money juggled with great care. Think about further out in time, perhaps upcoming vacations or holidays, possibly job or career plans, maybe even thoughts about the lives of parents that have come to an end or that are going to come to an end. We can think far enough out to consider our own mortality.

Then we can drop attention for a moment into the middle of our chest. We can let the bubbling and chattering of thoughts go on streaming through our headspace and bring a gentle, non-insistent awareness to the area of our heart. We can pause here long enough to notice what this is like, this being here. We can inhabit our bodies here, noticing, to whatever extent we do, the soft hum and buzz and energetic twinkling of the sense of our body below our neck.

Is it possible to think about tomorrow, or yesterday while our attention rests here? Indeed, is it even possible to think, in the sense of doing what we do most of the time, which is imparting exclusive reality to the thoughts?

Isn't it more true, when we rest attention in our heart, that something about the present moment undergoes a transformation? In headspace, where the world of past and future lives between our ears, the present moment seems almost irrelevant. But drop our attention twelve inches and the world of time falls away and the present moment becomes self-apparently luminous, infused with aliveness. We have moved into the space of *feeling*, and although this more subtle and delicate form of consciousness may not be familiar to us, it is clearly the great ground of being that is *now*.

We can explore this heart space some more. We can imagine for a moment that our eyes are transposed to the middle of our chest, that seeing is happening directly out of our heart. What is the visual world like now as we look from this non-habitual place? Do we perhaps experience the objects we see as if they are altogether less known and more curiously mysterious than the flavor of our customary looking?

We can go back up our head for a minute to provide contrast. We can fling away this absurd fancy that our eyes might be in the middle of our chest and look from the hardheaded place where thoughts tell us who we are and what the world is like.

Could it be that here, in our customary headspace, objects lose their luminous luster and become merely things, whose only consequence is utilitarian? Indeed, we might notice that alongside this somewhat bleak sense of objective things, a quality of straining at the forward edge of time becomes apparent. After all, this moment barely exists, does it, for the "we" that lives predominantly from thought? What matters to thought is time, not this infinitesimal present moment, so ephemeral, so fleeting.

We can drop back down into our chest space. We can become aware of how we are affected to do that—is there perhaps a slowing, a softening, an easing, a widening and broadening, a deepening? How are sounds when we are located here? Do we perhaps find ourselves listening with a curiosity that is mostly quite absent in the hurried space between our ears? Is the world not *now* a place that is felt, not predominately thought, spontaneously imbued with an entirety and completeness only rarely and fleetingly glimpsed, from the thought-mind upstairs? Is not time quietly reconfigured as the eternity we cannot not be, undying?

Oh, there is no time

…eternity is now. There is no time.

— Alan Watts

"There is no time" is the summation of it, a way of putting it into words, but the reality is *now*; absolutely the most obvious —and the most mysterious—element in eternity and infinity.

Obvious? All exists now: now is where our being is; now is the home of the real. However, this "now" is not the sliver of time between vast past and endless future, but our timeless fundament.

We have all been trained out of our identity with this ground of being; watch a two year old trying to grasp time and separate-seeming identity and you will see this same serene fundament convulsed by efforts to achieve and embody a mirage.

The universality of this possession-by-fugue is only rarely punctured by the presence of someone who has realized their true identity—the timeless and eternal fundament—and slipped back, no longer hallucinating separateness, into the serenity of it.

This "slipping back" is not in any way the action of someone separate, but the resumption of immemorial being, intrinsically possessed by all; indeed, the reality of all, inescapable and unending—and mostly dismissed by thought, which cannot apprehend it in any way at all, but supposes it to be the tiny fragment of time that appears to separate the figments of past and future.

We all recognize the primacy of *now* but find ourselves again and again propelled—by conditioning, habit and herd-mind— into the identity-misery of pretending to be solely suffering beings in time. Yet we remain what we always were, are and will be: unidentifiable and non-separate nowness, immemorial and still.

> *...just as there is no time but the present,*
> *and no one except the all-and-everything,*
> *there is never anything to be gained*
> *—though the zest of the game*
> *is to pretend that there is.*

> — Alan Watts

"Now"; "timeless fundament"; "ground of being"; these all imply a "something" (the ever-seductive imagination of words!)—when what is pointed to is the most existential of nothings, perpetually utterly present. This is what Buddhists call "the void," despite the inextricable and absolute intimacy of it with all seeming-things appearing as it.

But surely things must appear *in* a void, not as it? Indeed: were this "the void" offered by conceptual thought, separate and in time, then "things" would have to appear in it. But the true nature of *now*, where conceptuality has no power whatsoever, is utterly undivided in this way: the intimacy is total. As the only true journey—"back into" eternally-present undividedness—proceeds, timelessly, now becomes apparent as this intimate non-separateness of "void" and "things"; always here, and never not here.

Only now *is*

When we sit down quietly and go nowhere, then we are just where we (already) are; the only place that's effortless. This is more like letting go than making any kind of effort: we stop, cease, pause, relax. But it is not going to sleep, for curiosity stays awake: what *is* this like, this inescapable moment that everything exists in?

The question—*what is this like?*—is slightly tricky because thought composes it, and it would seem like thought could answer it. But thought can't go to this place, this moment of *now* that we can't get away from. This place is timeless, while thought is *always* operating in time, and the world it spins is a time world. "*What is this like?*" is therefore a question for contemplation, for being with, now.

We take time for granted, as if it is a feature of the universe. But time is only intrinsic to the human mind, an essential aspect of the magic theater where things can be remembered and anticipated, where memory is reborn as imagined future. Meanwhile at every moment, all along, and causelessly, timelessness lives, pristine and perfect. We are timelessness, misidentifying solely as time.

Immersing ourselves in this possibility of going nowhere, being in the only place we actually already are, the only place where no effort is required to be, and everything *is*, we may gradually discover the most profound relaxation we've ever known. As this deepens we begin to recognize this experience is bliss. This relaxation, this causeless timelessness is our nature, and it is bliss.

The blissfulness tells us we're on the right track, and we find ourselves letting go even more. We are engaged in the simplest of all possible activities—sitting quietly, doing nothing—and the fulfillment of everything we've ever reached towards, sought and desired is now ours, causelessly and unconditionally. This bliss is here already; always overlooked in the frantic pressured rushing of seeking, questing, desiring.

We recognize we have a word already for this unconditional causeless reality where thought cannot go, and where we helplessly are at all times and under all circumstances: infinity. And another word: eternity. Space and time are the avatars of infinity and eternity, their holograms. Only the indivisible original is real, existing without cause in the time before mind begins: *now*.

~

An answering hand

Of course, the mention in an earlier section of "an answering hand" is a metaphor: I attended the meditations twice daily, and quite often, after the meditation was finished there would be a recording played of a talk by Rajneesh (who changed his name to "Osho" not long before his death in 1990.) I could barely make out anything of his English amidst his strong Hindi accent—and I was just as puzzled by the invitations of the other meditators to formally join their group.

I was just there for the meditations—yes, I did get that somebody of the most immense compassion had composed them—for example, that they could be done blindfold, obviating self-consciousness; that I could dance, ecstatically and freely in a room, without alcohol, moved purely by life energy flowing out of nowhere; manifest, vital, blessed. But these were simply epiphenomena of the meditations—I had no interest in the teacher.

Yet as the weeks went by I began to notice that it was as if I was taking a journey. From where, to where, I could not say; I only knew that momentous, tectonic change was sweeping through me and my life, and it was both exhilarating and rather frightening.

No dimensions of measurement could be applied to this journey, other than it was the deepest response of my entire life to a longing I had never been able to give voice to before.

At the end of one evening meditation I put on my jacket and went out to the stairs that led down to the exit from the building. Over the stairs, at the level belonging to the meditation center was a large smiling picture of Osho, an inherently photogenic man radiating beneficence and warmth. I glanced at the picture, and then went down the stairs, out of sight of it—and was suddenly riveted by the realization that I had decamped from my familiar prior life, that I needed a guide in this profoundly unknown space— that Osho was implicitly offering himself as that guide —and that I wanted his company.

I'm telling you about joining a cult, because that's what the experience that followed was, from the outside of it. From the inside, it was utterly and radically differ- ent. Repeatedly in my life I've found myself living in the company of groups of people who are amidst some kind of deliberate consciousness-changing, often with a particular teacher—whose consciousness has powerfully shifted—at the forefront of the group.

We tend not to consider Jesus and his disciples "a cult," nor the gatherings of monks around Buddha "a cult," but that, no doubt, is how it looked to people outside these groups at the time. Except for the very first cult we find ourselves in, the draw of these groups, without exception, is a calling from the longing-space within us toward love, expansion, greater consciousness, less suffering, and more access to truth.

Within the very first or second cult we enter—our birth or adoption family—we absorb the cult-ure around us, including arduously inhabiting the system of duality we all mostly take for granted as reality. We receive many, many gifts in this process—and like any cult, pay a substantial price. We may emerge with sufficient life skills to drive a taxi, manage a bank branch, farm vegetables, work at a call center, acquire a PhD or play a guitar in a way that makes listeners dance, or weep—but some foundational quality of unconditional aliveness most likely has had to be relinquished along the way of this cultivation.

This relinquishment always includes the adoption of a view of reality and of who we are—that those teachers at the forefront of cults have somehow managed to wriggle free of—and it is this freedom that wordlessly beckons to our inner longing.

Just so, there were immense gains for me in participating fully in the loving community around Osho in the following years. The distrust of love radiating from my traumatized relationship with my mom was healed, in time. A certain kind of easeful embodiment infused me, where before I had lived predominantly up in my head. Participation in the community had costs, without a doubt, but the benefits were incalculable.

The very next day after my realization-descending-the-stairs, I went back to the meditation center and I asked the leader of the center to convey a message to (at that time) Rajneesh in India: I said that I had moved into no-man's land, and I needed a traveling companion in this utterly unknown landscape: would he be my companion?

There was a name for this in the meditation center culture—an important word, that: "cult-ure," because all of us belong to several of them, willy-nilly. In this cult it was called "taking sannyas," and it involved getting a new name from Rajneesh, wearing clothes the color of the rising sun, and having a locket around one's neck with his picture on it

(The story continues in *"Vehicle, gas, driver."*)

~

I don't know

I pretend I know what's going on. I pretend I know who, or what I am. We all do this. If you like, this is a personal statement; no disparagement is intended.

At the noticeable center of our existence—the life of every one of us—is a profound unknowing. This is a profound *unknown*, principally characterized by an open-ness with no limits. This is innocence, ease, relaxation—also sometimes known as "presence." Dogs, infants, lizards and butterflies seem to embody presence effortlessly.

This open-ness necessarily has to be overlaid, in the course of our human conditioning, by pretending to be someone who (seems to) know who they are. This pretending takes the form of a conviction that *I am my body and my biography.* Being able to occupy this conviction is essential to functional life in the world. But occupying this conviction *as if it is the only reality* is a highly-effective prescription for misery.

This convinced-overlay we might call "time-being," since *time* is the primary difference between the core of timeless being, and the overlay of the seeming-one who lives in time. The principal preoccupation of the time-being is *getting somewhere.*

Getting somewhere in all its forms is pretty much automatic for the time-being. The avoidance of what we don't like and our myriad efforts to have more of what we do like seem like our global *raison d'être.* Scale it up and billionaires appear, with power and wealth far outstripping that of ancient kings. Perhaps, even, something like rape of the planet also appears.

We can readily notice our core simply by slowing down or pausing our efforts to get somewhere. When chasing, seeking, searching, avoiding and dodging are disengaged from for a moment, we can notice the presence of something distinctly other than pursuit. We may not be able to name what this is (indeed, it is characterized by having no truly-definable characteristics whatsoever)—but that *this is* is unmistakable. We had just forgotten about it as our busy conditioning increasingly preoccupied our noticing.

Why did we forget it? There's not much to it: it has no face, no name, no gender, no time—yet, *it is,* in a completely different way than the coming-and-going of identifiable face, name, gender and time. It never alters one whit, by stark contrast with the endlessly dynamic dance of our perceptual existence.

Not it

Thus far, these reflections have been riddled by a major error; necessary as a means of introduction, but erroneous.

There is no "it."

If this referenced above as "unknowing" were truly an "it"—it would be known, but it (!) is the quintessence of unknowing, the source of the great mystery at our center-less center.

The most predominant feature of this *I don't know* is that it lives entirely in the moment. The moment, not coincidentally, is where thought cannot go; thought makes reference to "now" but what is referenced is always in the past. Where we intrinsically and inescapably live is always herenow—as we all, completely intuitively, know very well.

Without the slightest prejudice toward our getting-somewhere conditioning, miraculous in its power, and essential to inhabit, we can notice for ourselves that herenow is unknowing dynamic wellbeing. When we glimpse its eternality, we may also have an intimation it is everything.

A book of this nature makes reference to "it" hundreds of times, and could not make sense without such references. Many of the references are to the open space of noticing, universal and unceasing within us, and completely impossible to separate experientially from what is noticed—but for convenience this gets called "it," despite there being no such "thing." Just so, "*now*" as we live it is not in any way the conceptual and linguistic version of "now." We helplessly and inescapably live it, ceaselessly. "We" are this complete intimacy.

Home in the heart of now

That which cannot be cancelled by any experience is the real. That which cannot be transcended, beyond which you cannot go, is your Self. If you can go beyond it, then it was not your Self.

— Osho

(See the section *Negation*) The head freaks out, bucking and weaving wildly at "Cannot be me"—especially when there is the subsequent recognition, that "Cannot be me" also "Cannot be me," and there is a sweeping away of everything, into inexplicability, into the inner meaning of "Don't know." What is absolutely unchanged by this sweeping away? "Don't know" will probably be the answer that follows, but also "Impossible not to be."

Other terms for "Don't know" are undying, empty, eternal, and unborn, as well as the knowing (that we all have, implicitly or explicitly) that our original face, the one that never changes, the very same from which these words are being read, is this very inexplicability, on full display at all times.

But the heart already exists effortlessly and completely here, in the state that the head struggles against; the stateless state, our natural state. The wild gyrations of the head come to ease and peace when the heart is the channel.

We can readily see the "why" of this: the head deals, appropriately and solely, with matters that have time intrinsic to them. *Now* is, essentially, a mystery to the head—and the *only* "time" of the heart. There is no time in the heart; all is as it is, unfolding in sublime perfection, the orchestration perfect, the conductor having vanished into nothing at all.

"*Mind creates the abyss, the heart crosses it*" remarks Nisargadatta Maharaj.

Let's stop calling it "now"

I sat down this morning on my couch to be quiet for a while. My dog Tashi jumped up and lay down beside me, and the thought went through my mind "Ah, Tashi, so comforting."

A moment later I became aware that absent this thought, my dog was still here, but without the thinking I couldn't quite say what was happening. All was as before, just without the description. Without definition. Perfect.

My contemplative routine is simply to let myself inwardly gently be where I am as I sit, which is the same as "staying" *now*, in the present moment—all effort is relinquished. For a few seconds I relished the aliveness and vibrancy that is always here in now—in fact, the very qualities that tell us this is *now* —and then I realized that the same applies to "now" as applied to the thought about "my dog."

Why don't we stop calling it "now"? Why don't we do the same thing devout Jews do when they speak about God: confess themselves utterly unable to name divinity? Be at a loss, a complete, humbling and total loss in the face of it. Because we use this small word "now" to denote something that, were we asked to define it, we would be utterly and absolutely unable to give any kind of description to.

For one thing, this that we call *now* is always, always here. There is never a time now is not here. We can be absolutely certain that when the Big Bang happened it happened now, and no matter what happens, it will happen now, which would include the explosive disintegration of the universe and every event in between, no matter how minuscule.

The miracle that is *now* is hidden from us by a universal hypnosis we all completely believe-in: that we solely exist as a distinct "somebody," a separate "me." When this figment falls away for a moment—when we simply look for ourselves and see no trace of it—the immediate and uncaused peace, satisfaction and gladness of *now* is obvious, as it is.

Let's *really* stop calling it "now"

Strictly speaking, moreover, a past event as such has vanished once and for all; a future event as such is wholly inexistent. It follows that in thinking of past and future occurrences, we do so only with reference to a present time. But without a subsistent past and future we could not form any notion of the present. **There cannot indeed be a present**, *since there is neither a past nor a future time. Consciousness alone subsists and consciousness alone is ever-present.*

—John Levy (emphasis added)

Let's suppose that out of nowhere and nothing we are suddenly plunged into the reality we find ourselves in as we are reading this piece of writing.

We don't call it now, because we don't know what it is. We have been suddenly dropped into it. It is new, never-here-before.

Recognizing that there are a great many drifting skeins of story in thought-space about who we are, where we are, and what we are, we give ourselves a little shake to come alive to what this nowness is like. The stories are like waking dreams—only the nowness is real.

The vividness of everything is staggering. The sights, sounds, sensations, smells and tastes are nothing short of astonishing

—profoundly alive and without any conditions on exactly how they are, which is just as it is (this last is not poor grammar, but reality).

This vitality is everywhere: our body is a tingling field of alive energy and wherever it meets the room in which it is, there is simply a different kind of aliveness—but no real boundaries, just gradations of energy. The drifting skeins of story about our body are dream images superimposed on this absolutely-vibrant reality. We shake off the hypnotic effect of them, and continue noticing.

Where the world of feeling and sensation ends and the realm of hearing begins is impossible to tell, equally. Marveling, we move attention from the seemingly-outer sounds through the whole field of experience, and end up in the core of our body —but can find only gradations, not edges.

We notice the almost-insistent framing of everything by the clouds of thought and image, which keep on drifting through our mind space. The thoughts and images in and of themselves are utterly remarkable—what we keep shaking off is the compelling framing of reality by these unbidden visitors, who are inextricable from *now*.

Some of this framing—such as that "I am here" and "the world is over there"—has had to be faced down again and again, because this is not the directly experienced reality of this moment. Absent that framing—which is just the frame of conceptuality, but not reality—we don't know anything, but we vividly *are*. This "are," this Being, is causeless, and every-where, and a sheer miracle.

Infinity of the heart

*In the end, we will find that our heart holds the simple wisdom
and unshakable compassion that we have sought all along.*

—Jack Kornfield

Our heart relishes infinity; plays there, marvels there, is itself
the nature of infinity. This is easy to notice, in our own experience; we just go there, go to our heart, *now*.

Look into your heart. Follow your nature.

— Buddha

We can even call this heart-nature "now," but this would risk
infusion by the idea of time—and the marvel of the heart is
that there is no time in its infinity.

Trust in the heart is not-two. Not-two is trust in the heart.

— Hsin Hsin Ming

How could there possibly be time in infinity? Time is infinity's
miraculous way of making up separation—when there *is* no
separation, in reality. Reality is the heart—but we overlook it.

You overlook the heart, and fill yourself with desire.

— Buddha

Some amongst us live there; live as, in, with, through and by
the heart. They know nothing but the heart, until they are

uprooted into being solely mind-beings. Then, they are no longer children, but "grownups."

If my heart can become pure and simple like that of a child, I think there probably can be no greater happiness than this.

— Nishida Kitaro

"Our opening and Your entering are one"

*Ours is not the work
of seeking You here
or there where we
think You might be,
but of opening
the heart's door,
and when we do this
You cannot resist
coming in, since
our opening and Your
entering are one: You
knock and wait, and
when we open we
find that You were
there all along and
will not leave us.*

— Meister
Eckhart

Indeed, we *cannot* in any way be separate, not in all eternity, and that is our bliss, when it becomes consciously felt.

~

PRACTICAL POSSIBILITIES

Noticing noticing

Noticing noticing is very helpful. Everybody implicitly notices noticing, but explains it away as us noticing the presence of separate consciousness, believed to be enclosed within our skin envelope: this is what we have been taught we are, and we have assiduously practiced this belief our whole lives.

But *really* noticing noticing, in a curious and persistent way is a very profound exploration.

Perhaps it will help, in unfolding this further, to acknowledge that *noticing* and *now* are identical.

Also, although we deeply believe that being able to name something is to encompass and identify it—so we can glibly talk about "awareness," "now" or "noticing," the true reality of noticing is that nothing can be said about it. It simply is. If we are asked "Are you conscious?" our response will come without thought having to intervene: consciousness, or as it is called here, "noticing" is *intrinsic* to us, like now—and cannot be conceptualized. Hence, anything said here will be a fumbling pointer in the direction of what cannot be pointed at, but is the only enduring reality.

A similar conundrum presents itself in respect of "now." Nothing conceptual whatsoever is applicable to this limitless universal, the remarkable (and usually absolutely unexplored) center and essence of everything. We have always taken *now* entirely for granted, since it has never altered by even as much as an electron. So we ignore it—and thereby miss out on the most prodigious and inexhaustible treasure.

The moment there can be a glimpse that the noticing *is* now, or that now is itself the very same noticing, there can be moments of freedom in which the miraculous appearance of things is no longer possessed by some kind of I-center. This seeming-I center is made out of thought, sensations, and images. These seem to exist in time, and all of them are *noticeable*—which is radically different from the *noticing*.

The I-thought and all its accouterments (body sense; sense of perception proceeding from some center, etc, etc, etc.) go on burbling along, just like usual. But the extraordinarily persistent and utterly unchanging presence of *now*/noticing is in total contrast to—yet utter intimacy with—this burbling-along, which turns out to be the impermanent and ever-changing flow of life itself.

Once noticing notices itself, the immense, immovable mountain-like quality of it becomes more and more evident. *This* is our fundament—not the coming-and-going, the born-to-die appearance.

That one—the born-to-die appearance, wavering, appearing and disappearing—is made out of time. Noticing/now is outside time, and regards time with something akin to pleasure, at times sliding into deep love. *"Eternity is in love with the productions of time,"* remarks William Blake, accessing the inexplicable beauty and perfect configuration of this mystery-without-limits.

The gradual predominance of noticing/now is liberating. Where, before, I was constantly endeavoring to improve the separate-seeming one in time, there may now be blossoming freedom to enjoy the separate-seeming one as adventures unfold themselves by themselves. Arduous though it is to gradually peel away what cannot be identified ("noticing/now" is the inevitably-inadequate label offered here) from what is identifiable, the process in due course bears fruit.

Apocryphal remarks by Zen masters can be helpful in this respect: *"Let me repeat, the perceived cannot perceive,"* remarks Huang Po. His words are another, perhaps even richer way of pointing to the indescribability of what we are. "Time" is perceived, as is "the person" of Glenn. Neither can possibly be the perceiving itself: the perceived cannot possibly perceive.

So, we can turn attention back, as it were, to the perceiving; to the noticing. We can notice the qualities of the noticing—even recognize the most remarkable of these attributes, that noticing *notices itself.* Despite the paradox of it, the noticing, noticing-itself is the timeless outcome of recognizing that '*The perceived cannot perceive.*'

This noticing of noticing, by noticing is an implicit invitation to rest our attention in total inexplicability—and in the solidest of all realities. The purest reality of *now* is revealed: formless, utterly unchanging, causeless, and beyond all explaining. In this revealing, intimacy with the unceasing flow of form is endless: tingling body, current of sound, thoughts coming by themselves —and the unlimited depth of the noticing, noticing itself, in profound relaxation.

Explanations ebb and flow in the noticing. Concepts—"time" or "I" are noticed to be like bubbles in the immemorial flow that comes and goes amidst (or "as" or "within") the grandest of all immovables, noticing/now: imperturbable, unceasing, eternal, infinite.

In no particular order

We live in illusion and the appearance of things. There is a reality. We are that reality. When you understand this, you see that you are nothing, and being nothing, you are everything. That is all.

— Kalu Rinpoche

1. We can notice the direct, immediate experience of what seeing is like: turn attention backwards and notice the nature of where we see from. We can find out for ourselves, possibly ten thousand times over and more, what's really deeply true— that the seeing has no name, no gender, no nationality, no skin color; and exists immovably now. We can see for ourselves that there is no separate person intrinsic to this seeing—our body is seen, but the seen cannot be the seer. We can believe our own experience—not what we've been told.

2. We can notice the direct, immediate felt sense of our body from within. That it tingles and shimmers and is indistinct at the edges, no matter how it seems to appear to ourselves and others: in mirrors, and in photos. We can notice that wherever our body is in solid contact with the world—backside in the chair, feet on the floor—there should, in theory, be two sensations; but there is only one. We cannot tell, *except conceptually* where our feet end and the floor begins. We can believe our own experience, not what we think.

3. When thoughts claim to be us, we can notice that we are noticing the thoughts, so they cannot be us. In these moments when what we have supposed to be ourselves falls away briefly —"Oh, I thought that was *me*, and then I realized it was just a *thought* claiming to be me"—we can notice that we are still here, only now we cannot say *what* we are, only *that* we are.

4. Recognizing, howsoever dimly, that we never go away from now—and that *now* is utterly effortless—we can quit and relinquish, for a little bit, all and any efforts to get somewhere, go somewhere, be other than what we cannot not be. This is the easiest thing in the world—all of us are already here, where we are. Our principal distraction from it is the rushing, pushing, insistent momentum of the conditioned belief that we have to get somewhere in order for things to be alright, for "the problem" to be solved. We can give this momentum up for a minute. We can see what happens.

5. Notice that thought is completely incapable of conceptualizing this very moment of now, where we live all the time, effortlessly and without cessation. Notice that time and thought live together—conceptualizing myself as someone is to conceive of myself as someone in time. All "things" must necessarily have time as their theater—but time is a conceptual abstraction. Thoughts operate in time because it's the only way the marvel of concepts can possibly make sense—but when the future consists of things that have not yet happened, and the past, of things that are no more, nothing is left of time—except a thought.

6. Gradually become accustomed to the reality of existing—and the overlay of appearance on this reality: that the world seems to be divided the way thinking says it is—into separate-seeming-me and separate-seeming we, appearing to be wandering around a rocky ball hurtling through space, looking for fulfillment. Gradually come to notice the reality that is here *now*; nameless, timeless, edgeless; completely empty and without characteristics at the no-center of it; endlessly dynamic and ceaselessly changing at the periphery—and that the periphery is just a concept, an overlay of appearance dictated by thoughts. What we really are is the reality—at ease; unceasing, uncaused, timeless, magisterial, undying—and completely indefinable, except we can call it totality,

wholeness, infinity, one-without-a-second. And that all these big words are useless, yet, we are undivided reality, infinity and eternity, overlaid by an appearance of dividedness in time. We can find out what's true for ourselves.

Causeless love

"The causeless" can sound very conceptual, like an idea in philosophy. As we read this, we can see if we might be able to tentatively accept from the outset that the very source of this writing is itself the causeless, the most vivid and obvious reality at the core and center of each and every one of us. This reality is hidden in plain view.

We are not being asked to believe any of this: that would just add to the mass of confusion we are all tangled in. Rather, the writing here is about the causeless from direct experience. So we can see what we notice in our own direct and immediate experience when we follow along the way suggested. (Which is, incidentally, simply *that we trust our own direct and immediate experience*.)

Awakening noticing

In our noticing is an experience that is perfectly obvious and wholly remarkable. It has always been here, and is something we can't get rid of, something that's self-evidently prior to our mind and all our beliefs. It is causeless, and entirely free. If we like, we could treat this writing as a hypothesis that we are testing as we read. Like any good scientist, we can find out for ourselves what is true.

Let's start with reading itself. There are a couple of ways of experiencing what's going on here as we read these words. One of them is the habitual way of making sense we have all been taught and we all accept: these words are on the screen

or page and our video-camera-eyes translate pixels into meaning, through the astonishing capacities of our brains. Any
observer could verify this: "Yes, there's Glenn, I recognize him
and he's looking at the screen 3 feet away. There are words on
the screen and he's reading them and the words make sense.
His eyes are seeing the words and his brain is making sense of
them inside his head"

Radical awakening

The second way of experiencing is radical. A word of caution:
we may never be able to go back if we step into this second
way. We will proceed entirely alone and should we try to tell
anybody about what we experience, we will most likely be
misunderstood.

The misunderstanding of our listeners will be that they are
absolutely sure that the habitual way of making sense of this
reading is reality, "the truth." That our video-camera-eyes,
themselves an objective reality, are taking in the words on the
screen, another objective reality. These objects, eyes and words
on screen are real, distinct and separate. But direct experience
offers something else entirely.

Perhaps this already sounds a little odd to us. Or perhaps we
can recognize that how it sounds odd is because we are
querying—that is, gently questioning—that habitual first way
of making sense of reading: the one we all share, the one
we're all sure is true. But perhaps we are something of an
adventurer, and there's a frisson of excitement about stepping
into our own truth, even if it means there's no going back. If
so, let's go.

In our own direct experience what is taking in these words?
The crucial part of this question is *In our own direct experience.*"
What does that mean?

Before thinking decides for us

The invitation here is to notice what is so for us before every-thing we've ever been taught takes over and makes a determination for us. We are invited into the original meaning of meditation, which is to see what's here; freshly, presently, attentively, before thinking completely decides for us. This is different from trying to get our mind to shut up for a while.

Something is here in our direct experience—and we are invited to notice if this is true for us in our direct experience: something is here that's before thought-mind, and which notices mind, or in which mind and all its content floats. As said earlier, it is the most evident reality once it is noticed, and the best way to do that is to *see* it. There is a reason accom-plished meditators are known as "seers."

So what is taking in these words right here where our eyes are? When we recognize that we can look for ourselves, turn our attention right around and take in the reality, freshly and immediately from which we are looking, what is that reality like? When we put aside the habitual, conventional way we're all used to, of making sense of reading—and we notice for ourselves where and what we are looking from, what is it?

Remember, this is direct experience, so nothing we've ever heard or thought or believed will do here. We've stepped into our own sovereign being, and we are looking for ourselves, perhaps for the first time. We may notice great clouds of expe-rience floating by, possibly thoughts and irritated feelings that say things like "*This writer chap is full of it. The only reality is my eyes and the screen. What's he talking about?*" But we can keep on noticing, in our own direct experience, what the place from which we're looking is like; really, truly. It's like no other place in the universe.

~

Your experience is...?

Perhaps I might share my experience, and as we read along (for I will also be reading all this), simultaneously notice what your experience is, directly and immediately. See if there's any correspondence between what I'm sharing from here, where seeing is happening, and what is being noticed there, in that place from which you look.

The first thing—and it still takes my breath away to notice it, even after thousands of times of noticing it—is that there is spaciousness here. It is a strange kind of spaciousness because it seems to underlie all my experiences of distance and space, as if it is the intrinsic, within-most conscious essence of those experiences. This spaciousness here is paradoxically infinitely deep—and nothing whatsoever.

There is nothing—no-thing—here, to my own turned-around inspection. Yet this palpable nothing is brightly and vividly *aware*, alert to its own quality of infinite spaciousness. (Following along, alert to your own experience, will be the only true way to read this.)

This here is still. All movement—of my eyes, of the constantly changing scene of my gaze, of thought, feeling, emotion and body sensation, of breath or of the changing sounds in the room—are only discernible because this hitherto-hidden-obviousness is utterly still and has never been any other way.

This here is without characteristics (again, the only way to discover this is being turned around, into looking for yourself, into your own direct experience as you read this). It has no name, no age, no gender, nor any face, of the kind I can see when I look at your face. Although the *thought* of losing my identity can be frightening—no longer knowing my name, my gender, my age or having a distinctive face—by contrast this deepest of mysteries is inherently and wondrously without identity. No matter how much I dwell here, no matter how often I return to notice it, I marvel. This is uncaused. This takes in all the characteristics of every-thing I've always taken myself to be—but is itself entirely without characteristics.

Perhaps the marvel is because of the contrast: I'm so used to the characteristics of things, in that habitual, conventional way of seeing we all share and tend to believe in; the separated way, the video-camera-eyes way. Things have edges and names, they come into being and then eventually change, or die, or vanish. This has no edge, nor name. I can detect no possibility whatsoever that this was ever not here, and for this not to be here is inconceivable. It is eternity itself, and being absolutely no-thing is entirely impervious to changing in any way at all.

This is blatantly timeless—there is manifestly and obviously no time whatsoever here, or, this is the purest essence of *now*. I watch the second hand on my desk clock clicking away time, but here, in this intrinsic seeing that I cannot get rid of, there is no time at all, or purely *now*. Nor is there tension or distress, nor any possibility of those. There is inherent ease; all the time in the world, in the universe, then far beyond that.

This is the only causeless thing in the universe. Despite concepts, it's not a thing, not a "this," not "it"—but words are the only way of referring to it. Absolutely still, this is without cause. I can't go any deeper than this: this takes in everything I've taken myself to be; my momentarily-changing thoughts, mood, feelings, emotions; my constantly altering body, my life full of change. This is the real backdrop of all of that, the foundationless reality I can do nothing about.

This is the causeless. Our lives, increasingly as we grow more technologically sophisticated, are completely filled with cause. Everything that happens is explainable as being caused. Virtually the only times in our lives when our attention is riveted from beyond ourselves is when the causeless visits us. These visits come in the form of birth, love, death, creativity, and the truly sacred. And, it turns out, "visits" are nothing of the kind—these are glimpses of the only eternity, the only reality, of causeless love awake to itself, even momentarily.

An earlier section, *Not it* clearly stated that there is no "it." Exactly the same emphasis is applicable here: there is no "it," despite the many references to "it" in the above paragraphs. Investigating our own direct experience, we can gradually discover that this from which we see—that cannot be found, yet is unchanging—is the eternal. The intimacy of eternity with time is utterly indissoluble. They seem like two, but are not-two—and that is all that can be said with words.

I am conscious

Gazing with sheer awareness into sheer awareness...

— Tilopa

Being conscious is no big deal: everybody is conscious. If we are here—in life, alive—we are conscious. If someone asks us "Are you conscious?" we will not need to think *at all* in order to reply: being conscious is the most obvious aspect of us.

We are helplessly conscious—there's nothing we can do about it. We are conscious above all else. But we tend to think and believe we are solely *a separate I*, who is conscious; this is, after all, what we are all conditioned to believe from early in life.

After a while of *gazing into ourselves*, we can begin to notice that this I who is conscious is simply consciousness, helplessly conscious: the separate-seeming I is an appearance in, or of this helpless-consciousness.

Helpless? There's nothing we can do about being conscious— before we became a separate and identifiable I—Joe, Megan, Sue, Milo—we were conscious, aware, awake. We take it for granted that who *we* are is awake, as if there's *someone* who's awake, someone separate from consciousness. But all we are is simply consciousness, awakening to itself. *Gazing into itself*: consciousness noticing consciousness. The inexplicable, inescapably coming home to itself.

> *Realisation is a matter of* becoming conscious *of that which*
> *is already realised.*
>
> — Wei Wu Wei

These words are being written to consciousness—and natu- rally, the 'I' writing these words is consciousness. What else could it be? There isn't anything here except consciousness, so this is consciousness addressing itself. Each time I *gaze into myself* this becomes clearer: consciousness is being intimate with consciousness in this looking, because there is actually nothing else except consciousness becoming conscious of consciousness, consciousness gradually discovering there is just one thing here, marvelously aware, causelessly aware.

The provocative title of this section is *I Am Conscious*. If I said that the more accurate title is *I Am Consciousness*, we might think that I'm inflating myself—yet one more narcissistic person, proclaiming a new and separate identity; my separate self as the grand sweep of consciousness. The reality is rather the opposite: there isn't anything else except consciousness. Consciousness gets lost to itself, playing in the form of these infinitely-many identities: nonetheless, consciousness is all that's actually happening.

> *There is no such 'thing' to aim at, seek or look for, as what one is. On ceasing to seek or to look—one is present.*
>
> — Wei Wu Wei

From *gazing into myself, for myself*, the clarity and trust in what is noticed gradually blossoms. There can be a contemplative pausing, perhaps beginning with remembering, or recognizing that awareness miraculously notices itself, just the way Tilopa reminds us: "*Gazing with sheer awareness into sheer awareness…*" In the experienced-realization, in the contemplative pausing of the gazing, gazing into itself, resides an unmistakable relaxation and complete ease.

Certainly there may have been intimations of the truth of everything said above, but without the *gazing into myself* contemplation this doesn't really come to fruition—rather, there's an endless elaboration of the mind stream *about* this, not a revelation *of* this. The *gazing into myself* contemplation endlessly opens infinity to itself.

When we begin *gazing into ourselves*, we may immediately become frustrated. What we see, and what is gazing makes no sense at all, to the rational sense of ourselves. What is gazing is invisible—nonetheless, *it is definitely, and completely intimately us.* (It may take a while before what is being gazed at becomes apparent as also us.)

What a paradox: we are unquestionably looking—gazing at ourselves—but what is looking is completely invisible, yet completely certain: *we* are looking! That is the purpose of this contemplation, to look.

Dogshit awareness.

— Paul Hedderman

We are gazing into *ourselves.* We can't do this for long without noticing what it is that is looking: unquestionably, *we* are looking. After all, isn't this the practice, to look at ourselves? So, *we are gazing at the essence of ourselves!*

What we see, when we look, is equally invisible. Perhaps after a while we begin to notice that we have some nascent sense that the invisibility that is looking, and the invisibility that is seen is actually the greatest mystery in the whole of existence: something indefinable is looking at itself. Something indefinable is being seen, by itself, and seen immediately, outside time. Our subject-object language can't encompass this reality, that the looked-for is quite simply the looked-at.

> *THIS which is seeking is*
> *THAT which is sought, and*
> *THAT which is sought is*
> *THIS which is seeking.*

— Wei Wu Wei

There's no doubt about the situation of this *gazing at ourselves*: we've accepted the invitation. We've resolved, to *gaze at ourselves*; and we are determined to give it a try. The most significant part of the equation of *looking at* is established with complete certainty: WE are looking.

What do we see, when we turn attention backward and inward? With our conceptual mind we may say; nothing, emptiness, spaciousness, conscious luminosity—but if we hang out nakedly with the experience we may very well find:

that what we are looking at
is simply what is looking.

We take the radical turn back: turning *looking* towards ourselves, accepting the invitation to look at ourselves, we accept the complete directly-experienced-certainty that we are *looking at ourselves*. *What* we see makes no sense, because it is invisible. Because neither what looks nor what we see isn't any kind of thing.

If we were going to say anything about what we *see* in this looking, we would say that we simply see seeing. Which is very paradoxical, because the only thing we can say about our intention to look at ourselves is that *we are seeing*. Taking this one step further, we can only say that seeing is noticing seeing: we are looking at ourselves, and we are seeing ourselves, and these two are not separate from one another. Our word for the highest possibility of this is "love."

The natural state of nobody

Naturally, when we hear the phrase "the natural state" we think it must belong to *somebody*, to a separate-someone— perhaps a separate-someone who has "attained the ultimate," or some such gilding of the lily of life.

But there's nothing to "the natural state"—it is lived without cessation by everything and everyone in existence—except the humans, who are *searching* for it.

This identity; as the searcher, the seeker, the pursuer, chaser, hunter, has an unseen foundation, which is that the supposed-pursuing-person *does not exist as such.*

Only the natural state exists, the ceaselessness of being itself. Someone separate in this undivided being is a fiction, and can never attain the natural state because, most importantly, the natural state can be camouflaged by seeking it, but it never goes away.

This is obvious, to the heart of us. In the heart, there is nobody, just the natural state.

❧

Everything is perfect

The street door of the conference room clicked quietly shut behind me as I stepped out onto Piccadilly in central London on a late Sunday night in 1976. The conference—the notorious EST training*—was finally over, and I had departed quietly and a little shame-facedly at the end, gaze lowered and shoulders slumped: I had not "got it" the way so many others had, those who were now yelling and whooping in the meeting room behind me.

---

* EST was a transformative, intensive self-help seminar founded by Werner Erhard in 1971, using large-group dynamics for personal breakthroughs by teaching radical personal responsibility for one's life. The Landmark Forum today offers a modified version of the EST training.

Out on the sidewalk, I lit a cigarette, zipping up my jacket against the blustery damp of a central London evening. Then, out of nowhere, from no source in thought, or that I was conscious of, I relaxed.

The next three or four months I felt the most open of my entire life. I was barely conscious of it as a theme in and of itself, but I was aware of talking to strangers at bus stops with my heart wide open, and of being staggered by one monumental wave of insight after another into the nature of the universe and of myself. The seed of that relaxation blossomed, as if my soul was suddenly in springtime after the longest, hardest winter ever.

I knew without doubt that nothing had ever been wrong—that in fact, the nature of existence is that nothing ever could be wrong, that not even so much as an electron is ever out of place, to even an infinitesimal degree.

Everything up to the moment of realizing this formed a divine tango of the sublimest perfection. Walking down Golders Green Road one Saturday morning there was the sudden noticing of the obvious, that everything is simply made of love—the bricks of the houses and shops around me, the air and sky, the garbage littering the sidewalk and the shrubs and insects—different in appearance but palpably, directly, and obviously nothing but love.

I suppose discoveries like that change a person instan-taneously—it was not some sort of philosophical intu-ition or conclusion, but a commanding and indubitable re-perceiving. You can't really go back after something like that, even if gradually, as happened to me after several months, the bricks became bricks again, and the garbage garbage, and the habitual, habitual. Now, sometimes, I peer at things, as if their true nature as love might pop out (more of which later.)

Similarly, with time, the immediate and obvious organic-knowing that nothing is ever wrong began to shred and fragment, gradually morphing back into the kind of perception I'd lived in before, the state of being where a focus on the problematic or on the possibilities of the future predominates over the effulgent and overwhelmingly relaxed glory of what is here now. And still, that nothing is ever wrong, no matter what, rejiggered something deep within me that's never quite returned to its former configuration.

I found myself writing to my teacher in India: "I've never been broken, damaged, sick or other than exactly as perfectly orchestrated by the divine," I wrote, "and my intense efforts to 'get better' through meditation and by means of the groups and therapies I've done were all based on a mistake: I've never, ever been anything other than perfect, moment by moment, nor has there in all eternity ever been a nanosecond of imperfection in existence."

Nothing is ever wrong—everything is perfect.
Everything—no matter its appearance—is made of love.
There is—existentially—no such thing as being damaged, sick or broken.

This is not some kind of pretended transcendentalism

—some of the very same experiences cited above appear in R. M. Bucke's classic book *Cosmic Consciousness*, as well as in two chapters on mysticism in William James' *The Varieties of Religious Experience*. James' lectures in particular highlight the ineffability (the experience cannot be described, but only directly experienced), noesis (self-evidently divine truths can be discerned within them), transience (the experience is of limited duration), and passivity (the person having the experience has no control over the arrival or departure of the experience) of the occurrences. Just so.

To be still

Stillness is the sole requisite for the realization of the Self as God.

— Ramana Maharshi

To be still, we simply be what we are. We are already this, and cannot not be this—but mistaken identity is universally prevalent. (Oh, and "we" only exist as a concept.)

I think and believe *I* am exclusively some-thing in this spaciousness, a thing, an entity. The mirage of it is immensely persuasive, and universally believed, as if it is reality. But nothing could be further from the truth.

What we are is inexplicable—yet vividly discernable. The self-evident conspicuousness of it is obscured from us by our conviction that we are solely something—something explicable, some-thing born to die. Since we believe this fiction as if it's reality, we seem bound. Being still seems to take a certain kind of effort.

But being still is not an action! Being, still, is everlasting. Nothing can persuade, cajole, alter, or shift this causeless immensity. It is self-obviously what we are and cannot not be. Reading this is happening from Being, by Being, courtesy of Being, behind and beyond all explanation.

If we closely and with curiosity examine our own experience —perhaps the way Buddha did, resolving to sit under that damned Peepal tree until he either died or figured this thing out—we may gradually come to recognize that this spacious awareness, which is the fundament of everything existing, is intrinsically and inescapably "what we cannot not be." It is nothing at all.

But from long habit and practice we are more or less addicted to everything being objectified. (Just so, the previous paragraph objectified "what we cannot not be," and this cannot be helped, since language is being used.) Thing-if-a-cation is the skill we arduously learned as we inhabited language and concepts. Objectification is the biological gift we have become so expert at using that we now tend to entirely miss that which cannot be objectified at all, under any circumstances.

The words that we use to point to this that we cannot not be are dry and philosophical-sounding. "Void; emptiness; awareness" are immediately interpreted from within objectification —and then the real vitality, the infinite juice of what we cannot not be, gets lost from view.

But remember: this is impossible to lose. This is eternity; beyond harm, immortality—and stillness, without any opposite whatsoever. This is intrinsic to us, closer than heartbeat, breathing, feelings or thoughts.

We feel an inkling of the perfection and stability of eternity, for there is neither time nor space, neither before nor after, but every-thing present in one new, fresh-springing now where millenniums last no longer than the twinkling of an eye.

— Meister Eckhart

There is no point whatsoever in searching for this—indeed, any kind of searching diverts attention, from the real, true, essential nature of nowness to some *time* in which finding may happen (neither time nor such finding exist, although discovering our spectacles perched on our nose, never having left, is very real) and absolutely distracts us, from this, which we cannot not be.

This stillness, which we cannot not be, is meditation itself. It is absolutely the least effortful of all things in existence—and this can be clearly felt, as an intrinsic perception, as the self-evident nature of the highest, still-est, and greatest mystery of all existing. It is what we really are. Be still, to find out.

It makes no sense

It makes no sense that there is nobody here. Of course there is somebody here—my body is very visible, very apparent, to others, and to me.

But we forget that our bodies once appeared and will disap-pear, are known to us through inner and outer perception—and being the perceived, cannot possibly be the perceiver of them. We forget this.

Perhaps when we remember it, we turn our curious attention backwards, directly into the heart of perceiving itself. After all, we claim to be the one looking—should we not be able to look at our own looking? So we look at it. With our looking, we look at the looking. The looking, the seeing, examines itself.

It seems then to take some long time before we can begin to relish the flat-out miracle of what is thereby revealed: the astonishing causelessness of the place we look out of. We have to one-by-one dissolve—through our direct experience—all the things we were told and taught are reality: that we are solely someone separate, someone inside our enclosure of skin, peering out into a world made of matter. We have to dissolve our inhabitation of the world of time until we are radiant with remembrance of the timelessness at our core. Gradually, the misery lifts that qualified us to be members of the tribe, striving to be happy. We begin to know, causelessly, "*a thousand names for joy*," as one intimate commentator on the Buddhist *Diamond Sutra* said it.

Because it turns out that all those convictions, the things we were told and taught to be the nature of reality, conceal from us an astonishing truth: the entire world, every atom and electron of what we take to be the most solid material reality is nothing but this limitless radiant perceiving itself. Most intimately, this nothing-but-ness utterly includes our bodies, now known to be the radiant illumination of presence shining out, seemingly closer-than-close to what we have taken ourselves to be.

But despite this manifest closeness, we are not solely located there, within these bodies, although the appearance (and our conditioned conviction) is unmistakably of that. This radiant presence cannot be located anywhere, or, is everywhere. We intuit this in our backward-looking into presence, but in the stillness between thoughts, or in deep curiosity, or wonderment we know it without a shadow of a doubt: all we see is all we are.

All we are is *seeing*, but this is not the seeing-of-something-by-someone: *now* is seeing, and seeing is *now*. "Seeing" is a code word for "The Buddha-mind noticing the Buddha-mind." "Now is awake" offers itself into more and more grounded forms: "Now is seeing," as in "Now≡seeing," the mathematical way of saying "is identical with"— and seeing is simply consciousness, for there is nothing else.

> *All that is cognisable is part of the phantasy of living, all that we can think of as ourselves is an integral part of this hypothetical universe; sentient beings are totally therein and in no way or degree apart from it, as they often suppose when they imagine themselves as instruments whereby the objective universe is produced, for it is produced not by, but with them as one of its manifestations.*
>
> — Wei Wu Wei

Then "somebody" (somebody-separate being here independently of this entirety) becomes visible for what it is: a convenient fiction, an organizing idea—or most deeply, the effortless reaching of this which knows itself as itself to blossom into the love which is the core reality of it. For when this which sees— the indescribable, the ineffable, the undefinable—this that we simply cannot not be, gradually recognizes it is nothing but that which is seen, all that remains is love.

This love is wide open and without cause. There is nobody separate in it—truly, cannot be, could never be. That—the blatant, manifest *absence* of someone separate in it—is the source of the relaxation and joy that comes with it. Infinity has become aware, through suffering, that infinity never went anywhere; it just was camouflaged under some convictions, like separateness. Perhaps this camouflage was just the way infinity revealed itself to itself, via the illusion of separation.

In the separate-somebody world this makes no sense: that separateness is an illusion, "*...an optical illusion of...consciousness,*" as Einstein put it. The overcoming of this illusion, he went on to say, "*...gives us the attainable measure of inner quietude.*" And so it is.

Everything is in my heart

This is not a metaphorical statement: everything is in my heart. This is a statement of the blatant truth, of the undivided reality that appears divided by time and space. Inside my heart there is neither time nor space—but time and space are the means by which it appears.

Time and space do not exist, in the way things are ordinarily conceived to be, but are the exquisite means by which this heart becomes apparent to itself. The beauty, and the agony of what occurs in the space of the heart is unlimited. Life, love, birth, and death flicker and crackle here, like fireflies and lightning in a late summer sky.

> *The Lord of Lanka was then immediately awakened...realizing that the world was nothing but his own Heart.*
>
> — Lankavatara Sutra

Yet. This "in my heart" is in no way the personal possession of someone. It is impossible for it to be the personal possession of someone, because any and all occurrences of "someone" are effortlessly encompassed in this intrinsic heart.

This essence heart is itself the most radical and total emptiness—and this emptiness is indistinguishably intimate with everything occurring. This intimacy is so total, so complete that language cannot really touch it, only punt close to the edges of it with remarks like "Emptiness is form, and form, nothing but emptiness."

We ourselves do not need to punt close to the edges of it, for we live incessantly and helplessly, effortlessly and marvelously, in the location of this total intimacy, which we call *"now."* There is actually nothing else, despite language presupposing time and separateness—and then validating itself on that basis!

We can't get there

There's absolutely no point in meditating to attain some kind of spiritual state, some far off and fevered phantasm of enlightenment.

We are already here.

How to find this out for ourselves? Relax out of the stream of habitual thinking for a moment. Just an instant or two will do —to discover the entirety, waiting for us every moment that the prism, the illusory kaleidoscope of thinking, is not running the show.

A couple of things about the entirety: the first is that even while we are busy with a stream of thought we can see that everything that is thought-free in our surroundings is relaxed. Trees, rocks, fog banks, buildings, and the lump of concrete I'm sitting on, here, on this hilltop; all are totally relaxed.

The second quality of entirety really makes no sense to the stream of thought, but can be felt immediately when thinking is ignored for an instant. There is no existentially separate person in entirety. Separate-seeming persons belong to thought, to time. When thought is ignored, they disappear— and we are entirety; separate self vanishes and entirety appears. Miraculously, entirety is conscious, and it is this aware quality that appears in both entirety and the separate-seeming self.

Entirety must include mirages of separate selves at all times, or it would not be entirety. The thought of "I" is an unmistakable and real occurrence in entirety—yet what this thought refers to is merely a collection of experiences strung together: the rope on the ground that looks like a snake, the mirage of water in the desert.

Walking, I am surprised over and over again by the spontaneous effect of this non-practice. Reminded to drop out of the incessant stream of me-me-me, the pace, cadence, and feeling of walking immediately shifts into a different gear; softer, slower, more relaxed.

Despite the utility in this section of the word "entirety," the beauty of entirety itself is that no words can encompass it. This is the source of the ease of it, of the spontaneous cessation of going somewhere, of the relaxed expanded effulgence which is the hallmark of being where we already are.

This will fade from view

Since that time I have embraced and lived that revelation—and avoided and rejected it.

— Tony Parsons

I don't know if it's true that this remarkable discovering of essential awareness will fade from view (although both Richard Bucke, and William James said it will, having interviewed many realizers who said "Yes, it disappeared again, in due course"), but during the time it is vividly obvious, while the sublime veracity and inexplicable causelessness of it are palpable, I want to give it language.

But "I" as I am conventionally understood, as you see me, as I believe myself to be, could do no such thing. The singing of these words is Whitman-esque: a song of myself, celebrating the present-silent-stillness with words *that only mean something because the concept of time underpins them.* But the awareness is outside time entirely. (And, without time, these words could make no sense at all.)

Today's experience is an insight, let's face it. But it is also a deepening, a returning of a prior glimpse, now more palpable. Our identity does not shift in an instant (although I have yet to take my last breath, which will be an interesting moment of a potential radical shift). A mother, giving birth, is beginning a long transition into an identity totally unknown.

Hmmm, "Let's face it": with what will I face it? The first glimpse of face-to-no-face, as Douglas Harding titled it, was at least 50 years ago—and my no-face, just like your no-face, your "Original Face" is as timeless as ever. The non-separation of this no-face from the vivid quintessence of awareness itself —utterly unbound from a body, utterly invisible without a body—is the radical and vital meaning of words like "this" and "it" when the Zen teachers (and this book) exclaim "This is it!"

There are no moments whatsoever when this is not true; the miracle of awareness was never, ever, for a nanosecond confined within something, like a body.

The knowing of this truth is much more *seeing,* and vividly self-evident—to direct experience—than any kind of knowledge or knowing. The risk of putting this into words is it will seem dry, philosophical, or sourced in knowledge—when nothing of the kind is true. Because what is called here "awareness" is entirely without identity or boundaries of any kind whatsoever, nothing useful can be said about it: we have to see for ourselves. And, the present vividness of this seeing will probably vanish from view.

Radical stillness

Be still. Be absolutely still. In pure curiosity, stir not a muscle nor a thought.

Little by little, we can allow all the activities we call "I" to come to a halt. We can pause desiring, for anything, even this cessation. We can find out within ourselves how to benignly neglect the bubbles of thought, appearing and disappearing by themselves. We can be interested: what remains?

Perhaps we will discover ourselves to be where we already are.

Perhaps:

the hitherto-neglected moment of *now*,

the seemingly-tiny fragment of time

(that is nothing whatsoever of time)

that thought ignores because it's unthinkable

gently blossoms,

all by itself.

We are it: "It" is us.

We have always been at home.

"We" *are* "home."

We cannot not be at home.

But in the churning dynamism of desiring and thinking,

we found ourselves adrift, separate, lonely, and afraid.

It was a dream, a nightmare: now we are waking up.

∾

In quietude

Bodies don't last indefinitely. They deteriorate, in characteristic ways. The pursuit of "Now just where has that prostate cancer gone to?" has become very precise. A radioactive isotope is injected into the body, then there is waiting time while the isotope binds to prostate cancer cells, then there is a PET scan to detect the cancer spots, which glow on the scan.

During the hour of waiting, between injection and scan, I'm shown into a quiet room and seated in a luxurious reclining chair. I become quiet, and very still, and then the following emerges:

Total quietude and peace is the absolute relaxation of all and any effort whatsoever. This relaxation comes about in the dawning discovery that all and every effort is nothing but the momentum of time.
Time is installed within us early on, effectively camouflaging the total effortlessness and trustworthiness of the natural state.

This camouflaging was not in any way conscious; inspired by those we love, who love us completely, we follow their god-like lead; they are fully possessed by the madness of chasing, and we are conditionable beings, above all else. Chasing is the quintessential motion of the world of thoughts, and cannot be otherwise, since thoughts compose a world that appears divided—and surely, chasing will resolve this great abyss which separates us from nirvana?

So when quietude becomes the way, all chasing is recognized to be the momentum of the installation of the thought world. It is not our inherent natural being —that remains, utterly relaxed, only camouflaged by the habitual momentum of the pursuit inherent to the empty world of thinking. Our word for this inherency is *"now"*—and to the thought-world, to relax totally in it seems tantamount to insanity. But it is the only way.

The phrase "Loving to be" captures the lovely quality of this unresisting quietude. This is love without conditions—the famous "unconditional love"—as well as the energy behind "This is IT!" It is the ecstasy in dying, the sloughing-off of all volitional content (whether this is conscious, or not), and the purest form of *I am that*, shorn of any duality.

As I'm leaving the building, elderly people are tottering from their cars towards the various scans and medical test centers in the cavernous medical facility I've been in. I think of the phrase "Dead men walking," then laugh, because I am one of them.

Then, I remember something Osho once said:

Be herenow and grace comes of its own accord. Whenever you are herenow, suddenly you will find tremendous grace, harmony, equilibrium, a melody in your being, a tranquility - and a tranquility that has not been forced from the outside, a tranquility that is not part of any discipline, a tranquility that is not quiescence, a tranquility that is not a kind of managed stillness. If it is still managed, then it is not yet herenow. If by effort you have been keeping it there, then it is already past. Or, if by great desire you are holding it there, then it is already in the future. Only when there is no effort to maintain it, no desire to support it,

*unsupported by you, un-maintained, unmanaged by you, uncon-
trolled by you...it is simply there. It surrounds you like spontane-
ity, silence, benediction...then there is grace.*

— Osho

~

Be here now, redux

The title of Ram Dass' book *Be Here Now* contains the whole teaching of the entire book, with a sobriety unmatched by much of the LSD-inspired handwritten beauty and profound insight of the original text.

"Be here now" also inspired a generation of seekers—and tortured them, for the title, and the teaching have two utterly different levels and only one of them is obvious.

The exoteric, outer, superficial and obvious-level teaching is that each of us as time-bound individuals can do our best to live in the here-now, perhaps undertaking a practice of endlessly returning to this place (or seeming to, since we never, ever leave it, except in imagination....) I would only know about this superficial teaching because I've spent years trying to follow it, musing on it endlessly in an effort to...be where I already am. I know; it sounds foolish, but many of those drawn by their heart's yearning to come to the end of suffering endlessly recycle here, trying to be where they... already are.

We can clearly discern effort from the sense of our bodies, and *be here now* seems to take effort. Mostly, I believe myself to be someone living in time and made out of time. That is, after all, the lesson that I've been absorbing since I was about 10 months old, when the love-fest of early infancy naturally moved into the shame-fest of my mom painstakingly shaping me into believing "I'm someone separate." (This shaping has to happen, and is biologically and culturally inexorable.) So to be here now, from the perspective of this conditioning means to pause the flow of time—which I believe I am; which I am firmly convinced I am immersed in—and momentarily notice the presence of here now.

However, here now is a mystery because it cannot be conceived; somehow, I know intrinsically that it is dynamic and nothing but change. But it can't be conceptualized, and so it was seemingly left behind as childhood progressed, and my innocence fell away and was replaced by experience, in its increasingly elaborate conceptual matrix. This matrix—or perhaps it is more accurately termed "a maze"—is the thicket of interwoven ideas that seem to be *myself*, telling me who I am, where I am, and where I am headed, in time. These days, it takes effort—or so it seems—to step out of time and "be here now." However, that is the first level of the teaching offered in *Be Here Now*.

But there can be a quietly dawning intimation of the other, esoteric, inner, depth level teaching of this beautiful phrase, *Be Here Now*. This more intimate and inner meaning dives from the familiar platform of tortured attempts at the posture of someone...trying to be someone...who is here now—into the recognition that here now is all we actually *are*. At this deeper level, the invitation of the teaching is to be what we already *are*, which is the entirety of here now. "*Be this here, now*," invites this teaching, "for this is what you already are."

Yet we seem to be solely someone who lives in time, someone who perhaps makes efforts to "be here now," or a myriad other strenuous attempts to get somewhere—and can only momentarily be here now before we are once again bumped out of it by another swiftly-moving impulse from the gasoline of desire powering the vehicle of thought.

Oddly enough, at the very same time, we are implicitly and vitally aware that *our actual existing is never anywhere but here now*, and this actuality never changes, no matter what. As we inspect this here now, for ourselves, in our own experience, many, many times over, we may begin to notice that in the center of it (where we perpetually exist, entirely irrespective of circumstances) there is simply the entirety of here *now*—and anybody existentially, or actually separate in this is impossible. This is the open, relaxed, and effortless truth of the heart of us.

The heart never grows old.

— Neem Karoli Baba

This entirety we can readily be—except this "being" is now non-separate Being, wholeness—and when we recognize it we can feel the beneficence of it, for we are it, and nothing else, and the heart knows this from within itself. Relaxation is the keynote of this only-ness, and this is the benediction we feel as we gradually discover we are it.

The "separate I" we have always taken ourselves to be comes and goes in this wholeness; a complex potpourri of familiar thoughts, beliefs and bodily changes; hormone rushes, sensations, fleeting images and an immense trove of rapidly shifting memories. The process of this separate-seeming-I plays out in exactly the same light of consciousness that illuminates the entirety of non-separate Being—yet all of a sudden, amidst this beneficence, troubled questions are raised by separate-seeming "I" about the past and future of the fragmentary one —who does not enduringly exist the way the wholeness of here now simply *is*.

Time is intrinsic to this separate-seeming character, just the way early conditioning mandated it to be. Left behind by this conditioning is the innocent heart-openness of a little child, who knows, but cannot say—who lives it but cannot conceive it—that she or he has always been this here *now*, this only-ness, this one without a second.

Love is the strongest medicine. It is more powerful than electricity.

— Neem Karoli Baba

Children, until they are conditioned (and this conditioning is absolutely necessary for tribal membership), live in the innocence and openness that is our birthright: we come from love, then it tends to become covered over. Jesus is supposed to have remarked that we have to become again as little children, and "a mighty angel" says that in heaven, there shall be time no longer. *Be* this here-now, says the depth of this teaching, and then we are home; the home we never left, nor could leave. We are it *already*, and to *be* it is utterly, totally, and completely effortless. *Be here now* is the quintessence of effortlessness itself.

~

Every breath a blessing

Towards the end of a pre-Covid party in North Berkeley, I go into the kitchen. Only the under-cabinet lights are still on, and a single figure stands by the counter, a person standing amidst what looks like a walker, hung with bags and equipment.

Moving closer, I find myself standing next to a gaunt man in his early 40's who is breathing raggedly from a plastic nose cannula supplying oxygen from the portable oxygen machine slung on the walker. I guess, from the oxygen and from his rumpled appearance and shiny, sallow skin that he's seriously ill, and in an effort to be cheerful in the presence of such obvious adversity, I say "Hi, how are you?"

He takes another tremulous swipe at the piece of cheese he's attempting to spread on a cracker, and barely turning to me says, with some effort and complete sincerity "Every breath a blessing."

Following the breath

We firmly believe it is us—me, I—following the breath. A great deal of interior commentary is directed at our competence, capacity as meditators, the likelihood of our seeking bringing about the fruit we long for, and so forth, based on whether we are meditating successfully in this way.

But we overlook something essential: the essence of the breath, the guidance-offering of it is that it happens in the moment, only right *now*, and in this unceasing and undivided nowness there is no reality whatsoever to a side-by-side observer or breather. That separate-character is a concept-coming-after—a very useful concept, and one that each of us must learn, as if it is reality, as we grow up out of infancy. But still, the separate-seeming person is a concept, flickering like daytime lightning in the immense wholeness of the sky.

We are so bamboozled by this concept that meditation in the absence of it is greatly puzzling. Who, or what will watch the breath? Another conviction has tripped us up: that the consciousness is ours, that it resides within our skin envelope, that there is someone who owns it and can direct it.

All that is pointed out above as being conceptual—the result of conviction: without reality, or, more bluntly, bamboozle-ment—is *inescapable*. Functioning in this way *must* be adopted, or the individual will not be able to function as a member of the tribe.

To function in this way is an immense gift, with many dimen-sions. Becoming sensitive to the suffering of it, we can descend deeper and deeper through the layers of our conditioning. Gradually, our being helplessly and inescapably at home already is revealed. This is the ultimate gift of nowness—func-tioning as consciousness apparently-divided. "Time" is the divider.

The reality that consciousness is intrinsic to this undivided nowness seems to take a long time to sink in. For one thing, as this intrinsic undividedness is apparent more and more deeply, so life becomes a progressive relaxation; there is nowhere else to go. "*This very body, the Buddha, this very place, the Lotus Paradise*"—might these wise, poetic, and ancient words in reality be telling the truth?

Similarly, the marvel of the breath is its self-appearing nature. The immensely complex scientific account describing the myriad mechanisms comprising this biological miracle is abso-lutely valid—only the is-ness essence of it is intrinsically without a source; eternity, playing. And this can be known by "following the breath."

～

Vehicle, gas, driver

No-thought...and suddenly you are in. Without thought you cannot go out, without desire you cannot go out. You need the fuel of desire and the vehicle of thought to go out.

Sitting silently, doing nothing...not even thinking, not even desiring...and where will you be?

Going in is not really going in. It is simply stopping going out...and suddenly you find yourself in.

— Osho

I heard the above remarks from Osho in 1979. I was in my mid-20's and amidst what seemed like cosmic-catapulting: the sudden death of my mother in an accident, the seemingly-unstoppable grief pouring from me after that—and then, being drawn to India by an utterly unexpected opening to the purest love I have ever felt. The catapult flung me, and I found myself in the well of love.

But of course, my mind came with me. I knew, and trusted that I had been infused with sudden goodness —knew that the loving, dancing, singing and joyous energy of the community I was suddenly plunged into had something to do with the meditation that the teacher, now known as Osho, endlessly mentioned. But what did he mean when he talked about "going in"?

I didn't know, and I could not hide my ignorance from myself. Before my mother's death I had been a Zen student for some years—really, without a single substantial clue as to what I was doing sitting on the cushion. I had lived in a Zen priory in Northumberland, in the UK, cold and hungry and stumbling through the daily rituals completely unaware of how on earth it might dissolve my suffering. I still did not know what he was talking about when he said "Go in."

One day in India—now going by the new name he had given me, "Prem Vijen"—a lightbulb went on inside me: I could write to him and ask him about my perplexity. I heard about it all the time; people getting replies back from him in response to their questions about their lives. So I wrote to him. I sent in a piece of paper on which I'd simply written "Beloved Bhagwan," (the name he went by in those early days) "What do you mean when you say 'Go in'?" and signed my name to it.

This was the only innocent question I ever asked him. In the subsequent years I sent him a number of questions, all of them involving some element of calculation; some agenda, some secretiveness on my part. He responded to them, sometimes publicly, but only his response to that first, unflinchingly innocent question remains with me to this day.

His discourses in those earlier times were alternating days of sutras, and questions and answers. The day in question was a sutra day, and not a day when seeker's questions were personally addressed. I was afflicted with a terrible Indian head cold that morning, and sitting at the periphery of the lecture hall. From out of the fog of my cold, his talking about the sutra was suddenly interrupted. "Just the other day," he said, "Prem Vijen asked a question: 'Beloved master, what do you mean when you say "Go in"'?"

The essence of his reply was that watching the mind was like watching a road with vehicles trundling by on it. Thoughts are the vehicles, and desires their fuel. He said that in due course, through this process of watchfulness, the road of the mind slows down and empties. When the road of the mind is empty, he said, you are in.

When that reply was given, in 1979, the world was entirely different than it is now. But decades passed before I glimpsed for myself, in the resonant truth of direct experience, that he was pointing to something within me that is entirely accessible to everybody, right now, this very moment.

Uncharacteristically, he had paused a sutra discourse to reply to my question, and the paused sutra, from the foundational *Dhammapada* of Buddha, contained the lines:

> *Mistaking the true for the false*
> *and the false for the true*
> *you overlook the heart*
> *and fill yourself with desire.*

These days, I am simply astonished at what was overlooked for so long: when I rest attention in my heart, the world immediately unfolds into an altogether different version of itself, one that is totally different, yet completely the same.

Time vanishes; *now* is all there is. This version of the world is known, intuitively and immediately, to be the unconditioned reality beyond harm; the quintessence of "Be here now," the causeless stillness, the blessing of every breath.

(The story continues in *"You are here and nowhere else."*)

Driver, gas, vehicle

Ignorance is the identification of the Seer with the instruments of seeing.

— Patanjali

The vehicle is thought. Desire is the fuel—seeking, searching, hunting, questing, pursuing. Ignorance is the driver.

All this is entirely natural: quite early in infancy, as we gradually relinquished our connection to entirety and wholeness, to unceasing satisfaction, we took on the tribal mantle; necessarily and inevitably.

We became *thinkers*. Humans are uniquely conditionable and the desire to be one of the tribe is baked in by biology and by biological need: how to become safe? Become a member of the tribe. This isn't voluntary, but biologically inexorable.

Unfortunately (but very fortunately, from the perspective of entirety yearning to consciously discover itself) tribal-being involves complete identification with the idea of being someone separate. Ignorance takes over the driver's seat and reality gradually becomes ignored in favor of *an idea*: that we are, as the words suggest, someone separate; we *are* Mari, or Matson, Oak, or Olive. Because this idea is enormously fruitful, as well as being entirely erroneous—a universal illusion of immense power—it quite simply makes us absolutely miserable. If we are intelligent, the misery makes us search for the solution to our misery.

Most of a lifetime can pass before we gradually discover that the very same inhabited ignorance that distracted us from the intrinsic ease we were born with is now offering us the same mechanism to get out of our misery: seeking.

Seeking seems like the way out of our insoluble suffering; only gradually does it become apparent it is the same old ignorance, still in the driver's seat.

The ignore-ance is quite simply not noticing what's here when there is no seeking. Hardly anyone notices that when chasing, hunting, pursuing, questing and seeking pause, the separate-seeming driver vanishes, replaced by the direction of life itself. No thought is applicable in this timeless, undivided reality, so the vehicle has disappeared.

Pausing the flow of gasoline for even a moment begins a whole wisdom-cascade. With a little attunement—perhaps in the form of being intrigued and curious when we hear about the unending presence of eternity and infinity, right here, right now—we may unmistakably recognize that ceasing seeking is all that's called for. Spontaneous wisdom instantaneously dissolves ignorance from the driver's seat, and the vehicle becomes the ungoverned freedom of entirety.

> Osho's implicit instruction to have a silent mind (for so
> I interpreted it, correctly or not) hung me up totally for
> many years, as I struggled to be the kind of meditator
> whose mind could be sufficiently silent for realization
> to happen.
>
> All that "thought-free" preoccupation is not helpful, it
> now seems to me. What looks, what sees, right now,
> reading these words, is eternal being, cosmic

consciousness—and is the great dissolver of vehicle, gas and driver being anything else other than the sought, seeking the seeker, which it always was, is, and will be.

Three steps to where you already are

Time and space are thought's way of conceptualizing the eternal and infinite nature of Awareness.

— Rupert Spira

Three steps seem to assemble themselves over and over again on walks in the woods. At first there's the beauty of nature: the unfolding dance of trunk and limb and underbrush, the suffusion of leaves being born, living, and dying, and the symphony of dusty paths by trickling creeks amidst forested hills under a brilliant sky. Step one is seeing out—seemingly; because that's what we've been taught we're doing.

Step two is to see in. Attention turns backwards, to the looker, the seeing. This kind of turning of attention is profoundly curious. This reversed attention notices directly-experienced reality—as it was when we were born—and is, before we are taught anything. Turned 180° backward, noticing reveals conscious spaciousness without a name. Or, spacious consciousness that is the essence of the word "now," and the existential meaning of the word "here." Exactly this consciousness is taking in these words, right now, reading or listening.

Nothing can be done about this that is revealed in step two. Never changing, it is rarely noticed. Entirely quiet, devoid of birth, death, or time, this inexplicable spaciousness radically contrasts with the riotous display seen in step one. Step one reveals the florid presence of time and perpetual birthing and dying. Step two opens the door inwardly, revealing timeless deathlessness, never born. Nothing special, perpetually here, and so almost unnoticeable: the uncaused miracle of this presence is that it is the essence of being, of *I am*, of awareness.

Step three comes with the recognition that dividing these into "outer" and "inner" is entirely artificial. The means of dividing them—the miraculous human capacity for thought—isn't actually reality. It's like a grid of coordinates placed over territory that is fundamentally undivided. You can then point to square A, and square B, and square C, contrast them, and compare them, and pretend there are actually boxes there. But remove the grid and the territory instantly reverts to what it always was, and is: the undivided.

Step three implicitly acknowledges the profound power and utility of being able to—seemingly—divide the undivided. How else could you possibly notice the luminous emptiness of awareness itself, distinct from what it's aware of? Everything awareness is aware of comes and goes, birthing, living, and dying, and it is a miracle all its own to be able to notice the noticing, by virtue of this capacity to divide the undivided. Only thought makes it possible to take step two, and turn attention backwards. And only the yearning of the undivided then asks for step three, in which the grid of coordinates is deftly lifted away. It was never here to begin with.

The essence of step three is to undo step one and two. Step three recognizes that the division of the outer and the inner is only *seeming*-dividedness, dissolves the grid for a moment, and in thoughtless awe finds the territory of the undivided exactly where it has always been—here—and precisely at the only moment it really exists—*now*. Try it.

Staying

*All people know suffering which is as the mud in which the lotus takes its root: all people know the lotus blossom which gazes at the heavens. Few people indeed know how to nourish the root of True Religion within themselves in the mud of ignorance that surrounds them and fewer still know how to make that root flourish and grow the long stem needed in the dark water before the flower can bloom in the clear light of day.**

—Jiyu Kennet

Ordinary infinity is a delightful place. All of us live here, all of the time—but we don't notice it. We don't notice it because we're busy looking for something else. We are looking for happiness, satisfaction, ease, peace, energy, dynamism, or for money, sex, or power. But we are looking for something.

We were conditioned from our earliest life to look for things: to chase, to pursue. We have become so used to this entirely unnatural-but-universal state of being that we hardly notice the misery of it.

Chasing-after can only happen in time. Time is another profound conditioning, inescapably interwoven with chasing, as well as with the idea of being somebody. But time is essential to chasing. We hardly even notice our timeless nature, so great is the sound and fury of our pursuit of happiness and completion.

---

* Adapted from Jiyu Kennet, *Selling Water By the River*, preface to Book One; "people" has been substituted for the original "men."

Thing-time

Time also has the extraordinary capacity to allow the creation of desired things; could the sofa and the floor lamp, the computer on which this is being dictated, or anything else exist unless the concept of time made it possible? Obviously not—but we so deeply believe in the objective existence of things that we also believe in time as if it is reality, which it certainly seems to be. (None of this is in any way said to exclude the unlimited creative potential of time and things; certainly, my comfortable existence in this dwelling, dictating this piece of writing owes the entirety of its possibility to the creation of things in time.)

One of the most important "things" permitted to seemingly-exist by time is "me." The belief in the existence of this separate-seeming person isn't shared by newborn infants, who must gradually undergo the arduous task of inhabiting the belief in being someone separate. This inhabitation is inescapable. It has to happen to become a member of the tribe. We want with every cell of our being to become a member of the tribe. We can't wait.

Fast forward a decade or two and we've become fully fledged members of the tribe, functioning the way everybody else does, more or less. Unfortunately, although we were promised that all of this would make us happy, it has not. Something is radically not right, but the only solutions offered to us are more of what we've tried already: to chase stuff.

To the very end, loyal to the ideals offered by the culture, or because by this point we've taken on obligations to family that essentially leave us no escape, there seems no way out. In our spare time we may become spiritual seekers, because we have heard about a fabled state called enlightenment—and of course, pursuing it is all we know how to do.

We may try every method under the sun to get to what we have heard is possible by spiritual seeking; we chant mantras, whirl like dervishes, meditate for months on end, and starve ourselves half to death. We know in our heart of hearts that only the innermost essence of these practices is real, but we are desperately unhappy, and we will do desperate things to try to liberate ourselves. Walking on red hot coals, ceaseless prayer, total surrender to a narcissistic teacher—we'll do anything in pursuit of our imagined freedom.

The seeking glitch

If my example is anything to go by, it can take a very, very long time to notice the inherent glitch in this process. Gradually noticing that chasing is the problem, and has been from the very beginning opens a door to a new possibility, one that we effortlessly inhabited as tiny babies, innocent as the day is long. To be where we already are, and cannot not be.

Everything in existence except the humans manages this "being where we already are, and cannot not be" with immaculate perfection. This "being where we are" sounds ridiculously simple and totally easy; after all, if the rug on my living room floor, and the trees outside, the bugs sunning themselves on the deck, and the hum of the refrigerator are all completely at ease, how difficult could that really be for me?

Relax into nobodiness.

— Osho

Additionally, we know darned well—in some totally intuitive yet absolutely certain way—that we really only exist here *now*. But here now makes no sense, because we believe it is a sliver of time, the tiny temporal speck in between the immensity of the past and the endlessness of the future.

When we believe that now is a speck of time, we can make no sense of it, because anything that changes with such spontaneous and unpredictable dynamism cannot possibly be thought about: a cup of coffee (subtly different from every other cup of coffee that has ever existed); a sudden freezing wind, or Donald Trump for president—newness is unceasing. Thinking is about *things*, and this here-now is definitely not a thing.

Nonetheless, without an atom of a doubt, we are here, *now*.

As part of our seeking we may have taken up the practice of meditation. Once we get beyond the habit of chasing something in meditation, for example by simply being present with the coming and going of our breathing, we may start to notice a new possibility.

In the moments when thought pauses (between every thought and its neighbor is a pause, without exception) something very hard to describe occurs. We effectively vanish as separate-seeming people, instantaneously occurring instead as every-thing. This everything-ness is filled with energy, and we may gradually recognize that it was this natural state that we gradually lost touch with in our striving to become someone separate who belongs to the tribe. This natural everything-ness is quite profoundly at home, despite being saturated with dynamism.

Nothing is excluded from this entirely natural state; thoughts continue to float through the space of it, like bubbles in water. Currents of feeling are unceasing. The entirety of our body hums and shimmers in a way largely inaccessible to "mindfulness of the body" attempted by a separate-seeming person. We have vanished into an inexplicable restfulness that is inherently still and teemingly dynamic. "Vanishing" is a total para-dox, for our disappearance as someone separate-seeming is simultaneously the same as our sudden birthing as vitality itself, now liberated from the harness of seeming-separate.

Glimpses

The glimpses of this are moments of feeling it. Although ideas are being used here to try and convey some of the experience, the concepts have none of the infinite dimensionality that is felt as the natural state of *now*. Gradually through our lives training ourselves to be exclusively separate-seeming selves—the one I introduce to you when we meet, saying, as I put out my fist for bumping, "I'm Glenn"—we find our true reality whittled down to the flatness of things. Things are finite, and limited, exist in time, and can be encompassed by thought (or so it appears.)

Not only that, but my waking life is preoccupied with concerns for this separate-seeming self: how did I do in the past? Will the future be beneficial for me, or humdrum, or a nightmare? How can I get ahead? How can I steal a march on death, outwit the competition, outrun fate?

Inhabiting these kinds of streams of thought is to enter a seeming-reality a million miles from our natural state. We have left naturalness and entered time. Our being—saturated with dynamism, undivided inexplicable everything-ness, unthink-able yet utterly obvious—has been forgotten.

Yes, sometimes in the stream of thought we are imagining ourselves to be there is a splendid satisfaction; a win, a victory, and happiness briefly ensues. But we can't escape the obvious: the meaning of "winning" is entirely dependent on the meaning of "losing," and vice versa: there is no real getting ahead in the realm of thought, but the chasing of ourselves-as-potential guarantees misery. (Again, the immense utility of pursuing a possibility glimpsed within the miraculous theater of thought—iPhones, cooking pots, spacecraft, books like this one, sewing needles and nanotechnology—is in no way being dismissed or denigrated here. But when our open and miraculous being has morphed into exclusively a thing in thought, the tool has enslaved the toolmaker.)

So, naturally enough, with these glimpses of our true nature in sight, we wonder what helps to allow them more. We endlessly mull over the reality of our unceasing inhabitation of *now*, and how we seem to leave it: over, and over, and over, and over.

Stay

One day, a word occurs: *Stay*.

Stay where? Thinking leaves—that's the nature of thinking, to step into the theater of time and see what's possible, but to do this is to seemingly step away from where we unceasingly are. So great is the habitual momentum of this stepping away, this leaving, that most of us believe it's the predominance of who we are. What is here when we stay is the natural state.

If I remark here that the natural state is quite simply infinity and eternity it may seem ludicrous; pretentious, absurd, or worse. When we stay, we reside in complete inexplicability— but we can vividly feel the entire wholeness of it. The ease, the overflowing dynamic energy, the self-originating ceaseless changefulness of it can be readily felt. We are at home, the way the rug on my living room floor, and the trees, the bugs sunning themselves on the deck, and the hum of the refrigerator are at home; unruffled, undisturbed, living-being.

Stay is quite different from the seeming-instruction to "Be here now," because the latter is always taken to be something a separate-seeming person can *do*, or chase after. The reality, revealed by *Stay* is that any pursuing whatsoever hides the unceasing presence of our naturalness. In this naturalness there is nobody separate, and this nobody-separateness is quite obviously and palpably the nature of horses, rugs, bugs, clouds, trees—and everything, except within the imagination of the chasing humans.

Never having left

Stay is the cousin of Paul Hedderman's splendid book title *On Never Having Left*. Because we have, in reality, never left—but we sure seem like we have. Almost all of us (count me in here) feel as if we are separate, restless, unsatisfied, searching, seeking—and unhappy. Inspecting, and then perhaps gradually inhabiting the natural-state reality invited by *Stay*, we may find ourselves staggered: how did I miss this? How did I step away from the entirety that I am, the unceasingly dynamic wholeness in which the wind in the trees is myself in motion, and the tingling of my body is perfect peace in endless causeless flow?

"Loving what is" and the many teaching-book titles sharing this realization tend to elegantly reflect states of truth, but with few instructions on what to do—or rather, not do. Almost impossible to wriggle free from is the implication that someone separate-seeming will, by their actions, get to the place never left. The reality is that the separate-seeming self can do absolutely *nothing* whatsoever to bring about the realization invited by *Stay*.

Burst out laughing

Are we timeless ease, absolutely at rest, wanting nothing—or are we uprooted, anxious, disturbed, questing and wandering in time and space? Or perhaps we are both (*Each is Both*, announces a Wei Wu Wei book title), the "Two Truths" referenced by Zen teacher Steve Hagen.

If we *knew*, with complete certainty, that the only existent reality is this moment, exactly as it is, we would be free to die, would we not? Less dramatically, we would be free to be foundationally at ease with each and any moment, no matter whether such a moment is filled with ease and cheeriness—or anxiety and distress.

The only existent reality *is* this moment, exactly as it is. Nothing else exists. In this ground of being which *is* (inescapably and always), all sense of "timelessness," "infinity" and "eternity" carrying any special meaning dissolve; these words reflect the effortless simplicity of our true nature. These rarified terms only have their significance *from the perspective of separation*; from the 'normal' point of view which assumes that time is existent and therefore separation is actual. However, this is just a point of view: the whole is indissolubly limitless and eternal.

Timelessness is invisible to time. What cannot be thought is imperceptible to thinking. No-self makes no sense whatsoever to seeming-self. Yet the timeless, inconceivable no-self is the only reality, and time, thought, and the seeming-self are *appearances only*. Nonetheless, "Things are not as they seem, nor are they different," as the *Lankavatara Sutra* says; "Things neither exist, nor do they not exist," (and we "...might as well burst out laughing," remarks the sage Longchenpa.)

The heart of the matter

A book of this kind grows organically. The title, *Home Already*, and subtitle, *In the Heart of Now* emerged little by little; I hoped for a title that was a teaching, all by itself. What I could not know then, yet am gradually coming to realize, is that the title goes on teaching me.

I thought that the subtitle *"In the Heart of Now"* was something like a poetic metaphor. But in the *now* that is the *only* "time" of the heart is found our real existence: unlimited benediction, the entirety of being, unceasingly. There is nobody separate in the heart of now, nor could there ever be; now is unalterably home, and nothing else exists (except in the marvelous mirages of mentation). *The appearance of someone-separate-seeming in this home is an intrinsic part of home.*

Complete changefulness is the nature of this heart of the matter—which is, in actuality, the overflowing undivided cascade of energy we know as life itself—but the term "energy" is insufficient, for this energy is *conscious*. The awareness and the dynamism of life are woven together with such intimacy that they radiate a subtle blessing, which we might call loving-to-be, and this we can feel, in the heart of ourselves.

God laughing

The cosmic joke

The cosmic joke of all this is that what we seek cannot be gotten rid of, but searching for it hides it from us. When there is total cessation of searching—death would be a perfect example—we are revealed as infinity and eternity.

So, in actuality, every moment is quite simply infinity and eternity. We don't generally know this consciously, because there is an insistent momentum, seemingly in our heads, of conversation, dialogue, reaching, questing and chasing that only very rarely ceases. Nonetheless, every instant is infinity and eternity, despite the fact that infinity and eternity can very easily take

the appearance of limitation and time—which, it could sometimes appear, is for the purpose of discovering infinity and
eternity, now born as experience.

> *...you will be surprised: if you enter into the immediate, you will*
> *find the ultimate in it. If you move into that which is close by,*
> *you will find all the distant stars in it. If you move in the present*
> *moment, the whole eternity is in your hands.*

> — Osho

This is all readily discovered to be true in our direct experience. Anytime there is a pausing—even momentarily—of the
rushing forward, the habitual momentum; of the chasing,
seeking, searching, questing, and hunting, a particularly
marked noticing will become apparent.

The noticing will be of a distinctive quality, of unlimited
depth and extent. Time disappears as a consideration, and the
remarkable presence of eternity is palpable.

Nothing is different than it ever was—and everything is utterly
and totally transformed.

All of this can be quite readily noticed, simply by ceasing to
search. Then, we become, as it were, what we always are—
unlimited, uncaused: a cartwheeling miracle, unfolding by
itself, without the slightest design for the future. We become
again what we always are—which is quite simply eternity,
timelessness, the very same eternality we can notice behind
our eyes, out of the corner, so to speak, of our single apperceptive eye—timelessness that is astonishing for the limitlessness of it, and its totally uncaused nature.

And to come back to the beginning of this section: the joke.
The joke is quite simply that we were searching for what
cannot be gotten rid of. All our searching is to return to

finding we never lost it, and there is no "it," and losing "it" is impossible, because we are intrinsically and everlastingly it. This, surely, is divine humor, marveling at itself.

> *Please, please don't worry.*
> *How many times do I have to say it?*
> *There's no way not to be*
> *Who and where you are.*
>
> — Ikkyu

A wrinkle in the cosmic joke

An elegant and devilishly effective wrinkle in the cosmic joke is that the moment we notice our undivided state of being, the very next instant will likely bring grasping for it.

Undivided being is blessed. It is benediction. Of course, the mechanism in us that has always reached towards satisfaction, happiness, and pleasure becomes alert: "The goal has been reached; I must have it!"

Then, momentarily, there is the upwelling of grasping, chasing, seeking, searching and hunting—all of which take place in time, of which there was none in the original glimpse—and the space of unceasing satisfaction closes, or seems to: is essentially hidden from view by the activity of desiring, propelling, and grasping.

The discovery of uncaused perfection looks like death for the one who seems to be engaged in this reaching, grasping, pursuing and hunting. Curiously enough, the two are of a very marked difference in their character. The unceasing satisfaction and unlimitedness of the non-searching state of being is—seemingly—replaced by time and lack.

Time and lack are the hallmarks of the sense of being some-body separate, somebody who must quest and search; hunt, chase, and seek in order to have fruition. Yet Buddha's noticing of impermanence directly implies that this sense of a separate, long-lasting entity enduring in time, and needing fulfillment *does not substantially exist* the way we believe it does.

Because we take it for granted that we are indeed *only* these separate-seeming selves, we also take for granted that the activity of chasing is intrinsic to us. Undoubtedly, if we *are* fictitious non-entities then chasing will be absolutely necessary—indeed, will be intrinsic to this lacking and empty way of being. But the entire superstructure of this is built on top of a monumental misapprehension—that unceasing perfection is not already the case.

We might wonder if this remarkable construction, this arising in seeming-time and seeming-space is actually the grandest of all creations of infinity and eternity, searching to know itself, worship itself, and love the unlimited and ceaseless, causeless play of itself. We can't know this. I very clearly seem to be someone separate, hiking up a hillside in California, location quite well known, and destination—returning to my car—also supposedly quite well known (will I get there? Maybe).

But those are just what can be delineated about me. Behind my eyes is unlimited unknownness, or, consciousness, wide open, completely enrapt and marveling at the play of what seems to be limitation; limitation which is occurring as an appearance of unlimitedness.

Even more marvelously, the separate-seeming-entity is busy grasping every appearance of the unlimited perfection and eternity, and trying to make it his own, as if he exists; as if anything exists except this vast and undivided array that Wei Wu Wei calls "mind itself."

The seen is the seeing

The eye by which I see God is the same eye by which God sees me.

— Meister Eckhart

A kind of wonderment opens up when the seeing that is the open space behind our eyes becomes conscious of itself. This silent gazing, "…gazing with sheer awareness into sheer awareness" as Tilopa puts it—is unlike any other phenomenon in the whole universe. This that knows, knows its own knowing. Awakeness is awake to itself.

Yet what can we make of the world we see, which is surely made of material stuff, apparently quite different in kind than this miraculous seeing? Nothing, apparently, in this "material stuff" has the slightest awareness; even my hand, sensate though it apparently is, never, itself ever notices my eyes seeing it.

Our conditioned presumption is that the world exists objectively outside of us; for most of us, most of the time this is considered neither conditioning or presumption, but reality.

At some point, something may happen to soften or dissolve this seeming-reality. Perhaps it is reading some words of Krishna Menon, who remarks *"If form is itself seeing, how can one see a form?"* These words may have been read dozens of times—and one day, they land: form is just seeing—and nothing but seeing.

This is the inward, subjective, directly-obvious and indisputable truth of our own immediate and sovereign experience. The tension we have lived with since we first began our struggle to learn the system of dividedness—"me" here; "you" over there—begins to ease up. Reality is utterly and totally relaxed, and this can be felt in the recognition that form is itself seeing.

"The world that is seen" gradually resolves itself into simply the seeing. Form, it turns out—"that which" we always took to be objective; an externally-existing material reality—is *nothing whatsoever but the seeing.*

> *...our deepest and most enduring delusion is our resolute belief in substantiality.*
>
> — Steve Hagen

Transformative change in our seeing comes about through a directly-experienced recognition that *of course* form is seeing, despite our "...resolute belief in substantiality." We can become aware in our own direct experience—*see*, for ourselves—that form is nothing but seeing.

There are clear further implications: that sound is nothing but hearing, the felt nothing but feeling, taste only tasting, and smell only smelling, draw together into a single thread, for consciousness is the common theme of all this experiencing.

Consciousness is timeless—we can check again behind our eyes. No time can be found there, although when we look out into the world of clocks, all kinds of time are everywhere. But here, where the seeing lives, where the seeing itself is absolutely at ease? No time, or timeless *now.* And timelessness manifestly underpins hearing, feeling, tasting, smelling—even girds the vehicle of time, which is thinking.

The moment seeing is recognized to be form, there can be a stepping out of time; *time* is the foundation upon which the world of enduring material stuff rests. The concepts which are the discernible fabric of this reifying objectification (for example, "rug," "sky," "chair," "dog," "cloud," "window"—and "me") cement the sense of enduring substantiality. Then we appear divided, as if that *is* reality: "me" and "the world." But this is an appearance of consciousness, not the reality of a substantial world separate from us.

> *...thought is the apparent objectification of consciousness.*
>
> —John Levy

The world of seeing—the only world there is—turns out to be *nothing but* the open space of consciousness that has never not been here. The seeming-two are not-two, but are intimate without limits. Yet, they are certainly not "one," because turning in the interior direction* there is the unmistakable noticing of open spacious consciousness. Then, pointing outward, there is the appearance of seeing, which we formerly took to be the appearance of an objective world that is "being seen by someone separate"—but this misperception is gradually resolving itself into noticing there is only the seeing, and that is the entirety of what we used to believe was form.

> *Everything is clear to those for whom nonsubstantiality is clear.*
> *Nothing is clear to those for whom nonsubstantiality is not clear.*
>
> — Nagarjuna

We are tacking closer, as it were, in these successive realizations, to discovering *that there is nothing but ourselves*, and there

---

* Hitherto in these pages, the unmistakable duality of "pointing inward" and "pointing outward" has been accepted as reality. However, this seeming divide depends entirely on the completely-believed-in-idea that there is a "someone," a bodily-self who stands astride the boundary delineating the seeming-two. Nothing changes at all *when this is realized to be just an idea*—and yet everything is radically different.

never was anything else, except in the non-substantial, yet material-seeming perception into which we were conditioned.

Perhaps this was so that suffering was sufficient to propel the arduous journey of rediscovery, eventually arriving back where we began; now a divine child—no longer an unjaded and relatively unconditioned infant who is innocently setting out on the greatest journey of them all.

So, to recap: inwardly noticed, the remarkable presence of the seeing—without gender, name, face, or time. Pure open, conscious, timelessness, or timeless *now*. (To even give it a name like this is to make a graven idol out of something that is the purest divinity—but that is for consideration another time.)

Looking outward, there is the world of form, hitherto taken to be objectively existing; made out of material stuff—even if competent physicists have deconstructed it and found it to be utterly and totally insubstantial, down to the subnuclear degree. Our perception of objectivity in the seeming-outside world gradually melts into the discovery that this objective world is nothing but the seeing—and was never, ever, anything else.

The third step is the intimate joining, of the ineradicable seeing, and the world of form that is nothing but the seeing, now made manifest in the miracle that is the world.

There is, if we like, a potential fourth step. It is that in this entirely encompassing and unlimited miracle there is no room whatsoever for anybody separate. What is being glimpsed is entirely whole: utterly and totally entire, and never anything else. This is known with complete intimacy and familiarity by the heart of us.

Yet within this wholeness is a predominant identity of seeming like a distinct-seeming-entity, called "me," or "Glenn," who must be (seemingly) inhabited in childhood, and which is the miraculous instrument of creativity (the latter concept being indissolubly tied to, and meaningless without its twin: destructiveness.)

Eventually, it seems, with diligent inspection, with a kind of willingness to go on noticing things that defy logic but unmistakably *are*, the sense of things opens, and the undivided—acknowledged over and over again as the nature of *now* itself, where we never can not be—gradually offers the fruit of itself.

There is only this seeing, this open spaciousness, and the occurrence as it of the manifest world of seeing (which we formerly took to be the objective existence of a world.) There is no entity whatsoever remaining in this—and there never was: ever, from the very beginning, which was beginningless.

When there is realized to be absolutely nothing but this entirety, playing, with the most magnificent liberty—giving rise, moment by moment to every conceivable appearance, then there must and can only be love. This only comes into view gradually—there is a possibility of heart opening; glimpsed, sometimes.

Before the punchline

This final subsection is to mark two things. One of them is the absolutely dreadful and immersive misery subsuming me not long before these pieces of writing emerged. The other—we might say this could be seen as the upside of the prior downside—is that these pieces of writing successively unfold some of the aspects of this absolutely astounding and remarkable existence as it is. This existence is not in any way different, not by so much as an electron, from the ordinary existence in which we suffer.

Home Already

*Furthermore, there may be happiness or misery. Be equally indif-
ferent to both and abide in the faith in God.*

— Ramana Maharshi

The existence in which we suffer is sometimes called samsara, and the undivided unceasing miracle is sometimes called nirvana. It can be a mystifying, but gradually-clarifying remark from within the depths of Buddhism that samsara is nirvana, and nirvana, samsara, for the two are not-two.

The total intimacy of nirvana and samsara is something to be felt into and gradually inhabited—because the inhabitation of it is by itself. This that exists through itself is the way. These writing sections today, despite appearances of their emerging from somebody separate—seemingly coming from the action of dictating into a phone—nothing of the kind is actually true. This that exists through itself is giving voice to itself. This "giving voice" is distinctively human. Voicing, and the entire superstructure of conceptualizing, can be deceit and dreadfulness of the highest degree—and, can be creativity and caring of the most divine form.

This existence is fully alive from within itself, and there are no separate entities, despite the overwhelming appearance to every human being of their being solely a separate entity. This separative-appearance has to be learned—managed, if you will—and then the untold misery of it has to be pierced, for there is no limit to how much suffering is in samsara. Nor is there a limit to how much marvelousness there is in nirvana, and, samsara is nirvana, and nirvana, samsara.

Chasing two truths

We need to directly discover the truth of the total experience in the moment of now (through insight) and clearly see how it differs from the fragmented linear representations via the thought process. Without awareness of this distinction we cannot experience the actuality of what is occurring in our entire human process.

— Ligia Dantes

There are two ways to live one's life. One is to be preoccupied with the inescapable conceptual fracturing of the World. The other is to regularly acknowledge this apparent fracturing, while never losing sight of Totality.

— Steve Hagen

(NB: The quotes above, from utterly disparate writers, nonetheless reference some completely overlapping concepts: {*"Fragmented"; "Fracturing"; "Apparent fracturing"*} AND { *"Insight"; "Actuality"; "Sight"*})

Those who do not understand the distinction between these two truths cannot understand what the Buddha taught.

— Nagarjuna

Every morning I sit quietly on my couch, and contemplate "The Great Matter." This morning, I'm writing a piece about ceasing to chase or to search, but the blissfulness glimpsed in recent months, even yesterday, keeps on eluding me, and my state is of vague disquiet.

After about 15 minutes or so of this quiet angst I realize what's happening: I'm trying to *have* the blissfulness, and what's more, trying to have the blissfulness be here for longer. I'm searching and seeking; and I didn't even realize it.

The moment this trying stops—in the understanding that *it is the sole source of the distress I am experiencing*—the blissfulness is spontaneously present. It is simply the subtle dance of being itself, untrammeled by the buffeting of desire.

This dance of being is unconditional, has no beginning or end, is causeless, limitless, and completely beyond explanation. We are it, or, it is what we are; absolutely no words are needed or are adequate here, for this being-ness itself is the birthplace of words, but when the words subside, in the gap between two thoughts, the infinite being we helplessly and inescapably are is glimpsed, in a moment of miraculous wonder.

The moment blissfulness is glimpsed, or nanoseconds after the first apparency of it, another wave of grasping to have it and to hold it and to keep it ensues. Then the blissfulness is hidden behind the striving.

The striving seems to be by *me*. "Me," I have learned to believe, is small, separate, enclosed in my skin, and born to die. When I now read words written—just earlier today! —"This dance of being is unconditional, has no beginning or end, is causeless, limitless, and completely beyond explana- tion," the "me" sense coalesces around the mean and self- doubting thoughts that gather and call out:

See? You are full of it! You are just little you, exactly as I have always said! What nonsense is this that you are unconditional, causeless, and limitless? No wonder you go on writing this stuff—you are trying to convince yourself!

In a very well-respected contemporary school of inner work, Ridhwan, or the Diamond Approach, the initial years of deepening within are spent almost exclusively focused on coming to terms with these kinds of interior voices. Perhaps, even, it is necessary to allow ourselves to fall, willy-nilly down to these levels for there to be a glimpse of the nightmare of self-hatred all of us carry—because it is just beyond this depth that insight may happen of the true nature of things: that "me" is an appearance in wholeness, an appearance *of* wholeness, and *that* is the real backdrop of being.

We've forgotten the mist, the cloud of unknowing that is the birthplace of thoughts, even of self-hatred. We've lost touch with the tingling, teeming, streaming, shimmering feeling of being that only and ever lives immovably—and utterly imper-manently—here *now*. We are so habitually focused on what the thought process can pluck out of this cloud, distinguish in time within this miraculous womb of being, that only rarely do we settle enough to notice the genesis of everything.

Could it be we are the genesis of everything? We talk about self and no self as if it's a light switch, on, or off, but existing itself is grainy, pixilated, an unlimited dance of points of energy; infinite, infinitesimal.

This can be noticed, but only here now. When the shimmering streaming of our body sensations is gradually recognized to be intimately contiguous to what happens through hearing, and when the very same visual apparency, of teeming and tingling obviously composes every supposed-thing seen, we have most likely become very quiet and still for this noticing to happen.

What might it be that has become quiet and still? We can no longer say; it is causeless, unstoppable, effortless. The quieter we become, the more apparent it is, and the depths of the quietude of it are self-existing and without cause. No words, no thoughts can describe it, for here *now*, where this luminous essence unceasingly is genesis, is the no-place and the no-time where we live unceasingly, where this illuminated true-nature intuits its own presence; where thought can never go (including this thought!) Here the heart is at home.

If we clearly apperceive the difference between direct apprehension in Whole-mind and relative comprehension by reasoning in mind divided into subject-and-object, all the apparent mysteries will disappear.

— Wei Wu Wei

In the beginning was the word, so it is said. But that cannot be, for only in the world of words is there anything like beginning. Words open wide the door to suffering, and then the searching begins, the turning and turning, deeper and deeper, of what we cannot not be illuminating itself, the suffering calling out bliss, and the end of searching being where we already helplessly and unstoppably are.

Countdown to luminosity

Truth is that which lies in a dimension beyond the reach of thought.

— Wei Wu Wei

From sitting quietly:

Let me repeat. The perceived cannot perceive.

— Huang Po

"The perceived" are known quite clearly to be such; the rug before me, the sensations of pressure, backside on couch, drifting thoughts; clock ticking, dog next to me snoring and twitching, bird song outside.

But, "the perceiving"? This cannot be known—or it would be

"the perceived." Nonetheless, there appears to be perceiv*ing*, otherwise, what could "the perceived" possibly mean?

> *Although I am in front of you, in you, and behind you, it is better first to look behind and try to see Me there.*
>
> — Krishna Menon

Let's intuit something vaporous, impossible to give name or form to: something never not here, never absent; the eternal aware backdrop of all experience.

> *I am always standing behind you witnessing your varied activi-ties. You can see me so without much effort.*
>
> — Krishna Menon

To be specific, this is "the seeing," noticeable behind our eyes; the hearing, listening to itself behind our ears; the feeling, alert to everything showing up as "my body."

> *Through our eyes, the universe is perceiving itself. Through our ears, the universe is listening to its harmonies. We are the witnesses through which the universe becomes conscious....*
>
> — Alan Watts

This seeing is behind *our* eyes, this moment, reading these words: this seeing *that notices itself* (and is thereby *totally* different than everything perceived. No rug, pressure, backside, thought, clock, dog, snoring, twitching or song *ever* notices itself.)

Home Already

As soon as you turn behind to see Me, I will take you into the inmost core of your being and there you will see Me.

— Krishna Menon

Let's (realistically) pretend *this* gossamer intuited presence, knowing itself by itself, is the meaning of "perceiving."

Later on, you will see Me in your thoughts and feelings.

— Krishna Menon

We are poised for the tripartite countdown: there is "me" who is writing this; "the perceived" in the form of all and everything showing up sensorially—and there is "perceiving."

Still later, you will see that the thoughts and feelings are none other than Myself.

— Krishna Menon

All of these are present. "Present" means "now," as in, "present now."

Since all objects are mere thought forms, they will also be seen in the end as Myself.

— Krishna Menon

Yet now, as we have already established, is inconceivable. No concepts ("me"; "the perceived"; "perceiving" are all concepts) can possibly apply here, where we live at all times, effortlessly.

...the experiencer and the experience are one and the same, that is Myself.

— Krishna Menon

Realizing this, like swift stage magicians, we pull away the underpinning *thought* of three, and what remains is "what is," now momentarily self-illuminated—liberated from the known: Unmistakable. Intrinsically perfect. Self-existing. As it is. Luminous. This is the inmost (and outermost) world of the heart, just as it is, now.

...it is only looking straight out of your eyes, it is nothing far off, mysterious, out of touch, imperceptible at present: it is what is there now.

— Wei Wu Wei

This isn't about taking on comforting concepts. This is reality at its most raw. Nothing can be blocked out anymore. It's the end of control. It's a love affair with what is.

— Jeff Foster

There is no thing to attain, no where to go. There is only acceptance of what is, on the deepest possible level, and even that only happens if it happens.

— David Carse

Reading the above three quotations, we may notice each realizer differently reflects on the complete homecoming of "What is." There is "what is there now"; "a love affair with what is"; and "acceptance of what is." J. Krishnamurti, in a remark quoted elsewhere in this book, said: *"When there is understanding of "what is" then there is no need for control."*

Wouldn't it be amazing?

Wouldn't it be amazing if we knew we were entirely and completely free—entirely free of all the travails of life, and, just as free around the triumphs?

Wouldn't it be amazing if "we" and "free" were—correction: *are*—the obvious reality, evident when we point backward within ourselves and rest more and more deeply in the eternity thus noticed?

Wouldn't it be amazing to find that this eternity is immediately accessible at all times to our own direct experience— when we trust a certain kind of in-seeing that has never gone away, only been camouflaged, then covered over completely, by convictions, opinions, and beliefs?

Wouldn't it be amazing to discover, more and more deeply, that this eternal nature has always been here, in full view—but we were solely turned outward, to the perceptible (and conditioned) version of the world, seemingly made of matter and separateness, with "ourselves" another separate-seeming thing?

Wouldn't it be amazing to realize directly, through our very own heart space, heart-seeing, or heart-knowing, that each of the seeming-two, of "outward" and "inward" are actually each other, in an undivided intimacy astonishing for its closeness? That another term for this intimacy is "love," love that never ceases, has no causes, and is without conditions?

Wouldn't it be amazing to come to realize that the entire world of time and things is only and ever this sheer nondivided intimacy with eternity, and that this arrangement (and every fragment of experience coming through it) is inexorable perfection, and can be nothing else whatsoever?

Wouldn't it be amazing if we realized, with an endlessly-deepening certainty—a palpable and entirely trustworthy surety—that this perceptible life of ours is complete perfection, every moment, and in every electron of every atom of itself?

Wouldn't it be amazing if we realized that we are not this life, not in any way this life, yet our intimacy with it is unstinting: effortless, total and complete; and this loving and indivisible closeness with it cannot be undone at all?

Wouldn't it be amazing if we realized this total indivisible closeness nevertheless absolutely includes our complete invulnerability to harm of any kind? (The body known as "Glenn," "my" body, will still die eventually.)

Wouldn't it be amazing if we realized that this intimacy with our life is the greatest possible gift—that of all gifts, this one, *this* very life, *exactly* as it is, could not in any way at all be a greater present to us than it is?

Wouldn't it be amazing if we understood that relaxation is our true, free, entirely trustworthy nature; that what we are, inherently, and without cause, is perfectly relaxed, and that there are no limits to this relaxation?

Wouldn't it be amazing to come to realize that no matter the tensions populating our perceptible life, the utterly relaxed knowing of them is as undisturbed as the sky is by the clouds scudding across it?

Wouldn't it be amazing if we realized that this relaxation is nothing whatsoever to do with effort, but is inherent to us, is our ceaseless true nature; uncaused, timeless, and *never* other than perfect, in itself?

Wouldn't it be amazing that the deepening of this realization increasingly led to complete freedom to be ourselves, just as we are, in every minuscule detail of our lives?

Wouldn't it be amazing to realize that this freedom to be utterly relaxed is exactly the same freedom liberating our life to move precisely as it does?

Wouldn't it be amazing to realize that the more deeply we die —which is realizing, more and more deeply that we were never, ever solely the living, but were always the purest undying essence of living—the more our unique life itself is free to live fully?

Wouldn't it be amazing if this freedom were nothing like licentiousness; had no abuse in it, but was the kind of loving care for the world and every tiny fragment inhabiting it that could *only* come from realizing the world is myself, and nothing else?

Wouldn't it be amazing to realize that this world being myself has always been the nature of the world, but could not be realized until the blossoming of my own true, essential nature as nothing but the seeing of what I'm not?

Wouldn't it be amazing to realize that this "myself" is the purest possible absence, liberating the world to be exactly and precisely as it is?

Wouldn't it be amazing that, even facing the inevitable death of our seeming bodily-self, the one that all these years we identified with as solely ourselves, our uncaused, untrained, natural-state of equanimity remains as it is; still, curious, loving, and unfazed by time and space?

And, wouldn't it be amazing if all these amazing things were true—which they are?

INFINITY

Infinite now

To repeat: *now* is unlimited, which is the simple and clear meaning of "infinite": "unlimited." This very moment of now can only be defined, or boxed by conceptual limitations by using time. Time itself is an abstraction from now, and such abstractions are concepts, not this very moment of now itself.

The source of the goodness of this very moment of *now* is that it is infinite. This moment is infinite. This can be known and felt simply by noticing what now is really like. This kind of noticing is non-conceptual, which is to say that any thoughts that come out of this kind of noticing are like froth on the ocean's waves; they are not the ocean itself, but they have no reality without the existence of the ocean. Any reference to "now" utterly fails because the language and the labeling have their source in infinity and can only lumber along behind the dance of the limitless.

So we can know and feel the nature of this moment of *now* because we are never not here, where this nature is brilliantly on display, forever and ever. We are never for an instant away from this, our infinite home, unless we are pretending we are exclusively separate from it.

This pretending to be separate is very carefully conditioned into us in early life by people we love the most in all the world. We *must* learn this pretending—so deeply that it becomes as if it is reality. But it is not reality. We remain infinite. This infinity can be noticed at any moment, because now is where all of us live, all of the time.

The noticing of infinity is by infinity; this sounds complicated but could be said as "What you truly are notices what you truly are."

Discovering what we truly are means to go via the route of gradually noticing what we are not. The arduous conditioning we underwent in the first two years of life, in which we stepped into the miracle of being separate-seeming-creatures existing in time, leaves us indelibly stamped with the belief-as-reality that that is indeed what we solely are: creatures in time, born to die. Nonetheless, this, and everything else which we are convinced is reality is only known from the imperishable citadel of infinite *now*, which we truly are, which is impossible to leave, which cannot die.

This infinite now is the birthplace of finite-Glenn—not just the moving and sacred marvel of biological birth, but the emergence into possibility of the infinite astonished at itself in this new world of form, then forgetting itself, camouflaged by the conditioning required to join the tribe. The suffering of this forgetting is so powerful—for the infinite has arranged to forget itself—that for some people, such as Glenn, the entire biological span of life will be preoccupied with this one incipient seeming-forgetting: that I am infinite.

Always home in the heart of now

Whether we like it or not, we are always at home in the heart of now. Whether we are up in our heads, worrying about something to come, or dismayed about the past, our being is always home, in the heart of *now*.

But our ideas about ourselves say otherwise: we believe we are exclusively creatures in time, made out of past and future. Not only that, but we believe we are solely separate creatures, and the mirage of this is extraordinarily potent, drilled into us in early life, when everything goes as deeply as possible.

So to be at home in the heart of now is completely effortless; we are always at home there—or, to be more accurate, here. Being at home in the Heart of now is already the reality of everything, and of every creature—except the humans, and their incredible cognitive capacity for creation and destruction. This capacity is a tool; a servant, a gift that has run amok.

The ancient traditions all have stories about the servant usurping the queen or king. It can be simply astounding to notice that when effort ceases, and attention drops relaxedly back into heart space, there is complete fulfillment. The looping yammering of our familiar state of being in our heads seems like it has purpose; we need to get somewhere, and fast, otherwise it seems like we may miss out on fulfillment. Only relatively rarely does a contemplative person notice that in the heart of *now*, there is fulfillment already. Even more rarely is there enduring inhabitation of this never-not-here reality. The head doesn't like it. Its job has become less important.

This dislike by the head has good reason. The head works exclusively in the realm of thought, which is the realm of time. The heart lives exclusively in timelessness: in the existential, in the real; the undivided, the whole and entire. This reality can be clearly felt whenever we drop contemplative attention into heart space. Then, timelessness reigns.

Dropped into heart space, there is the marvelous, direct and immediate knowing that the nature of *now* is eternity, in the light of which time plays out in concepts. Yet eternity is real, and time a superimposition, a pretender. A marvelous servant, no doubt about it—but a dreadful sovereign.

A curious paradox obtains in respect of head and heart. The head objects to the reality of the heart, because time is the only *lingua franca* it possesses—and the heart is forever immersed in now, and no other time: in the purity of the heart, there is only eternity. But the heart has no problem with time; indeed, in the end has no problem with anything that occurs, and time is one of the most obvious existential occurrences, despite the fact it is made only out of airy concepts, and nothing whatsoever besides.

So the subtle gradations of living-experience that are the perpetual delight of the heart, such as the infinitely altering light that accompanies our days and nights, are flattened by concepts to "light" and "dark," or the effortful (or poetic) discernments we might try to make between one or other phase of diminishing or growing light.

Finally, the most important aspect of this: we imagine ourselves to be exclusively distinct and separate creatures in time—but there is no time, other than concepts. The existential is now, the no-time of the heart. Perfectly clearly, in this no-time space, immediately available by dropping attention into the energetic reality of our heart, we are nothing but *now*. Our reality is the entirety. There is nothing and nobody separate, nor could there be, in timelessness. For there to be dividedness, time has to pertain; dancing with its bosom-companion, concepts. Otherwise, there is only home, in the heart of now, always home, forever and ever.

~

You are here and nowhere else

Osho was my first true teacher but I could not begin to absorb what he was teaching me until I was no longer

in thrall to him, until his magnetizing charisma faded
with his death, and I could begin to discover my own
spiritual authority. This leaving, while painful and difficult and uncertain, left behind a root in my heart from
which this book has blossomed.

Osho insisted that this moment of now is where God
lives, and repeated this insistence thousands of times in
various forms. He was a thoroughly inconsistent
teacher—indeed, used inconsistency as a method to
shake up our mind-centric certainty—but about now,
he was utterly consistent.

I didn't get it. Like most of us, I was hypnotized by the
belief that now is simply a relatively insignificant and
momentary fragment sandwiched in between past and
future. I could read and admire the truthfulness of
Buddha's remark that it is easier for a single man to
defeat an army of a thousand men than to defeat the
habits of thought, but I was utterly bamboozled by
thought and often still am. "Hypnotized by belief"
means that I don't even see it's a belief, because it
seems like reality.

I did dimly glimpse that seeking was the problem, or to
put it another way, that following the siren call of
other-than-now, a.k.a. my mind, consistently kept me
both running on a treadmill of the future—and not
finding what I sought.

After Osho's death, I traveled to Lucknow in India
where lived a truly enlightening teacher, said the
excited buzz in the spiritual circles I inhabited. His
name was Sri H. W. L. Poonja, known fondly as
Papaji, who awoke to the infinite depth of his own

reality while a student of perhaps the greatest sage in modern India, Ramana Maharishi. In Papaji's company I had two experiences, one of which went on circling in my mind's confusion, and one of which went straight into indubitability, where I can feel it in my heart to this day.

Up next to him, in front of a meeting of about 40 people, I asked Papaji directly if I could finally stop seeking now. He responded to my question with great sincerity, kindly and earnestly pulling out a pad of paper and a pencil and drawing a circle. "You are here," he said, indicating within the circle. "Seeking is looking for yourself somewhere else—but you are here, and nowhere else." His forefinger tapped the interior of the circle he had drawn. "Do you understand?" I did, but with my head, not with my heart and my whole being. I returned to my seat having made polite noises that yes, I had understood, although I really had not in any deep way.

In this swirl of confusion, understanding intellectually, but having experienced no foundational shift of the kind I hoped for, I passed the next 24 hours and went back to sit with Papaji the next day. I happened to be sitting on the floor, Indian style, at the edge of the small group of people at the gathering, and Papaji came out of his room and, elderly as he was, began his somewhat infirm and tottering walk towards his seat at the front of the audience. In passing me he reached out to steady himself by putting a hand on my head.

In this unanticipated moment I experienced myself being touched more lovingly than had ever happened in my life before. This entirely unfiltered perception was unaccompanied by any of the expectation, wild celebration, and hoped-for transformation that went with being more ceremonially and intentionally touched by my teacher Osho.

Papaji put his hand on my head to steady himself and in his touch I could clearly feel, without any inter-posing thought getting in the way, that he touched me that lovingly because everything without exception was nothing but himself. And I am expert about touch: at one point during my successful 15 year career as a professional bodyworker, my role in the therapeutic center where I worked was to evaluate the services offered by other bodyworkers in order to see whether they were suitable for our center. Something about touch speaks to us with wordless elegance, if we are capable of listening, and Papaji's touch on my head that day said everything there is to say.

Throughout this book it will gradually become apparent that there is in fact a specific location in time in which it is obvious that everything without excep-tion is nothing but ourselves. This "specific location" is *now*, before thought springs up to claim it, and it turns out to be outside time and never not here. It turns out to be the essence of who we are, and what everything is. When everything is ourself there is nothing but complete intimacy, or as we put it when we speak from our heart, love.

~

Not realizing

Clearly, we are inside infinity already: at the very least, the very existence of the concept of infinity—unless the concept is completely fanciful, or misconstrued and nonsensical—means this writing must be it. Nothing is outside the unlimited.

There's just energy.

— Jean Klein, personal communication

Then doubt comes in, and habituation, and being in thrall to concepts (not enlivened by them, like the unlimited vibrancy of the concept of infinity.) I forget for a while, amidst this dull habituation, that all I have to do is turn attention to what's here in this immanent now, the flash moment, the instant of being alive which is inescapable. Then discover, once again the tingling, thrumming, churning river of experiencing which is the essence of changefulness, the entirety of what we are; in particular, as we get used to being this being-what-we-are— when we are manifestly and noticeably not ("not" being a summary of Buddha's most foundational discovery about the nonsubstantial nature of our thoroughly-impermanent reality).

It's all energy.

— Tony Parsons

A later noticing is that doubt, habituation, and being in thrall to concepts must also, by necessity, be the infinite. It plays how it plays. With complete aplomb, total skillfulness and blithe indifference to consequences, the infinite pretends a "me" that is remarkably beautifully wrought. "I" am made with a perfection that unmistakably signals divinity at work.

This perfection includes being able to turn noticing back upon itself and examine what the immanent *now* is like. The flash moment, also known as eternity-now, is quite clearly composed of a shimmering, tingling, ever-altering dance of energy. Nothing is excluded from this, and the noticing can start in our own body, taking in the directly-experienced indistinct shimmering of it, and then expand outwards, noticing meanwhile there is actually no boundary between this shimmering-tingling and the apparently material world which, examined closely, turns out to be utterly insubstantial: energy, actually, and not much (if anything) else.

Energy is delight.

— William Blake

"Infinity" is an explosive concept, but we tend to like our concepts bite-size and seemingly, controllable. Nonetheless, "limitless," which is the meaning of infinity, can only mean that this writing is it, this reading is it, that my imagination of myself as someone separate is it, and likewise all of our seemingly-own imagination of being someone separate is it. Any seeming-boundary encountered ("Yes, but....") is inevitably also it, as is the presence of a preference for concepts to be bite-size. Everything is it, no exceptions. Even we, filled with our conviction of our separate seeming-nature—yes, that too is it.

Does anything remain? Wei Wu Wei remarks on "*...the perfect peace of the presence of absolute absence.*"

Occurring by itself

When chasing ceases completely, life is noticed to be

happening by itself. Actors? There are none in this panorama —miracles, plenty. In fact, all of it is a miracle.

It is occurring by itself, and the more this relaxation is entered into, this absolute ease is inhabited, the more apparent becomes the miracle.

We could say it is consciousness that is absolutely relaxed—but that would require the effort of understanding, and when this understanding falls away, the extraordinary nature of the perfectly ordinary is vividly revealed.

This humdrum, daily life intimately partakes of awareness— but in this utterly relaxed closeness there are not-two. It is a miracle, entirely defying explanation—even though it is the simple and obvious reality of our everyday life, all the time, without exception. It is occurring by itself.

> *What we are required to do…(is)…to lay everything down, to be nothing, to know we are nothing—and thereby to leave behind the whole process of conceptualization. So doing, we cease to be that which we never were, are not, and never could be. That, no doubt, is nirvana.*
>
> — Wei Wu Wei

The undying heart
of the now-moment

I am descending into time. Please help me.

> — Ramakrishna

Oh, I know this is insane: how can it possibly be said that "There has never been any time"? What kind of madness is this?

Try as it might, the mind cannot understand any of this. But the heart full-well knows.

Glimpses of this before, moments of sudden and inexplicable insight, resulted in essays with titles like *"Oh, there is no time."* But this time, the source is evident. This time, the source is the heart.

We have discovered the fountain of timeless awareness.

— Ramakrishna

Because the heart knows there is no time. There is only *now*— the time of the heart—and everything changes. In the no-time of the heart, time appears.

One of the marvelous productions of eternity is time, or the appearance of it, for there *is* only eternity. Eternity getting to know itself is time. Time is a fabrication, an appearance, making possible the eventual dissolution of time and the unmistakable knowing of eternity, by eternity.

We are now being drawn into the very core of timeless awareness.

— Ramakrishna

Eternity is, and is the entirety of what is. There is nothing else, although a thoroughgoing descent into seeming like a being made of time will be needed for this to be realized. But there is only this sovereign, impeccable, timeless knowing, utterly undisturbed by anything.

Knowing, timelessness, impeccability, and eternity are all the intrinsic qualities of the heart. This quality of the heart is still: indeed, beyond stillness, and peaceful entirely outside the confines of any concepts of peace. It is, if you like, the quintessence of the now-moment.

And, it is entirely immaterial. Material, or corporeal existence is the way it appears, or appears to be. Time is intrinsic to this seeming-to-be—and there has never been any such thing as time. Time is a conceptual abstraction from events. There are not even "events," for only now is real. Even "now" is an idea the reality of which can never be grasped, because it is nothing but change; a dazzling flux, the inward nature of which is undying stillness. And all this is known through, and only through, the heart.

O spaceless, timeless One.
O boundless bliss of Knowledge,
a drop of which intoxicates
the manifest universe.
O Radiance without beginning.
O ecstatic Lord of Love.
O King of kings. Life of my life,
unveil Your Countenance
as clear light within my heart.

— Ramakrishna

What this is like

It is only when you seek it that you lose it.
You cannot take hold of it, nor can you get rid of it;
While you can do neither, it goes on its own way.

— Yoka Daishi

This that can't be gotten away from, cannot be chased, cannot be possessed, is the whole and entirety of everything we've ever wanted—what is it like?

It has one brilliantly obvious characteristic—that it is an unceasing river of change. Behind the verity of the illuminated remark that our true nature is "*...in highest truth, devoid of any trace of objectivity,*" as Huang Po puts it, is quite simply that there are no *things* in the river of experiencing (and neither are there not, states another venerable sutra.) There is just a ceaseless flood of experiencing, a river, a torrent. This is sometimes called "impermanence" which is offered by contrast with the apparent solidity of things, which, when you get very close to how things are now, does not exist as anything substantial.

> *We are deceived if we allow ourselves to believe that there is ever a pause in the flow of becoming, a resting place where positive existence is attained for even the briefest duration of time. It is only by shutting our eyes to the succession of events that we come to speak of things rather than processes.*

> — A. K. Coomaraswamy

Impermanence isn't an alternative to substantiality, some sort of altered perspective—rather, it is the entire totality of what we have, what we are, what we cannot not be. But we are always trying to be something we are not, which is solid, substantial, and enduring. That will not work. Nothing substantial like that truly exists.

Impermanence, non-substantiality, the flood, the river of experiencing does exist, but the moment we feel it we clearly recognize that no language can encompass it. We can be it quite simply because we *are* it, but terms like impermanence, totality, Buddha-nature or "the one without a second" can only be place markers denoting the infinite.

Obviously, once infinity is in the picture (it never is not) all this could *only* be infinity noticing itself. There is no other possibility. Hence, as the venerable *Lankavatara Sutra* puts it, *"Things are not as they are seen, nor are they otherwise."*

Non-duality is the mothership

The original title of this section was going to be "Non-duality is the mother of duality." However, it was too long; true, but lengthy.

We believe duality is the only game in town. We believe this as if it's reality, although Steve Hagen, in *The Grand Delusion* says: *The things and thoughts of this world appear compellingly Real. And for most of us, that's all there is to it. We believe in all of it. And so, believing, we live for a while, suffer because of our beliefs, and then die.*

What is said here will be impossible to say because it is about non-duality, spoken in the vehicle of duality; words and ideas. Nonetheless, we live perpetually and inescapably in non-duality *because there isn't actually anything else*; there just seems to be something else, something like duality.

Where is this place we live inescapably and perpetually? Here, *now*. Can anything be said about it? Absolutely not, other than helplessly remarking that it is undivided, infinite, inexpressible, utterly impermanent, suffused with consciousness as an intrinsic aspect, and never not here.

This is the mother. Out of her is born dividedness, finitude, expressive definition, seeming-permanence and the observer: the observer seemingly distinct from the observed. Duality.

All of the characteristics observed in the prior paragraph we believe to be real, but they are the children of the mother. These chimerical children are referenced in Buddhist teaching by mysterious remarks such as "*Things neither exist, nor do they not exist.*"

We are the mother; and we are the children. Per the warning about impossibility-of-expression earlier, this will inevitably be misunderstood as a statement about duality, when it is, in truth, a statement about actuality, which we are.

Being here now...again

What was never lost can never be found. Your very search for safety and joy keeps you away from them. Stop searching, cease losing. The disease is simple and the remedy equally simple.

— Nisargadatta Maharaj

Here's a remarkable truth: our existence in actuality is completely and utterly safe, totally assured, beyond harm and absolutely effortless. All we have to do to realize this is be exactly where we already are: here *now*. (Since we are already here, and cannot *not* be here, this is not remotely effortful. The clouds, bees, flowers, dogs and pebbles are impeccably effortless.)

But another version of "Be here now" clouds our minds. In this version we are someone, a person in time, endeavoring to be here now. This version is utterly and totally fruitless because it is based on a fiction, namely, someone separate.

It is your mind only that makes you insecure and unhappy. Antic-ipation makes you insecure, memory—unhappy. Stop misusing your mind and all will be well with you.

— Nisargadatta Maharaj

Our actual existence—the safe one, the one beyond harm—has no separate person in it. A separate person is a *concept*. Concepts inherently involve time, itself an extremely handy cognitive human abstraction. In truth, there are no *things* in existence the way time and concepts imply there are. There is only the wide open infinite existence, and we are that, and could never be anything else.

> *You need not set [the mind] right—it will set itself right, as soon as you give up all concern with the past and the future and live entirely in the now.*
>
> Questioner: But the now has no dimension. I shall become a nobody, a nothing!
>
> *Exactly. As nothing and nobody you are safe and happy. You can have the experience for the asking. Just try.*
>
> — Nisargadatta Maharaj

This is not to deny the experience of separate things, nor the compelling appearance of what we've been trained into, namely being someone separate. But all of that is the play of concepts; *actuality* is unbroken, whole, and always undivided.

We are a gift of the infinite

It seems like I'm always going somewhere. At any moment, amidst the many actions of daily life, I'm rushing from one thing to another, completely unaware that there is anything but haste and hurry, rush and pressure, and anxious end-gaining.

The paradox of this is that whenever I realize this is happening, and I pause with momentary experience, I am suddenly filled with an uncaused sense of being the infinite. This sounds very inflated, until we try it for ourselves, and notice that in the complete subsidence of going anywhere, there is the blossoming of a dimension of being that is completely quiet, absolutely sacred in nature, (whatever the circumstances of it), and always here, no matter what.

The speculation is tempting that the rushing, the hurrying, the endless anxious pursuing is because the entity that is seemingly doing all that knows it does not actually exist—hence, it must hurriedly chase after every momentary target, in the deep fear that by pausing it will vanish.

There is indeed vanishing in the pausing, although it is actually the spontaneous, immediate, uncaused, and effortless appearing of the infinite, instantaneously replacing the separate-seeming person.

But the vanishing is not permanent—which is to say, the separate-seeming person springs up again, and again, and again, and indeed, we may speculate this has no end, seeing how it, too, can only be infinity playing, since the definition of infinity —unlimited—remains unvarying, and inexorable.

Where we find ourselves when we pause is now. We think now is a momentary blip in between past and future, but that would be conceptual-now; this *now*, here, in pausing, is sometimes called the eternal now, and is the only verity, the rock of ages, the great undying ground of being. We are it; and it is infinite.

Possibly, the above remarks prompt some exploration of our own immediate and direct experience; we may find ourselves experientially exploring the fact of our infinity, every moment of now.

Perhaps this "fact" sounds surprising to us; we know ourselves only as the finite, the time-bound, the born-to-die. But time is an abstraction from eternity, and only our identification as solely a separate-seeming creature in time hides this from us.

When I first noticed that every moment is infinite, it definitely seemed as if I, separate-seeming me, was behind the noticing. What ensued then was, predictably, an effort to maintain this noticing; to continue it—the sheer paradox of time trying to control the timeless.

There is, of course, no control of this kind; everything happens as it happens. When this is recognized, suddenly or gradually, there is total relaxation, for everything is realized to be the same no-thing functioning—as it ever was, is and will be.

This flies completely in the face of our mind-centric certainty that I, we, me, you, are in charge of our lives. I completely imagine I am writing this essay—even though the promptings that lead to this very sentence, written here, come from the most mysterious of all "sources," which we call "my mind." Thoughts appear by themselves, as do moods, sensations, sounds, the vagaries of the visual world, and all and every memory and anticipation. The persistently adamant interpretation of all this as the possession—and even the agency—of somebody who is separate appears by itself, and persists by itself.

I only ever write to myself, really—and only yesterday, I was flooded with the realization that in the heart of everything (which is *now*, the inescapable centerless core of all that exists, no matter who, where, or when), there is the love-ly utter certainty that *this*, knowing itself as *this*, is bliss. "The observer is the observed" is the dry way this is usually rendered—but that is the mind's version of what the thought-world of the head can only reach dimly toward, never be. Only the heart can *be* it—and we are the heart of it, and cannot not be.

And the nature of "we," in the title of this section, "We are a gift of the infinite"? The most mysterious of all mysteries has been pointed to repeatedly, elsewhere in these pages; the seeing behind our eyes is known to itself, by itself. This revelation can only be a brief glimmer in the mind, but when this knowing knows itself via our heart, there is a blossoming into wonderment.

In the only-nowness that is the domain of the heart, there is neither hearer nor heard in the distant sound of traffic, but a knowing, knowing itself. The rug upon the floor is perceptibly awake to itself, by itself, for in the no-time that is now, forever *now*, the nature of all things is felt to be intrinsic, unborn; infinite. The glimmer in the mind becomes a resonant chord in heart-feeling—then there can be a turning toward what "we" might be.

No such thing as "we" can be found, in our direct experience —a total and complete zero: absolute emptiness. The intimacy of this open space with all the things of the world, with the sights, sounds, feelings, tastes, smells and thoughts, is total: an intimacy so close it brings a thrill, a subtle vibration known as *"ananda"* or bliss in Sanskrit, and called "loving to be" by Sailor Bob Adamson. This absolute closeness is the purest gift; of the infinite, to the infinite, by the infinite (that we are).

Everything is included

Just a moment of life without thought reveals infinity, and the endless immensity, majesty, and wonder of it.

"Life without thought"? Not really so absurd: all it takes is a moment of slipping out of our heads, momentarily shucking thought—then we are being exactly where we already are, all the time without exception—and that's the joke of it.

We just tend not to notice what the moment is like, because thought goes burbling on, as if it could really encompass life, which it absolutely cannot.

What thought goes burbling on about is not at all this completely and utterly inclusive moment that we can fruitlessly try to encompass with words like "infinity" and "eternity" (or, "here-now," "now-here," or "nowhere"....)—this is the reality, and the supposed-version in thought is nothing at all like this reality.

One of the most obvious differences between reality and the thought-world is the predominant presence, in the thought world, of somebody who's supposed to be separate: that would be "I," along with "me," and "mine."

Yet the moment thought subsides, or is wriggled free of for a second or two, what remains is the essence of I-ness, now the totality, the undivided wholeness we've always intuited we are anyway. Because all the misery is only happening to the one who is seemingly-exclusively-separate; the fantasized one, the one who only exists separately in time-bound thought—and nowhere else.

Everything is included in the reality, the seamless wholeness, the moment-by-moment miracle that all of us live, all of the time, without exception: mostly neglectfully.

Included is the tingling of our body, now clearly known to be indivisible from the susurration of the furnace pumping out warmth on this cold winter day, non-separate from everything in the room; except now there are no things, because they belong to the thought-world. Here, where all of us live, all of the time, without exception, as a great Buddhist master put it: *"From the very beginning, not a thing is."*

Everything is included—and there are no things, because they belong to the world of time, and we are the timeless. We are helplessly the timeless, and *we* are not; nothing can be done about the immense blessing of it. Nor is it possible to alter the complete and total inclusivity of it.

The system of things, and of time is a remarkable human capacity, and probably undergirds our predominance of the planet. No other creature here seems to have developed this neural technology to the degree we have—and surely, no other creature is as profoundly miserable as we are. No other creature, we might speculate, is busy with the version of themselves that exists exclusively in conceptuality. Yet, no other creature suffers so deeply that they find themselves turning toward the misery to pierce the mystery of their own being, and awaken.

All creatures other than the humans seem to live here-*now*, sometimes turning their astonished gaze, as my dog does, to a laughing or weeping human.

But make no mistake: this piece of writing could not be recorded without the fantastic capacities of that neural technology being highly developed. It is intrinsic to human beings to conceptualize the possibility—in time—of creating something that subsequently comes into being. Yet the very same technology has run amok and claimed separate "I" as the author of all our accomplishments and the observer of the rest. And while that, the separate-seeming "I" is absolutely gathered in to the "everything is included," it is not real. But it is the suffering-vehicle for awakening to the inclusive reality.

The heart of Buddha-nature

Buddha-nature is nonduality.

— Hui Neng

Hui Neng is one of the old grandfathers of Zen; an illiterate woodcutter who awoke just hearing the teaching. We could spend thoughtful hours making a mental mishmash of the sense of what he meant when he said *Buddha-nature is nonduality* —and get nowhere.

But there is an alternative to that torturous process, and it is readily available to all of us. This option is to drop down into the space of our heart, and notice the nature of being there— or, to be more accurate, *here*.

We may notice, for example, that in this easeful lowering of our attention just 12 crucial inches, time disappears because within the heart, it is purely and only *now*. There's no need to worry about the disappearance of time—the app is available, whenever we need it. But it's an app, and our real being is not in the thinking machinery between our ears, but in the heart of us.

We can also notice, dropped into heart space, that there is no dividedness; time is needed for dividedness, and immensely useful as that functioning in time is, there is none of it in the heart of us, and so, there is no dividedness.

In this undivided heart there is no longer someone separate— that was a conditioned apparition, belonging to concepts and the world of time. The mirage of actually seeming like someone separate is enormously useful—but if that's the totality of who we take ourselves to be, we will be in substantial difficulty until there is an opening to the immediate, deep, and entirely palpable truth that can be found in our heart.

This possibility, of attention resting deeper, in heart space, is surely where we originally lived before we had to undertake the inevitable upward elevator ride (we call it "growing up") into the more and more elaborated ideas of ourselves as conceptual beings.

Then desire cements the deal; the misery of seeming solely like something that we're not—a conceptual creature that is made out of time and ideas—promises us a solution, in the form of more, better, and different. We helplessly step onto the treadmill of becoming, sure that somewhere out ahead of us in time is the fruition we seem to have lost. But we have been prior-persuaded that we are solely the mirage of separate selfhood. This persuasion has to happen, and we have to fully accept the functional idea of being someone separate. Unless we accept this we will not be able to join the tribe in any kind of satisfactory way. So we accept it.

Meanwhile, neglected by the increasingly complex and sophisticated web of concepts forming the separate-seeming one that we have been persuaded we solely are, our original Buddha nature becomes invisible to us. It has no name. It is perfectly formless. Time is in no way intrinsic to it, or, it is timeless *now*, and helplessly and eternally so.

There's no point searching for this original nature, Buddha nature, for it is completely involuntarily accompanying these words, reading them; the origin of creating them, and everything in between. No boundary can be discerned where this wide open nature comes to a stop and the world of seemingly material things begins. Such a hypothetical junction exists only in thought, and in any thought-free instant, the marvel of the undivided entirety is vividly apparent.

Another remark of Hui-Neng's can then complete this section:

> *I at once became thoroughly enlightened and realized that all things in the universe are the essence of mind itself.*

> — Hui Neng

Infinite identity

Just like matter, space, and time, location and motion are simply constructs of Mind.

— Steve Hagen

All identity is conceptual, or, as Steve Hagen puts it, *"constructs of mind."* At the root, this has to do with time being a conceptual abstraction from now; time has no existence, as such, since there is, in reality, only now (which ceaselessly changes by itself).

Although this conceptualizing itself is an intrinsic part of the ceaselessly changing flow of *now*, it is nonetheless the weaver of the dreaming of substance which composes our supposed material world.

All identity hinges on the presupposition of some kind of enduring, substantial entity in time—but once time is seen through, all entities become what they are; appearing to exist, but not existing. Consequently, to say *I am Glenn* is to claim identity as some-thing that appears to exist, but does not, in fact, enduringly exist; only now exists.

All the above, explained via a web of profoundly abstract concepts, is known directly by the heart of us. When we drop attention into heart-space—relocate ourselves, as it were, from our habitually head-focused nexus into our heart—crystallized identity as any-thing becomes obviously absurd. Existing, or being, is quite simply the nature of everything, and we are that.

In this heart-existing, we can certainly recognize (and give conceptual voice to, like this here) the presence of an undying spaciousness entirely without name or form. The intimacy of this spacious sentience with all that is illuminated by it, with all that is born and dies, is total, complete, and unceasing.

"All that is illuminated by it" is the familiar world we know as material reality; there it is, spread before us, the customary world of matter, time, space, location and motion. We can conceptually divide the aware-spaciousness from what seems to occur in it—but the heart knows this dividedness is unreal. This undivided knowing of the heart is intrinsic, luscious, nourishing and fulfilling; it is more like being at home, all the time, no matter what, where, when or who.

In this feeling-full heart-space, the absence of identity is an easy, simple joy: a naturalness, like the warmth of sunshine or the wetness of water. There is a quiet flow of something like subtle sensation to it: the simple feeling of being, as it has been called. There is nothing to this: no cause, no past or future. When existing and consciousness (which was spoken of above as material reality and aware-spaciousness) rest undivided, in and as the heart, there is bliss, or "loving to be," as Sailor Bob Adamson calls it.

It turns out that to come down out of the head is really a misnomer; a mistaken identification. We have never been that one who seems to live in our heads, because "that one" is composed only and entirely by a complex concatenation of various bodily experiences—sequestered by concepts. And, "that one" is a pure and glorious production of the infinite one we cannot not be; a marvel, really. The intrinsic-infinite, known without thought by the heart to be simply the undivided nature of *now*, has arranged itself to be Glenn, appearing in time and space, made out of matter, in California, typing these words. Marvelous.

Intuition

Intuition is the present moment communicating with itself. Since in reality there are not two things, "the present moment" and "itself," intuition is the infinity we are, in sacred communion. This is inescapable intimacy; our heart knows it from within itself, from within timeless immediacy, or, reality.

Intuition is the means by which we know the present moment is infinite. There is a sensing of this infinity; we know it by the momentary relaxation and ease experienced in the moments of simply being here-now. The most marked characteristic of this relaxation and ease is that it is absolutely causeless. The palpable sacredness of it comes from the clear and obvious, infinity-deep sense that nothing whatsoever needs to be done for there to be complete ease, even blissfulness.

Although all this can be said in thought, it does not have its source in thought whatsoever. In fact, the relaxation is marked by the complete absence of thought, or, by the way thought is irrelevant to it.

~

SEEKING

Built-in benediction

The benediction is built-in; we just became conditioned so we no longer notice it.

The conditioning is inescapable and implacable; we *have* to learn to identify ourselves as solely someone separate. Because this separate-seeming-self makes us miserable—remember, necessary, but miserable-making—our lives become about chasing the happiness we have lost, or seem to have lost.

Our entire thought process is essentially dedicated to finding what will give us back what we seem to have lost—but we have not lost it.

The chasing hides it from us, and the chasing is always in the form of somebody running after something; I am empty, sad, lonely or ashamed, and I yearn to be filled, happy, connected and proud. Chasing, seeking, hunting, pursuing, searching; all of these preoccupy attention.

This preoccupation leads to a good deal of drama and trauma, for the energy of chasing is prodigious, a firehose of actions squirting everywhere. All the while, back at the source, where we live without a nanosecond's interruption, there is the benediction, built-in, waiting for us to be at home where it is —where we are, as it is. This "back at the source" is the unending residence of the heart.

Nonsensical benediction

> *In short everything appears to be wrong in me because the funda-mental idea that everything is perfectly, eternally and totally posi-tive, is asleep in the center of my being, because it is not awakened, living and active therein.*

> — Hubert Benoit

We won't know this is here until looking for it pauses, or ceases. The revelation of it comes in the cessation, the quietude of not chasing anything. Then the thoughts are more like fish lazily playing than like arrows hurrying to their destination.

There is no sense at all to this that is revealed, this benedic-tion: obvious when the chasing after anything else ceases for a moment. Then we are quite simply infinity—which was always our nature anyway, but which was hidden from us by the chasing, and the conviction that thoughts reflect things.

To repeat: "*From the very beginning, not a thing is,*" says a venerable Zen teacher, speaking straight from the center of the nonsensical benediction where all of us live, all of the time.

We just *believe* there's somewhere to go, and someone—separate-seeming-I—who has to get there. Neither of these are the truth, where the heart of our true nature lives, beyond sensibility, immaculate and never-not-here.

Home free already

We ourselves are not an illusory part of Reality; rather are we Reality itself illusorily conceived.

— Wei Wu Wei

No way round this: we are home free already. We have just been distracted by searching. The I-thought is the seeming-agent of this searching, but the stillness that is the real source of it is home, free, already—and we are it.

~

Stephen Levine: "Pretending to be real"

As a teenager I was vividly and uncomfortably aware that every other human being appeared more substantial than I—that everyone seemed solid by comparison with my own internal experience of myself. Teenagers, of course, are so beset by the troubles of their hurtling transition toward adulthood that it would take a rare degree of presence and awareness to ask questions about these esoteric matters, or come to that, find a suitable adult to ask. Still, it was not until some 30 years later, with the publication in 1997 of Stephen Levine's book *A Year to Live* that I found somebody addressing this head on and exactly in the terms I experienced it:

"We go through life pretending to be real. We are told from every guarded corner that we are supposed to be a solid citizen, someone of merit. We are relieved that no one seems to notice that we hardly exist, that we are only a thought here and there, some feelings floating through, a few frames of color-faded memory, a tingling in the fingertips, a bewilderment of opposing desires and beliefs."

He had got it; and sharing it in his book, he allowed me to get this universal truth, and not have it be just my own singular peculiarity. This experience is everybody's, whether they know it or not.

When they do not know it—the way I was so uncomfortable about it as a teenager—then imposter syndrome is rife; all of us, I suspect, go through life pretending to be real, but we don't talk to one another about it, in case we should seem peculiar. This is a pity, since the almost universal distress of imposter syndrome is in actuality a doorway to a much larger reality. Further along in the chapter in question in *A Year to Live*, some of the following extracted remarks appear:

"We turn inward and like an absolute beginner…see who is doing all this thinking and what is observing it all…we examine everything…we find that nothing lasts very long…But then something in all this catches our eye…That there is an unchanging spaciousness in which all our changes float…When we look directly at this…when we enter it, when we sit quietly within it, we discover that it is endless…It is the formlessness upon which form depends, the deathless which dies again and again just to prove it never dies."

— Stephen Levine

∼

Effortless

What was never lost can never be found.

— Nisargadatta Maharaj

Although many seekers struggle to "Be here now," everyone without exception acknowledges the obvious fact that we exist NOW, without a doubt.

Nobody can voice or explain this existing-NOW sense, but universally, all acknowledge the intimate and immediate truth of existing NOW.

We already exist here. No effort *whatsoever* is needed to be here. However, we are *seekers*, and seekers seek. Seeking is effortful.

Effort takes us away from the essential peace enjoyed by everything that exists. We can see this very clearly in the rocks, trees, clouds, lizards and dogs. The table next to me sits upon the floor with exactly the same total ease enjoyed by the rug, and my computer bag. All of it is enjoying complete relaxation. Except me.

"Me" is searching. There must be some answer to this whole universe of mystery and my place in it, and with enough time, effort, gathered-wisdom, meditation, grace of teachers, or of God, etc, etc, etc, I will find it. There must be a state of sustained ease that can eventually be reached by my efforts. Enlightenment, surely, can be sought after—and found.

What is hard to notice in all this flurry of activity is that "I" exists only as a bundle of concepts woven together with some very familiar body sensations. Taking time and space (which are purely conceptual) to be actual makes the weaving of sensations and concepts seem completely real, with a life of its own: me. My predominant mode of being is *seeking*.

But prior to "me," in the gaps when no effort is being made, I *am*. Existing entirely and seamlessly encompasses me, in the form of effortlessness. The moment I do absolutely nothing (releasing even the miniscule effort to "do nothing") effortlessness completely embraces me; and there is no "me."

What is there, in this effortlessness? (Or, of course, rather, "here"?)

"Am-ness" is one of the phrases used to describe it. "Globality," "One without a second," and "Non-duality" have all been offered as possible titles. Tinged with more feeling and emotion are words and phrases like "wholeness," "uncaused ease," "benediction" and "happiness."

Why "Stop searching"?

At first, stopping searching is a desperation move. Every other rock except this one has been turned over and found wanting.

Only *now* itself is left to examine, and "stopping searching" is the key.

But once we begin to notice where consciousness lives—notice that consciousness *is* now itself—our desperation gambit becomes a wisdom move: the only game in town.

Want to be consciousness itself? Be now. But all instructions ("stop searching"; "be now") are bizarre because they derive from the seeking mind, and although we are that also, being that is a transient phase on the way to wisdom. No instructions are pertinent in this timeless, causeless, ineffable perfect existing that most of us may remain ignorant of until we die. We *are* that—or, as Nisargadatta Maharaj famously said, *I am that*.

What you're pursuing ain't it

As simple as that: anything we are pursuing is not it. Or, as Gangaji puts it, referencing thoughts, *"If you have not stopped, you are still searching."*

When we stop searching, the entire cosmos presents itself, utterly and totally without effort (and, the effort of words has to happen for these lines to get written).

Practically, this means that any kind of chasing, questing, pursuing or seeking is quite simply *going away* (or seeming to) from what we are. What are we? Stop pursuing and find out.

This can't be searched for

This can't be searched for because it is here, all the time, no matter what. Searching, remarks Wei Wu Wei, *"...is precisely that which, by externalizing itself, turns itself away from this which it is."*

This "it" is us, precisely, effortlessly, and exactly where we are, right now, before the thought of "I" or "now" grips us.

~

RELAXING

Thinning veils

Things are not as they are seen, nor are they otherwise.

— Lankavatara Sutra

Symmetry…refers to any dynamic transformation within a system that leaves the overall system unchanged…It is woven into the fabric of Reality.

— Steve Hagen

This moment is eternality. This moment is forever and always eternality. The ease of eternal being—ask the rocks, trees, sky, flowers, dogs and bacteria—expresses the foundational peace that is the absence of the concept of time.

This peace is intrinsic. We can consult the material of our shoes; it is fundamentally relaxed, is it not? The fabric of our clothes is surely unlimited at-ease-ness. Objects at rest near us; they are surely in let-go, entirely and completely absent effort? Extending outward, the building we are in, the ground upon which it sits, and every pebble and scrap of earth beneath and around it are intrinsically at rest, are they palpably not?

"Peace" is not static, but the bedrock experience of being when the time-concept is laid aside. And since Being endures, in the form of this moment of *now*, but concepts come and go, the experiment of laying aside the time-concept is always available to us.

In this experiment, "this moment of now"—conventionally, an inexplicable speck squeezed between past and future—becomes quietly obvious as "the eternal now." We have never (in all eternity!) been anything other than this, and never could be. What we are, what we cannot not be, vividly and palpably, has no definition whatsoever, yet the intimacy of it is inescapable.

These realities are experiential, and indubitable. The power accompanying the words of those who have awakened and lived this reality, which is ordinarily hidden from conditioned viewing, comes from this bedrock of being, which we are and cannot not be. The play of everything that accompanies it is not as it is usually seen—nor is it otherwise.

I had no earlier clue whatsoever that the preoccupation with time, dogging my entire adult life, was this upwelling of Being. This morning, sitting in expanding wonder, even quiet astonishment at the revelation of eternity, right here, right now; *that* gnawing at the time-mystery is obviously *this* timelessness, the very same, with the intimacy of a fungi breaking the soil's surface when the moisture of the fall makes things just right.

I always believed it was *my* preoccupation, but when the time-concept is laid aside (once it is clearly seen "time" is nothing but *a concept*) there is no exclusionary *my*, there is only spaciousness without explanation: intrinsic, at ease, sourceless, nameless and free. "My" is not at all precluded, but included: just no longer the source.

Just as the *Lankavatara Sutra* says, it is neither as it seems, nor different; for the profoundly-conditioned sense of separate-seeming-self is an appearance of this eternality, a wave upon the ocean's surface making no difference whatsoever to the ocean itself: a play, a game of appearance-and-disappearance. "Symmetry," one of the foundational characteristics of the laws of physics, is exemplified in just the same way; in these illuminated moments, the entire system of existing is utterly transformed—and completely unchanged.

I am is relaxed

Everything is relaxed. The cup of tea beside me, and the rug beneath my feet are completely at ease. The sky overhead, the bark of a distant dog, and the clatter of recycling bins in the next valley are all totally relaxed.

The presence of our own relaxation can be a little difficult to notice. Something essential in us intrinsically partakes of this ease, indeed, knows this ease to be itself; yet we seem to be something else altogether besides this easy-is-right nature.

This something-else-altogether is generally called "I." There is no doubt in my mind that I am solely something separate from the general ease. From my earliest life I was taught that I am someone distinct and particular, someone who must make their way to peace and happiness through my own efforts.

I was taught this by people who were not themselves happy, and certainly not peaceful, but who were sure this effortful formula would succeed—eventually, surely, for someone?—because they themselves were failures at it. But everybody believes the formula, and since everybody is taught the method of striving for happiness and peace by someone they deeply love, who deeply loves them, surely it must be true?

The method does indeed bring results; I look around the clean and quiet room in which I am writing this and reflect gratefully on the fantastic amount of ingenuity, creativity, labor and dedication necessary for it to come into being, and house me.

But enduring happiness is not to be found in results; results come from the method. We imagine or conceive possibility, action occurs, results are the outcome. The technology of the method is astounding in its elegance and divine in its design, but the results that come are simply results, not happiness or peace. Happiness is already in residence before any results-producing project begins in time.

Of course, there is a long (or short...) period of satisfaction when results are achieved. We could even call it "happiness," but if we look more deeply we can recognize that in the moment of our desire being fulfilled, we are simply suddenly freed, even if momentarily, back into the state of ease from which it all began. In desire's natural cessation, our real being is obvious, even if we can only be in wonderment about it, for it cannot be sought, only found.

If we are spiritual seekers, who are, in a way, the most persistent and dedicated chasers-after-results, we may look everywhere, even for a lifetime, for the result we would like to produce: liberation, enlightenment, and moksha: grace. We use the method of searching we have been taught—how could we not?—and sometimes only in exhaustion realize that what we essentially are is here all along, in exactly the same relaxation enjoyed by everything else in existence.

There is just nobody

Any identification with any object is an absolute hindrance, because 'I' am totally devoid of objectivity, or of any trace-element thereof.

— Wei Wu Wei

Reality is the way the heart knows it is, whole and complete, moment by moment; there is nothing else. It is only *now*, always and forever.

Appearing as an integral part of this reality are *thoughts*. Thoughts make no sense at all without the theatre in which they play, namely time. Time and thoughts imply a reality that is divided; that is their game. This seeming-dividedness appears amidst undivided entirety, or reality.

The realness of reality is nothing but entirely momentary changefulness, altering unceasingly, and conscious.

> *Every concept is a thing, but, as such, is not. Neither 'God' nor*
> *'I' is as an object.*

> — Wei Wu Wei

Consequently, enduring things appear to exist, but are nothing but this unceasing seething change. Enduring (and endearing...) bodies appear, exist like energy clouds for a while, and then vanish. The substance of seeming-"I" is one of these bodies, and the soundtrack that accompanies it—the voice much like Siri, or ChatGPT—insists that "I" am someone separate, but that cannot be so. Reality is whole and complete, total perfection, moment by moment, and can be no other way; there is nobody separate in it, and this is not only self-evident to the heart, but the heart is completely at ease with it.

> *I said that the universe is I. You can say it, every beetle, every*
> *sentient being can say it—what else is there that it could be,*
> *where else is there for it to be? Movement, space and time are*
> *only concepts. There can only be 'I'—and I am not, no matter*
> *who says it.*

> — Wei Wu Wei

∽

There is only now

Scott Morrison was a lovely man. Having traveled by way of the most desperate and pitiful form of alcoholism, and been a lifelong seeker and a Zen Buddhist student along his path, Scott was one of the kindest people I ever met. He was absolutely and genuinely uninterested in having students and enthusiastic about having friends, who he called "Dharma-buddies." Such people might have come to him initially as aspiring students, as I did, but Scott immediately and unpretentiously disarmed any such formality simply by how he was. His manner simply said I am you, and you are me.

Scott's first book was called *There Is Only Now.* In the introduction he writes *"There is only now. Everything we call the "past" is absolutely nothing but present memory. Everything we call the "future" is absolutely nothing but fantasy, that is, present memory rearranged. If we continue to pretend there is some other time or place to be besides right here, right now, we are cruelly and pathologically deluding ourselves. Now is the only "time" we can be awake and free, honest, wise and compassionate."*

I visited Scott twice in Puerto Rico where he lived. We took hikes into the rainforest and he gently made the suggestion that we might walk in nature without being busy thinking and talking, which resulted in some of the most gorgeous walks I've ever taken, amidst the freshness of relatively untouched wilderness and the calling of the birds and tree frogs.

We rowed boats out to the edge of the mangrove swamps where the night was made magic by bioluminescent plankton—then got lost, me with my girlfriend perched on the prow of the boat, Scott hunting the darkness for the harbor which we eventually only found when we were completely exhausted. As we rowed, seemingly forever, Scott's delighted chuckle kept coming through the warm moist night.

And in complete good humor he proposed, and we spent hours elaborating a new 12-step organization called *Liars Anonymous*, for recovering addicts of the disease of having a self. All of us are liars about this, and we go on lying to one another about it, a game of *The Emperor Has No Clothes* in which nobody will step into the role of the child who says "But the Emperor is naked!"

Scott had the kind of childlike innocence able, with laughing kindness, to point to the fact that the moment we really notice now—because there is only now—we may also notice that our supposed separate self is just a concatenation of thoughts, images, hormonal impulses, bodily sensations and energies woven together and taken for granted as an entity of some kind.

Scott wrote *"Whether it is called Consciousness or Emptiness or Pure Being or whatever, when there is no longer an infatuation with a separate "you," with its needs, wants, desires, hopes, fears, histories, futures and so on there is nothing but the intense joy and elegant silence of What Is."*

~

Easy is right

What is the easiest thing in the world? To be precisely and exactly where we are. But this ease is unlike anything in the world, because it has no opposite. This ease is unconditional, and without cause. This ease is, if you like, the hymnal offering of the never-ending and unceasing center of our lives, the one we label by the word "now."

Abundant confusion surrounds all of the above, especially for seekers (and we are all seekers, of one sort or another). The possibility that our longing for peace, ease, and causeless happiness is intrinsically fulfilled when we do nothing—absolutely nothing—blows the fuses of our ordinary time-bound thought-stream seeking-mind. It makes no sense.

We are sure that happiness and satisfaction are to be found in time; eventually, by effort, which essentially means "It's not here already, buddy." If you, too, have been handcuffed by this belief since you were about 18 months old, when the time-concept began to seem real to you, join the club; my 26,000th day on the planet happened recently, and only in the last few weeks has it begun to be obvious to me that peace and ease are simply and only to be found *now*. No effort to "be now" is of any use whatsoever, because it is where we all live all of our lives, with no exceptions.

~

REFLECTIONS

This which it is

Every sentient being — being nothing but mind itself, can find mind itself, mind his, her or our self, just by ceasing to search, for the act of searching is precisely that which, by externalizing itself turns itself away from this which it is.

— Wei Wu Wei

This-which-it-is is ceaseless, and wondrous. To be it is a miracle, for then timeless perfection reigns.

You only exist as existence itself.

— Wei Wu Wei

This-which-it-is cannot be sought, had or held, for any such action constellates a separate entity or person—thus seemingly-sundering the relaxed wholeness of this-which-it is.

One must become identified with non-being and mirror the whole, for the truth is one and final.

— Hsieh Ling-yün

The only possibility is to be it—amidst the total and complete paradox that *we are it already*—but unnoticed beneath the incessant chatter and stress accompanying identification as separate-someone, seeking.

Then, another remark of Wei Wu Wei can make more sense:

I am notoriously invulnerable simply because nothing in conceptual phenomenality can reach what-I-am, since I am already all that it is.

Hence, this section could be called "All that it is," just as well as "This which it is."

The dilemma of the heart

The heart is timeless *now*. No matter the immaterial source of the mentation-marvels of time and dividedness, called "the head" elsewhere in these pages, these tend to predominate: our identity as exclusively the divided one seems like our only identity. Our heart is forgotten.

Yet these are clearly both here; for the head, either-or is the dilemma, often posed to myself as "*Why is it so difficult to stay in my heart?*" This question, and the strands of feeling accompanying it include a subtle flavor that there is something more right about the heart's perspective; that it is always true: it is always now—which it is.

But the fact that it is more right simply signals that we have head and heart upside down; nonetheless, they exist together. One cannot be here without the other. However, most of the time the head is predominant, dividedness reigns, separateness seems like the entire universe—and we are uprooted and miserable.

Tony Parsons remarks "*There is a subtle feeling of risk and serenity in presence.*" He is unmistakably talking about pure perception through the heart, living directly from the heart center. *The risk* is the sense of quite simply being on the wave of the moment, the next instant unanticipated. *The serenity* is that life is always right, no matter what, and our heart quietly knows this.

Yet there is another dimension to life, and the very fact of being able to reflect on it here, in these words, confirms this profound plane of existence. This is the sphere of time and separateness, which we ordinarily take to be solely the nature of life itself. But it is not.

Life itself is *now*. An integral part of this unceasing spontaneous unfolding of momentariness is the dance of free-spirited creation that is the world of concepts, the dance of time in the timelessness of the heart. The crucial—and predominating—aspect of this part of life itself is the way it gives rise to things: seemingly-permanent things, existing things, independently-existing things, like "you" and "I."

In actuality, this independent nature is impossible, since there is only now, and nothing else. Nonetheless, nowness gives rise to the appearance of time—and here we are, courtesy of the marvels of time and dividedness, writing this book, or reading it. But nowness, or timelessness comes first, or is the backdrop upon which time appears, and this order, timelessness and time, heart and head, is the right way up.

The dilemma of the heart is not actually a dilemma of the heart, but of the head. The heart is infinity, unfolding by itself, moment by moment; we call it "now." The momentous unfolding of it, exactly as it is, instant by instant, is unmistakably vast; it could be no other way than how it is.

There is a stillness here, in the heart, completely intimate with an unlimited dynamism. Time would be the hegemony of sequence, a subtle tension, a framework of conceptuality in which the pure unknown of the next moment is anticipated, orchestrated, pushed and pulled. Then, "the known" seems to replace the view of totality, bringing with it habituation and predictable dreariness.

"The dilemma" in the most stark terms is quite simply that I believe *I am* the source and cause, the real nature of all that pushing, pulling and orchestration. All that cause-and-effect seems to be what I am: a being in time, doing stuff. Seeming to be solely this is rather miserable.

Yet, rather marvelously, purely in the realm of the heart, I am not and everything is; everything happens how it happens.

This absence ("I am not") is not experienced as any kind of loss; on the contrary, marvelousness becomes apparent, for the entirety is happening on its own, a divine unfolding without any kind of discernible orchestrator.

Purely in the space of heart, this absence highlights the nature of the separate-seeming-one that I primarily (and mostly, solely) identify as: this separate-seeming-one is conceptual; in time; divided from wholeness.

How hard can it be to be still?

Be still, and know that I am God.

— Psalm 46:10

Be what you cannot not be.

— Karl Renz

How hard can it be to be still? That would depend entirely on who, or what, we are—or believe we are.

If we are someone moving around, busily thinking most of the time; born to die and fretting anxiously about it, then being still can be very difficult.

But what if we *are* stillness itself? What if we have never been anything else other than stillness? What if stillness is our real nature "*...as the Masters of all the doctrines never tire of telling* *us…,"* and we, stillness, merely forgot; distracted into another identity altogether by the fabulous torrent of life?

Nothing other than our *being stillness already* makes sense of the ease of noticing; the complete lack of effort that is seeing; the effortlessness of hearing; the inherently relaxed receptivity that makes feeling possible—and the openly welcoming spaciousness of thoughts being noticed.

Inescapable us

We are effortless. We are discovered when we die, always; effort falls away in dying, and what remains is us.

I am discovered in letting go; not as an effortful activity but simply in a kind of falling away, the easiest possible exploration of what is here when effort ceases entirely.

What is discovered is effortless; I am, you are. What falls away? For one thing, time disappears, in the ordinary way we live it. Thinking falls away, as the subtle effort of it is relinquished.

What remains? Impossible to say; after all, thinking has fallen away. There are no words here; painters and poets punt the edges of this ocean, but it is the immensity of ineffability.

What's here when there's no effort whatsoever? The intuition —the obviousness—that we never, ever leave this we call "*now*" really does invite us toward itself; what *IS* this remarkable, unsung, never-ending, completely reliable, inexplicable causeless presence?

As Wei Wu Wei so elegantly puts it, *"The direction of measurement of this essentially timeless dimension is—within."* The whole idea of "the inner," the within can remain really puzzling for the

---

* Wei Wu Wei

longest time. It is the haziest of concepts. Yet it is the agony and suffering of exactly this interior world that brings people to psychotherapy, and scour spiritual teaching for an end to their misery.

At least, so it has been for me, my entire life. This morning's contemplation began, I now remember, somewhat earlier in the wee small hours waking from sleep and realizing how miserable I was feeling. A million threatening stories of imminent catastrophe floated in the dark, every one of them subvocally muttering the unavoidable termination of death. And at some point, the stream of problems and impossible solutions completely changed their orientation and the thoughts began to focus on my beloved, and how to get her to solve *her* problems—and I laughed, at the transparent ridiculousness of it: misery over me, then misery over her.

For quite some time now, "meditation" for me has meant allowing or prompting a certain kind of sitting quietly and going nowhere. This can sound like the familiar "be here now," and indeed, when first undertaken, that was the spirit of it. But something has transpired, evolved, transformed, the way a tiny black dot no bigger than a period in this sentence can unfold into the unique beauty of a poppy flower. The "going nowhere" has metamorphosed into the purest being here. All along, the call of this meditation instruction: to go nowhere—was—is—in actuality the calling of what cannot go anywhere.

But because my predominant identification was as someone separate, someone searching and seeking, the intuition of direction to explore could only take the form it did: someone, meditating, dimly following an intuition that what I seek is *now*, and that effortlessness is somehow intrinsic to it. "Go nowhere," became the instruction of my practice.

So, in my bed before dawn, amazed (and truthfully, a bit horrified) by the amount of misery, moved to laughter by the abruptly-shifting focus of it, I lay on my back and wondered *What's here when everything is let go?* In particular, what happens when no energy whatsoever is given to the thoughts?

This cessation doesn't happen all at once; when we stop pedaling the bicycle—when we cease giving our energy to our-selves-in-time, a.k.a. "the ego"—it takes a while for the momentum to become still.

Or to put it another way, we gradually discover we don't die when there are no thoughts; and, fish-like free-divers, expanding our lung capacity as we go deeper and deeper, we little by little find the water is our true home. In different words, the ocean was always ourselves—*is* always ourselves—but we were sure we were a particular wave in the ocean, and only that.

That's the rub: "only that." That's who I was this morning, amid the flood of misery; I was solely a separated wave, the ocean forgotten.

How to return to the ocean? Only the separated-seeming wave could hallucinate its divisibility from the ocean! The thoughts, astonishing marvels of creation, and so, so well practiced they seem entirely real, compel separateness. In actuality there is no separateness, no matter the appearance, the seeming. The thoughts are the highest play of this that we are, truly remarkable for how things can be brought into being via the thought process. Like "I."

This separated version of ourselves, "I," lives in time. Because it is predominantly body-based, the terror of death is built into it. Built into *us*; until we gradually discover eternity, living unfazed, unflappable, immovable; precisely and exactly where we have always been and cannot not be.

The words lead and mislead us; "eternity" connotes time, but there is *no time* where we inescapably (and eternally!) live. *"There shall be time no longer,"* avers "a mighty angel" about heaven—and this can be *felt* when effort winds down, when inherent-existing is glimpsed, causeless and free in total relaxation-without-an-opposite.

This can also be noticed in our immediate experience of seeing right *now*; we hardly ever notice (and even less, trust what we notice) the basic screen upon which all experience occurs. Yet it is available for our intuitive inspection at all times; "it" (in quotes, for it can never be an "it") is empty, free, dimensionless, nameless, genderless—and entirely without time. Time is written upon the inherent nowness of it. When time stops—in death, orgasm, great beauty, or total grief—this is apparent, just as it is noticed when all effort comes to an end.

> *You can only be the real, which you are, anyhow. The problem is not mental. Abandon false ideas, that is all. There is no need of true ideas. There aren't any.*

> — Nisargadatta Maharaj

~

THE HEART OF REALITY

Immersion

We stand, sit, lie down, walk, work, breathe and love totally immersed in a creation out of nowhere that has never existed before.

We don't realize this because we are so convinced that we are solely separate creatures, wandering a landscape that we may love, but which is essentially alien to us.

As we wake up we may periodically realize we have never been separate from any of it. Only our conviction that we were solely the center of it all—for "ourselves," for the "I," "me," "my" of our conditioned beliefs—hides the miracle from us.

This gradual awakening is to something that has never not existed. It was and is here all along, all the time. We knew it implicitly as children—and the time-jaded adults around us marveled at the innocence of our playing amidst it. But we knew it was good.

Our heart is still the abode of this goodness, and never is it not so. Whenever attention drops into our heart, centerless *now* is our reality, just as it is.

We can live again as this miracle; indeed, the marvel of awakening is that the doors of perception open and we gradually find ourselves once again infinite, and find the sacred, the miraculous, never left; we were just distracted.

Our distraction—the universal conviction that I am solely a separate center of consciousness enclosed within my body, striving for fulfillment that never really arrives—can gradually fade. Gazing long and persistently enough at reality, undistracted by conditioned convictions, aided by realizing again and again that the heart is our natural home, beauty and magic gradually break through the tight shield of belief. We find ourselves immersed in a miraculous creation without a center, one that unceasingly changes in exact synchrony with immemorial and total changelessness.

A million times

A million times a day this real-I is here. Every time a thought ends, and before the next begins, real-I is all that is. Real-I is life, just as it is, without conditions. Real-I is at ease and content. All of us know real-I because we are it.

Synthetic-I is the one we have come to believe is solely me. Synthetic-I is the *thought version* of real-I, and it always, *always* comes after real-I. It also, being made out of thought exclusively, is in time.

There is no choice whatsoever about developing a synthetic-I. To join the tribe, and capably function with time as a basis, synthetic-I is a must. Synthetic-I is the highest expression of our cognitive capacities to remember, and then to project new concatenations of memory into a non-existent time called "the future"—this writing is courtesy of this very means: an idea whose existence has unfolded in time.

Synthetic-I implies the existence of something out of this moment—*now* being where real-I lives, all of the time. In actuality, nothing exists outside this moment—but synthetic-I claims to live there. We take ourselves to be exclusively synthetic-I, not recognizing that real-I is never not here.

There is nothing for anybody to get in real-I; "getting" belongs entirely to synthetic-I. Real-I wants for nothing. Real-I has nothing to do with thought, where synthetic-I is made out of thought. And, synthetic-I is a miracle; a Mozart, a Spinoza, a Nelson Mandela—but it cannot help also being a Hitler, a Stalin, a Mao Tse-tung.

Douglas Harding and the open space of seeing

Douglas Harding was a most unlikely spiritual teacher (in the sense that he was a professional architect, married and with children, living fully in the ordinary world), one who spent some 50 years of his life encouraging people to turn the direction of their attention back to the place from which they look —and pay attention, in direct experience to what they find there. We can do Douglas's basic experiment ourselves: point our forefinger at our face.

We can notice what our finger is pointing at when we ignore all the answers that come from the past. What is that finger-pointing at when we don't refer to what we're thinking, or believing, or feeling? When we dismiss everything we've been told, or learned, or believe conceptually about what that finger is pointing at: what is our direct experience, now, of the place we are looking out of? We can attend directly, in the present moment, to the experience occurring where the finger is pointing to.

Aren't we looking out of nowhere, in our own present moment direct experience? Without reference to the past or to any conceptual or mental images or definitions of ourselves, can we find any trace there of a person, where our pointing finger directs our attention? *Without thinking about it* (and we are still there, aren't we, looking uninterruptedly, even when we're not thinking?) can we say if we are man or woman, or specify our age, or even our name? Is there any time at all in that place from which we've always looked? Could there even *be* time in that place?

Isn't the realm from which seeing happens—the realm in us that notices—nameless, genderless, timeless and changeless, with no characteristics whatsoever, except intrinsically possessed of this most mysterious of all qualities, awareness?

~

The Headless Way Mini-Kit

"Send for the free Headless Way Mini-Kit," said the small ad buried in the back of a London magazine. It was 1974 and the spirit of inner adventure was very much alive in me and the culture around me, so I sent away for the intriguing freebie. And received back a large white paper bag which, unfolded and with the bottom slit open, formed a paper tube, together with a small booklet of questions mimeographed in the primitive copying technology we had then. Douglas Harding had sent me the kit.

The inquiry suggested in the booklet said to place your face in one end of the tube, with someone else's face in the far end, thus looking at each other.

I was too embarrassed to involve anybody else in this strangeness, so I simply imagined another face in the far end of the tube, and asked the suggested questions about my end of the tube.

Question 1: "In your direct present moment experience, without reference to what you think or believe, or have been told, without reference even to what you feel, is your end of the paper tube open or closed?"

It was open. It still is. This quiet mystery lives on, untouched by time—or by anything, come to that—in the midst of a busy life filled with thoughts and beliefs and feelings to do with who I am. Nonetheless, my end of the tube was—and is—indubitably open, in direct present moment experience.

Question 2: "In your direct present moment experience, without reference to what you think or believe, or have been told, without reference even to what you feel, is there anything at your end of the tube with the colors of the face at the far end of the tube, pink, brown, gray, blue, white; anything at your end of the tube with those contours you can see at the other end of the tube, nose, eye, lip, cheek, chin; is there anything, in your direct present moment experience at your end of the tube that has name and gender and age, the way the face at the far end of the tube has?"

Beyond the staggering and enduring mystery that was discovered that day and is here unchanged as I write this, I could find nothing at my end of the tube other than—what shall I call it?—awareness?

It took me about 15 years to integrate this amazing discovery, to come to terms with the fact that in the center of my being, closer to myself than my breath (which it seems to be the noticer-of), closer to myself than my thoughts (ditto), closer than anything I could identify as myself, there is simply pure aware spaciousness.

Our own direct experience awaits us.

~

God is right behind our eyes

Find within you something which is uncaused.

— Osho

In all the world—indeed, in all the universe—nothing can be found that is uncaused: except the no-thing we really are, and cannot not be. We could call it "the seeing." We can notice it.

God is the subject. He is the seer. Don't concern yourself with objects that can be seen. Find out who the seer is.

— Ramana Maharshi, to Papaji at their first meeting.

This seeing—reading these words, as well as being the source of their writing—is nameless and faceless, as well as being the very quintessence of now, effortlessly present. Other than this, no option exists *in reality*. When attention rests gently downward into heart-presence, everything is known to be nothing but this nowness, entirely uncaused.

The past and future are both far from God and alien to his way.

— Meister Eckhart

The seeing, the noticing, is timeless, or eternal. Everything else can go—even breath, heartbeat, thoughts—this remains.

Gazing with sheer awareness into sheer awareness, habitual, abstract structures melt into the fruitful springtime of Buddhahood.

— Tilopa

We have never not been it, only distracted from it by the conditioning of people we love, who love us, who cajoled us into solely believing we are inside a body, born to die. This is an idea—an abstract idea—that gradually becomes so deeply installed it seems like reality. This believing *has* to happen in order to join the human tribe. Some time later, the seeing notices itself; either while living, or, with utter certainty, in dying.

> *The observer is the observed.*
>
> —J. Krishnamurti

This never-not-here calls to itself. The call sign is great perfection, great peace and great wisdom, all of which are intrinsic to us. We can turn our attention backwards and notice it right *now*: the seeing, exactly present. We can drop attention gently into our own heart and realize unseparated eternity, right here, right now, without the slightest objection to the presence of time.

> *I—luminous, open, empty Awareness—am the truth of your Being and am eternally with you, in you, as you, shining quietly at the heart of all experience. Just turn towards Me, and acknowledge Me, and I will take you into Myself.*
>
> — Rupert Spira

A venerable Upanishad tells us how to "*spring out of the mouth of Death.*" This is the "how": turn noticing backward to the uncaused Seeing, which can never die. We are it, and we are the inescapable intimacy of it.

Keep your eyes open, and try to keep the mind unshakenly fixed on That Which Sees. It is inside yourself. Do not expect to find that "That" is something definite on which the mind can be fixed easily; it will not be so.

> — Frank Humphreys, Ramana Maharshi's
> first Western student.

We don't recognize "ourselves"

We look, and assume that "I," the one looking, is like all the other apparent-lookers: defined by name and form, time-bound, and therefore aging towards inevitable death; limited in time and space.

Almost inevitably, we hardly notice the real nature of the seeing; our own seeing—that it is nameless, ageless, timeless, causeless—and is absolutely no kind of either an "I" or an "it."

This directly-experienced obviousness is completely unfamiliar to our conditioned understanding of ourselves. All we seem to know is what we have been told. We believe we are one "it" amongst many.

We call this that we have been told, and that we helplessly believe "identity"—and identification is perhaps the quintessential human process. We assiduously learn what we are (supposed to be) in infancy; the "terrible twos" manifest this, and from there on out, we live lives of rampant confusion until such time as we resolve to find what is true, no matter what.

Part of the difficulty is that in those very same "terrible twos," we begin to partake of the miracle of conceptualization. The blurry, initially randomly-moving flesh-toned object waving in our vision gradually becomes "my hand." Watch a two-year-old become a five-year-old, and emerge into a seven, 12, and 17-year-old, and we will see the gradual inhabitation of the misery of increasing identification with someone separate, someone conceptual, living in time, who seems solely to look out at a not-self world that is alien and other. (There is a great deal more to the process of development cited in this age-progression, but something happens to turn amazed two-year-olds into jaded and cynical adults, and it is the essence of this turning-away from goodness that is exclusively considered here.)

> *Just imagine living in a world without mirrors. You'd dream about your face and imagine it as an outer reflection of what is inside you. And then, when you reached forty, someone put a mirror before you for the first time in your life. Imagine your fright! You'd see the face of a stranger. And you'd know quite clearly what you are unable to grasp: your face is not you.*
>
> — Milan Kundera

This process is splendidly-well adapted to the aspirational progression of a separate-somebody ambitiously trying to make their way to fulfillment and completion.

They—believed-in separate-somebody's—attempt to make this progress because they generally believe themselves to be deficient—wrong, broken, empty, and lacking—and it can take a very long time and a good deal of attentive effort to notice that this belief is a nightmarish phantasmagoria, possessing almost everybody until they begin to awaken.

The effort to awaken comes entirely from the misery of the mirage—or, as it is more precisely termed here, "identification."

What, in particular, has become identified in this way?

It can only be the quintessential namelessness.

Only this realization brings relaxation. Only this realization relaxes the core belly-sense of ourselves back into the embrace of reality. Only this dawning, expanding, and then burgeoning discovery gradually fills us with a sense of infinitely-expanding completion. By and by, we realize our heart intrinsically has this entirely right; that home is what we already are, and where we are.

> *You should get to know the spirit of your own heart, whose essence is far from being split into death and the everlasting, whose nature is without purity or defilement, profoundly complete, in which ordinary and sacred are equal.*
>
> — Shitou

This completion begins from knowing we are home already; quintessentially and inescapably. This is completely unlike the effortful-progression-towards-happiness that terrorized earlier epochs in our lives, until we gave it up and resolved to discover "Who am I?" even if dying was the price.

> *We don't experience consciousness, because that's what we are.*
>
> — Ajahn Sumedho

Let's reorient: none of this is to imply that anything about any aspect of life is other than perfect. All of it tends to be lived in its own terms, which is exclusively as if the separate-seeming self is the sole reality.

The fact that it's absolutely not the sole reality can upset the applecart, so to speak; Jesus consorts with prostitutes and lepers, and angrily overturns the tables of the money-changers. Apparently, he is in touch with a reality that has no interest in the customary dividedness infesting our lives with injustice and depredation. Something else altogether moves him; he calls it "love."

The immense energy of it comes down through the ages to us, infuses the vision of his (and our) heart and being; a vision so powerful, so real, true, and right, that when his life is taken from him on the cross he has a brief crisis of faith in which he cries out the anguish of his possibly being forsaken by what he really is. Then he is welcomed, without reservation or hindrance into the infinity of love; into eternity, into deathlessness: into God.

Jesus' quest to know who he is—what he is—is willing to die in the process. Jesus knows unquestionably that he has outgrown the definition of himself given in his earliest identification in infancy; now, in mature life, with biological death on the near-horizon he wants to know what and who he is. His quest, his question is on behalf of us all.

The greatest mystery

There is no greater mystery than this: being reality ourselves, we seek to gain reality.

— Ramana Maharshi

This is the greatest mystery of our human life: we are exactly and precisely where (and when) we are all the time. Somehow, we know this. We know it without a shadow of a doubt. Yet we spend our entire lives in a more or less constant agitation to get somewhere else. We seem not to know we are home already.

Perhaps the discovery of Buddha, and a myriad other explorers of this great matter was that there seem to be two "we's." Our familiar "we" is taken utterly for granted, since it is the "we" of everybody: separate from each other and from our environment, making its effortful solo way through life in time, from birth to death, and filled, almost always, with a vague sense of unsatisfactoriness which drives it on to find the remedy for the dissatisfaction.

The other "we"—the one we know for sure? There's only one way to find out for certain about this "we": be where we are, and see what it's like. (An earlier section, *A million times*, termed these two "we's" respectively, as synthetic-I and real-I.)

But there are some difficulties with this already-accomplished project. ("Already-accomplished" because we are irrevocably, helplessly, effortlessly, always and unchangingly here, *now*, home.) No thought can go here, *where we are*, simply because thought is a vehicle for getting somewhere. (These thoughts here, for example, are expressive of the urge to give voice to the matter of the greatest mystery.) We will have to not go anywhere—where we are already. We will have to be still, which we already are. We can sink attention into our heart, where we are already home.

> *From questing inward in the heart comes knowledge which destroys all false illusions.*
>
> — Ramana Maharshi

One of these "we's" is already still, and going nowhere; this is known intuitively and immediately in heart-presence. This quality of going nowhere is so immense, so utterly and totally immovable—never, ever not here—that we tend to ignore the presence of it, despite the fact it accompanies us with total faithfulness from birth to death. We even tend to ignore its eternality, supposing ourselves to be only what everybody else says we are: born to die. "Going nowhere," through some divine trick of language, is also rendered as "Going NowHere."

Going NowHere

When we make the effort to be still (how much effort can it be, to be where we already are?!) we discover something we may not have noticed before: we firmly believe, as if it is reality, that our mutable and ever-altering thought stream is *us*. We do, indeed, seem to be the one always going somewhere!

Indeed, "seem to be the one" is much too tentative—we are convinced we *are* solely that moving one; otherwise, how could we be so unhappy? Dissatisfaction is our *raison d'etre*; missing seems to be our true nature: seeking what we have lost, inevitable and unending!

Yet the still one, the one who lives where we always live, unchangingly unperturbed, is clearly possessed of a kind of ease that accepts misery with as much grace as ecstasy is welcomed. At the joyous birth of a new baby, there is welcoming; at the last struggling breath, and the agony of a body suffocating, there is welcoming. Nothing is rejected. In this welcoming, no trace of effort whatsoever is found.

So when, perhaps, we sit to meditate, resolved to be the still one, our very effort reveals who we think and believe we are: *we are not already the still one*. We are solely the moving one, who must make effort to be otherwise. We could not possibly be the still one, could not possibly be already the perfect welcoming, the imperturbable and inconceivable immensity our heart says we are.

Inclusive immensity

In the above, we have picked out one characteristic of the "still we": that it is unmoving. But we have mentioned in passing that no thought can encompass it (although all and every thought is encompassed within it, and welcomed.)

What cannot be encompassed by thought, with its inherent imposition of limitation, must, by definition, be unlimited. The inconceivable still "we" is absolutely unmoving, and has no limitations whatsoever. Yet the great mystery is that despite it being inconceivable, it is what we are, and cannot not be: it is limitless; so by definition (and intuition) it intimately *includes* the "chasing we," *but is not solely that.*

Another way to put this is to say that when the "chasing-we" is less prominent in attention, when we glimpse over the shoulder of "chasing-we," or even when "chasing-we" falls entirely silent for a moment, still-we is absolutely unaltered; it is what we are and cannot not be. Still-we *knows absolutely no other time than now.* This "absolutely no other time than now" is the only "time" of the heart.

Still-we has no trace of time in it, or, is timeless. Time belongs entirely to the world of the chasing-me, where it constitutes the marvelous theater where thoughts can dream. Time is foundational to the world of the chasing-me; an extraordinary appearance, *only possible* by virtue of the eternality of the still-we.

In just the same way, space is another appearance within the world of chasing-me, and only possible because still-we is limitless, or infinite. Time and space are this boundless and effortless intimacy of the immeasurable and the finite; we could also call this intimacy "home," and here we are, at all times, already.

Intuition is the way still-we knows itself. Intuition is immediate, and timeless, requiring no process of logic to arrive at the truth; it is intuition that provides the absolute certainty that "We are exactly and precisely where (and when) we are all the time." This latter truth is obvious, even prosaic (and certainly almost completely ignored by chasing-we)—but is provided by the intuition inherent to still-we, and most certainly, by our heart-knowing.

We firmly believe ourselves to be solely the sound and the fury of chasing-we, as if it is reality itself. All that coming and going, all that writhing and changing, birthing and dying, that must be *us*.

Yet all that drama and unhappy story (there are happy bits, but they exist in precise balance with the unhappy ones) occurs within the unconditionally loving welcome of still-we.

Still-we never changes, and is limitless; still-we utterly and effortlessly includes within itself the entire play of chasing-we. Still-we loves, even, the play of chasing-we. Still-we watches the play of chasing-we and gradually realizes itself; notices the contrast between its own inherent deep fulfillment and the equally inherent dissatisfaction of chasing-we. Still-we over time becomes aware of timelessness, because the theater of time is so dynamically different than that; discovers intrinsic infinity by studying limitation—and comes home to itself, as intimate-everything, never having left.

Searching for what cannot be lost

Our efforts to understand and enact realization are driven by realization.

— Shinshu Roberts

Zero effort—absolute effortlessness—and the complete absence of searching reveals still-we. Nothing whatsoever is thereby revealed; and the term "nothing" is provided us by intuition, as is the obvious "everything," its beloved unseparated twin, equally illuminated in effortless no-searching: nothing-everything is revealed, the immediate heart-realization.

We have arrived back, as it were, where we already are and cannot not be; what we call "now" in chasing-we terms, turns out to be the only reality of still-we—a ceaseless chiaroscuro of energy in a totally free symphony that is being, or nothing-everything. *There is no separate still-we*, only this. The I-am-being of "Glenn," like a river meeting the ocean, is gone, gone, gone into the inexplicable immensity which is all there is. And, the I-am-being of "Glenn" is here, here, here, and remains.

"Zero effort" connotes some kind of contrasting exercise, stretch, reaching or project to chasing-me. This is natural, since chasing-me only knows how to chase. What cannot be sought, *because it cannot be lost*, is quite literally inconceivable—but is all that is existent, in reality. What cannot be sought, *because it cannot be lost*, is already utterly and totally relaxed.

This relaxation is not the opposite of tension (as in, tension-relaxation) but an entirely different realm of being, which we might approximate by talking about "godliness." It is what we *are*, gradually more and more obvious as what-we-are-not is seen through. It is still-we, gradually noticed by contrast with chasing-we. "It," (despite being, in truth, no kind of "it," for it is entirely beyond all definition or limitation) is infinite-we, sublime-we, unperturbed-we and eternal-we; omnipotent, omniscient, and omnipresent. This is "heart-we."

All references to the opening of the "inner eye," or the "third eye" point toward this seeing, which is of the invisible, unseen to the clouded vision of chasing-we, which is intent on the goal and misses the miracle that is inherent in immediacy, in each and every moment.

It is not a thing, but the source of all seeming-things. All seeming-things are the intimate concatenation, the miraculous assemblage of apparency manifesting as the nothing-every-thing we helplessly cannot not be—the still-we that we barely notice, until, despairing of chasing, we turn to examine with curiosity the nature of *now*, through our withinward heart-eyes.

We hardly notice, in the start of this exploration, that we have found infinity, blatantly-present in the core of our lives: inescapable, utterly still, absolutely without effort. Only little by little does it become obvious that this is what we cannot leave, nor lose; we have found our intrinsic-ness, and the felt-restfulness of it gives sensate meaning to those siren-song words "infinity" and "eternity"

> *Therefore, experience takes place only in the present, and beyond and apart from experience, nothing exists. Even the present is mere imagination, for the sense of time is purely mental: formless consciousness alone exists.*
>
> — Ramana Maharshi

Oh, it's love

> *At first the words "I am love" would seem nonsense: at the last they alone mean anything.*
>
> — Wei Wu Wei

When the emptiness behind my eyes was again pointed out to me, decades ago, reading Douglas Harding's *On Having No*

Home Already

Head at 35,000 feet, on a flight returning from India, a question was also born.

How is this inherent translucent marvel—even closer to me than breath, heartbeat or thoughts—in relationship with all the things of this world: with the clouds, the sound of traffic down the valley, with the taste of tea in my mouth and with the ideas briefly flickering, and then disappearing in mind?

Is there blissful union, somewhere in my being—in *our* being—where the radical translucency that never changes is intimately interwoven with every changeable *thing*? Surely, the complete intimacy of timelessness and time must have a birthplace, a locus of being?

It does. This birthplace, this intimacy of the formless and form, is the heart of us, literally and metaphorically.

And just as wetness is the nature of water, and heat the nature of fire, just so; love is the nature of our heart.

Our name for the indissoluble union of translucency and existing is *love*. The moment this is recognized—the moment there is the clicking into place that emptiness and form only make true, felt-sense when they are recognized as love itself—then there is also a coming home, a never-having-left: a being-home-itself-already.

> *There is no escape from Love,*
> *There is no East or West*
> *for Peace and Freedom.*
> *No matter where you go,*
> *It is always with you.*
> *Wisdom…*
> *is the reminder that you are at Home,*
> *That you are the Home itself…*

> — Papaji

Coming up out of infancy, we naturally tend to lose touch with the actuality that we are love, and cannot not be. This gradual losing touch with ourselves is the womb of suffering— as well as the beginning of the journey of rediscovering our nature as love.

We are love, but have forgotten it. The most marvelous thing in the universe, and far beyond it, gets forgotten as the identification as some-separate-thing—as Marie, Zoe, Mano, or Jorge —gradually predominates. Our thinking head becomes our center, and our heart is overlooked and then neglected.

This moment exactly as it is is love without conditions. As it is. What is, as is. This is the real meaning of loving what is—not somebody separate, loving something apart from themselves, but the ceaseless, faultless love that is the unmistakable causeless nature of every moment, particularly when it is recognized that only this makes complete sense through our heart, in the very core of ourselves that not even death can get rid of. Here (where we already are) the observer is the observed; the seeker is the sought; the longing is the longed-for.

Calling this "love" may seem like a stretch, because our conditioned, dualistic version of love is only constituted by the implicit presence of hate. But when attention rests in our heart, moment by moment, only one word has sufficient luminosity. "Love" fits exactly, when the radiant nowness that is the entirety of reality is noticed by the inherent nobody that is also the nature of our inescapable essence.

Only one means exists to come into this form as a human, wandering through the woods, dictating these words into a tiny tile of plastic and electronics. I can't be sure of this, but intuitively I know it to be so: as the sperm enters the egg, there is ecstasy. As the egg opens to the sperm, there is the ultimate thrill of being, blossoming. *Now*, each is both, and as the avatars of this contemplation have unanimously opined, this each is both is love, and only love. And this, inescapably, dear reader, is what we are and cannot not be.

The journey of return

The so-called journey of return is universal. We never for a moment depart from our origin, nor is there any possibility of leaving. Our origin is sheer blessing, and can absolutely be no other way—but this is only discovered as returning happens.

How can there be returning, when there is no leaving? Our origin dreams an astonishing dream, the most exquisite of all creations. In this dream there is time, and space, and every element appears separate from everything else. A central character is at the hub of every dream; known universally as "I" — and also known, seemingly-separately, as Marlies, Mike, Janelle, or Joey.

Appearing to be a separate-seeming character is inescapable; taking name and form is the only way the dream is dreamt. Conscious existing bodies forth, but as the form of it gathers increasing depth and complexity with language and experience, the blissful loving-to-be of its origin becomes increasingly suffused by the problems of time and space.

Yet at the center of all of this is a core without dreaming—the hub we universally call "I." When sufficient despair gathers at the insuperable problems of time and space, there can be a turning backward toward this core.

In this reversal of the direction of attention, there is a gradually growing recognition of the essential true nature of "I": it is absolutely and utterly empty. It has neither time nor space intrinsic to it, although, somewhat marvelously, all of time, space and experience are totally welcome to it.

This emptiness is truly remarkable for its complete absence as every-thing, indeed, as any-thing—yet it is effortlessly present without cessation, unlike every experience which comes and goes, all of which have about them cause and effect, movement, time, space and change.

But we can't really call this emptiness "it," for it is, above all, quite simply not. As this utter not-ness grows more and more apparent, there is a blossoming marvel: all of experience is taking place by itself, inseparably from the emptiness, which turns out to be nothing but the experience.

The experience is home itself, and could be nothing else. The experience is perfect, to the infinite degree, and could be nothing else—for there is nothing else—certainly no actual separate-somebody blundering about in the experience, imagining themselves existing independently of it, and causing all kinds of trouble.

This finding the experience alone to exist, perfect in all respects, is the legendary awakening. The absolute simplicity of it, the totally given nature of it, the fact that any kind of seeking for it is utterly and completely absurd; these all announce that there is nothing else but this.

And, this has to be forgotten, camouflaged, and lost to view in order for the journey of return to happen.

> *Those who have awakened have noticed that the selfhood functioning within thinking is like smoke or a cloud — a temporary appearance without actual selfhood. This very insight brings peace and joy to the thinking activity's futile efforts to make sense of its own existence — it simply doesn't exist as a self, it exists as a selfless stream. It is now 'liberated' from the suffering of mistaken selfhood.*

> — Yoshin David Radin

Only one way

There's only one way to learn about emptiness and form, to distinguish our inherent and unvarying radical translucency from the quadrillion changeable things that seemingly occur in it.

There's only one way to commence the journey of return that is life's invitation to learn as deeply as possible, if we find ourselves inclined to take it.

This 'one way' is to learn language, and it's bosom buddy, time. Then, there can be separate seeming-things—like emptiness; and all of the forms.

Marvelousness vanishes as the system of concepts completely colonizes our world. In particular, the presence of someone seeming-separate, namely 'I' can make the whole enterprise of life a kind of troubling grind, with only the end point of death seeming like a way out. After all, 'I' and 'my' life are the main problem—and supposedly, the entire solution.

Along the way of this life there can be some fantastic adventures, the greatest of which is to search for the absolute peace and freedom that the system of concepts and time tell us will be ours, eventually.

But perhaps we missed something, as we were quite naturally hypnotized by the marvelous powers of the giant parental gods surrounding us. They beamed love to us, along with their miraculous capacity to make us feel safe. To them, the search for peace and freedom was the only game in town.

What we missed is that early on in our lives, peace and freedom *themselves* were abandoned in favor of the search—for peace and freedom.

This missing happens to everyone; is natural, and inexorable, and has to occur, for the way forward to open.

There truly was (and is) only one way to go forward, and there was no choice about it at all: the system of time and concepts had to be learned; is essential to learn, and without this learning there can be no adequate tribal membership, for the whole tribe lives as if the entire point of life is to *be* this system of time and ideas.

This very moment of now is love

Nonetheless, every single one of us, innocent children suffused with peace and ease, once knew in the very essence and core of ourselves that this very moment of *now* is love. We only seem to exit this reality by learning language and all the gifts it brings.

"This moment of now is love"? Perhaps the conventional meaning of the word "love" has contaminated the sacred truth of it, for this moment of now contains the bombs raining down in Gaza, the rapes taking place across Sudan, and the terror of children forcefully separated from their parents, on planes to faraway countries.

One of the greatest avatars of this love himself seemed to lose faith completely amidst the ultimate extremity; Jesus, tortured near death on the cross, asking beseechingly if he had been forsaken by his own intrinsic source.

Perhaps each one of us inevitably travels this same road, for the moment of death is guaranteed in every life; of facing the end of time, and thereby, the dissolution of all ideas.

Any notion of our being in any way separate inexorably vanishes with the inevitable evaporation of time, and then we once again know ourselves as the unceasing, unstinting, never-ending and unconditional love that brought us here, into form, with a name.

On this journey of return, now with a form, and a name, we may have learned to distinguish the empty translucent backdrop of all experience from the experiences themselves.

We may, if you resemble me at all, have spent years and years questing the edge where these seeming-two might find each other.

Perhaps, again in the fashion this has happened for me, there's been a gradually dawning realization that there's only one place in our physical being where the union of these two is anything like blissful, and that is the heart of us.

The only time

But location alone is merely a good clue. The main hint provided us by heart space is that whatever is being looked for must be here *now*, known intrinsically by heart space to be the only time. For whatever is here now was never left to begin with, and must unceasingly be here this very moment, else it simply partakes of the appearing and disappearing nature of everything in time.

Quite clearly, *now* is the only time of this remarkable location-clue, inherently midway in our bodies between absolute transcendence and the most grounded earthiness.

What might we call the quality of being most evident in this domain of non-separateness?

Only "love" will suffice.

There is inherently nobody separate here, nor can there be, for this is the realm of intrinsic non-separateness. The cascading fountain of life upwells spontaneously without ceasing, The marvelousness of it is now reborn by the vanishing of someone-seeming-separate: it is happening by itself.

This happening by itself is intrinsically marvelous. Noticing it, we can again feel the wonder in the eyes of a very young child, before they take the arduous journey into being someone, looking at some-things.

The great perfection of things—because they can be absolutely no other way than they are, occurring moment by moment—completely melts the fuses of any way in which the structures of time and ideas can go on pretending they have any foundational influence here.

These structures of thought were always imagination; immensely potent, capable of dreaming up this astonishing device on which this text is appearing from a voice, while hiking in the woods, but like the clouds of the sky, only appearing by virtue of the vastness giving birth to them.

And, the journey of return has intrinsic to it the loving misdirection of these structures; our parents only *ever* intended to help us become adequate members of the tribe, all of whom are searching for peace and freedom.

Yet, as this conditioned overlay of belief and ideas undergoes gradual dissolution, what could never be left is gradually revealed, now as if for the first time: exactly and precisely now, just as it is, miraculously self-occurring, and perfect. We are home already, in the heart of *now*.

Your blind groping is full of promise. Your very searching is the finding. You cannot fail.

— Nisargadatta Maharaj

Notes

Acknowledgments

Many contributors to this book have cheered from the sidelines, or do not even know how they were being in support, often over many years. I'm grateful to Gary Buck, Marsha Fields, Mallory Geitheim, Mary McBride, Alia Lesko, Geneen Roth, Richard Shapiro, Jeff Tipp, and Doug Wallace, amongst many others.

Helpful conversations unfolded, sometimes over years, with Kat Adamson, Stephan Bodian, Peter Dziuban, Gay Hendricks, Shai Lavie, Francis Lucille, Brett Lyon, David Mars, Riyaz Motan, Scott Morrison, David Parrish, and Joan Tollifson.

In the realm of writing and providing reflection on writing, Ethan Barnes, Mona Coan, C. Shoshana Fershtman, Helga Herman, David Maxwell, and Susie Melnick have all given sterling support. Kay Brooks has perhaps read as much of my writing as anyone, and her steady championing of the book's emergence has been invaluable.

Encouragement to write, and to publish this book has come very consistently from Premsiri Lewin; in many, many ways, it would not have come about without her.

Willow Whitcomb's precise and discerning editorial expertise, and her loving companionship have contributed more to this project than even she can possibly know; I owe her an immense debt of gratitude.

As the project gathered steam, Ritu Esbjorn wholeheartedly gave her meticulous and discerning skills as a reader and copy-editor. The book began as a collection of pieces of writing that I enjoyed, and one day planned to send her. The 200 paper pages of the eventual manuscript traveled back and forth between California and Maine: every carefully-read page displays her thoughtfulness and encouragement to keep going.

Joel Lesko has been extraordinarily generous in support of the evolution of this project—to the point of it actually being published. He encouraged me endlessly as the book haltingly took shape, as it got a series of titles, and even when the wake of my reluctance and reticence seemed to capsize it. He found the right software to turn the manuscript into book form, familiarized himself with it, then taught me how to use it. Collaborating closely with him on every aspect of the book has been a pleasure that has only deepened as the book has gradually emerged. I feel wholeheartedly grateful for his collaboration, leadership and close company.

If I have not mentioned you here, please accept my gratitude, and quiet regret for any such omissions; this book is our universal immensity in motion.

About the author

Glenn Francis, Psy.D., is a psychotherapist, teacher, and writer whose work lives at the intersection of psychological depth and contemplative insight. He holds bachelor's, master's, and doctoral degrees in psychology, along with post-graduate training in psychotherapy, and has spent decades working closely with people as a therapist, coach, educator, and bodyworker.

Over the course of his professional life, Glenn has accompanied individuals through every kind of emotional suffering, relational challenges, and periods of profound questioning about meaning, identity, and presence. His approach is grounded in careful listening, respect for lived experience, and a deep trust in the intelligence already present within each person.

Alongside his clinical work, Glenn has studied with spiritual teachers across cultures and traditions, engaging deeply with Zen, Buddhist, Taoist, and nondual teachings. These influences inform his writing—not as philosophy or doctrine, but as lived inquiry. Rather than offering methods or prescriptions, he is interested in what becomes apparent when striving softens and attention returns to what is already here.

His writing reflects a lifelong engagement with the ordinary and the profound: the ways suffering points beyond itself, how seeking both serves and exhausts us, and how a quiet, unassuming freedom can be discovered in the midst of everyday life. He writes from experience, humility, and empathy, meeting readers not as students, but as fellow human beings.

Home Already: In the Heart of Now grows directly out of this terrain, offering a contemplative space for readers who sense that what they are looking for may be closer—and simpler—than they have been taught to believe.

For more information: https://www.intheheartofnow.com